T0204232

Summer Reading Clubs

Complete Plans for 50 Theme-Based Library Programs

by

MARTHA SEIF SIMPSON

McFarland & Company, Inc., Publishers
Jefferson, North Carolina, and London

British Library Cataloguing-in-Publication data are available

Library of Congress Cataloguing-in-Publication Data

Simpson, Martha Seif, 1954–
    Summer reading clubs : complete plans for 50 theme-based library
programs / by Martha Seif Simpson.
        p. cm.
    Includes indexes.
    ISBN 0-89950-721-2 (sewn softcover : 50# alk. paper) ∞
    1. Libraries, Children's—Activity programs.   2. Children's
literature—Appreciation.   3. Children—Books and reading.
I. Title.
Z718.1.S57   1992
027.62'5—dc20   91-51231
                                                                            CIP

Manufactured in the United States of America

McFarland & Company, Inc., Publishers
  Box 611, Jefferson, North Carolina 28640

For my parents,
Sam and Dorothy Seif

Table of Contents

Acknowledgments

I would like to thank the following librarians who took the time to answer my questions and offer comments: Lynda Frattalone, Kathy Lescoe, Elizabeth Thornton, Phyllis Dacorte, Michelle Jacobson, Deborah Prozzo, Pat Balfe, Antionette Charest, Debra Carrier-Perry, Jennifer McKinlay, Valerie Harrod, Bea Piersa, Carolyn Freeman, Bette St. John, Jeanne Smith, Constance Cleary, Janet Gourley, Julie Clapp, Delice Feinn, Sally Schultz, Marcia Trotta, Karen Smith, Louise Bailey, Shirley Rayner, Marian Lattanzio, Pat LaTerza, Marilyn Beattie, Sandra Davis, Coral Lindenfelser, Kristin Retigliano, Beverly Crompton, Joan Yanicke, Carol Terapane, Joan Rossi, Pauline A. Cole, Elizabeth Perrin, Annette Ouellet, Phyllis Hedberg.

My special thanks to Dr. Victor Triolo and Barbara Freedman for helping me get started on this project; to my husband, John Simpson, for compiling data and offering support; and to Ron Gagliardi for his good advice.

An Open Letter to Public Librarians in Charge of Youth Services

Oh, no! It's already spring, and you haven't put together a summer reading program yet. What will you do?

You could purchase a kit or attend a workshop to learn about this year's fad theme. You could pore through educational journals and sourcebooks and try to adapt a teaching unit for the public library. Most likely, you will sit down—alone or with co-workers—and rack your brains until you come up with an idea that interests you and will (you hope) excite your young patrons. And somewhere in this process, you'll probably wish you could find a book written specifically for public libraries, just chock full of summer reading club ideas.

Well, you are not alone. Many other librarians go through the same process and make the same wish. And that is why I have written this book. Although teachers and school media specialists will also find these units helpful, this sourcebook was written primarily with you in mind—the librarian responsible for the children's summer program.

It has been proven in numerous studies that children who develop good reading habits tend to perform better in the classroom. A reading promotion based on a fun theme is a great way to get children into the library, and to fill the educational gap left by the closing of school for the summer. While researching this book, I spoke to many public librarians about their summer programs to find out what they did to entice children into their libraries. I noted which ideas seemed to be the most successful, and incorporated many of them into the following units. In addition, I have included some general observations and suggestions. Please feel free to adapt the information contained in this book to meet the specific needs of your own patrons. And have a wonderful summer!

Introduction:
The Summer Reading Club

Children like to have fun, especially in the summer. I have found that the most successful programs attract children by creating a "kid's club" environment to which they would want to belong. Having a summer theme, and making sure the entire children's area reflects that theme, is the best way to promote this club atmosphere. The bulletin board, a welcoming sign at the check-out area, and other theme-related displays all add to the excitement of the program.

Each of the fifty units contained in this book is based on a theme, to which every part of the unit is related. Each unit is presented in the following order:

1. An introduction, which may be reproduced in publicity materials.
2. A list of promotional items (such as bookmarks or cut-outs) to carry out the theme.
3. Fifteen activities, including a bulletin board idea, a reading incentive game, a closing ceremony idea, and various individual and group projects.
4. A suggested book list.
5. A list of theme-related children's films and videos.

One of the goals of the programs in this book is to help children experience a feeling of accomplishment. In my research, I discovered a great deal of controversy over whether there should be a minimum number of books that a child is required to read in order to qualify for an end-of-the-program bonus. Many librarians noted that slow readers often dropped out of the summer program because they could not manage the indicated number of books. Therefore, I have suggested reading incentive games which are based on the entire group's performance, not on individual reading skills. With a group goal, the slower readers will not feel pressured to compete with the super readers. Each child can read at his or her own level and still have a chance to win the game. The number of books (indicated in game descriptions by the phrase "every X books") and the number of spaces for each game can be varied according to your number of club participants and the length of your program. *Always make sure the game goal is attainable.* Children will welcome a challenge, but if they cannot succeed at reaching the goal, they will not want to return next year.

1

Many librarians have found cut-outs useful for creating the club atmosphere. I have suggested a theme-related cut-out for each unit. Each time a child completes a book, have him write his own name and the title of the book on a construction paper cut-out. Post these cut-outs in the children's department. Children love to see their names displayed, and will want to read more so they can cover the walls with cut-outs. This visual incentive has raised summer book circulation tremendously in libraries that have used it. Although any book read can be listed on a cut-out, you may want to place stars or theme-related stickers on book titles related to the summer theme, making them more noticeable to your readers.

Another good way to keep track of accomplishments is for each child to keep a reading log. Each unit suggests a theme-related name for this log, but you should adapt its format to suit your preference. Some librarians have children list the titles and authors of books read. Others prefer a contract system whereby a child agrees to read a certain number of minutes per day or pages per week. A reading log in which children can place a sticker or color in a spot for each accomplishment adds to the fun. You may want to file the reading logs in the library so that the children do not lose them. At the closing ceremony, you can place an official library seal or theme-related sticker on the logs and present them to the readers along with their certificates of participation.

Many librarians like to start off their summer programs with a big "kick-off." Children who have not previously registered for the program may do so at this time. I have not provided any specific kick-off suggestions in this book, but I can offer some general comments. First and foremost, *make sure it is fun!* A carnival, parade, or live performance related to the theme always works well. Give each child a Reading Club Packet to introduce him to the summer theme. This packet should include the reading log, a bookmark, and the membership card (unless otherwise noted in the unit). Other packet items might be theme-related coloring pages, picture puzzles, and a small prize; a calendar of events; club rules; and a suggested reading list. Enthusiastically describe the reading incentive game and other special features of the program. Get the word out that the library is the place to be for the summer!

As with all the other elements of the summer promotion, the suggested book list should be theme-related. In the lists provided with each unit, "Younger Readers" refers to fiction for children in grades pre–K to 3, and "Older Readers" refers to fiction for children in grades 3 through 6. The core group of reading club participants is K–6, but your own situation may be different. The nonfiction section includes factual books for children of all ages, poetry and riddle books, as well as craft and sourcebooks which may be of interest to the program planner. Of course, there are many more theme-related books available then those I have included— these are just a few to get you started. You may want to display suggested books on a separate shelf to draw them to the attention of your readers.

I have also included short lists of theme-related films and videos of varying lengths. These may be shown as part of a summer film series, or during a specific activity, as suits your needs. The names of film and video distributors are abbreviated in the lists; full names and addresses are provided in the back of the book.

Throughout the summer, you should be building up enthusiasm for the closing ceremony. By then, the reading incentive game should be completed and the walls of the children's room covered with cut-outs of books read and artwork created by the children. I have included various suggestions for closing ceremonies, but there is one constant for all of them: *Be sure to acknowledge all children for a job well done.* The closing ceremony is more than an excuse for a party; it is a celebration of the readers' accomplishments. Every child should be praised for taking part in the program, regardless of his attendance or number of books read. The certificate of participation is just that—a reward for taking part in the library's summer program. Hopefully, the children will have completed the reading incentive game and will receive their game prizes; if not, you had better revise your book requirement so the goal will be met the following year. Above all, let the children know how proud you are of their reading skills. It's good for their self-esteem and will encourage them to become lifelong readers and library patrons. And isn't that really what it's all about?

General Procedural Suggestions

1. The instructions for bulletin boards and reading incentive games tell you to post cut-outs or draw pictures of various items. Use whichever method works best for you. An overhead projector may be used to enlarge a small picture and allow you to trace it onto a larger surface.

2. Visuals are great motivators. In addition to the cut-outs for books read, post drawings, mobiles, and other artwork created by children around the area. It adds a festive spirit to the library, and communicates the message that the children's department is a vital and thriving element of the community.

3. I have suggested the use of oak tag rather than construction paper for many arts and crafts activities because it holds up better. Acrylic paints can be used for most painting activities because they are simple to use and clean up. There are many arts and crafts materials on the market which are fun and easy to use, such as Art Tape and Scratch Etch Board. You may want to consult an art teacher or art supply store for other ideas.

4. It may be a good idea to invest in a camera that takes instant-developing ID photos. Several units mention using headshot photos for activities such as membership cards, bulletin boards, and crafts. And children love to show their pictures to parents and friends.

5. Many collage ideas are included in these units. The directions say to supply lots of old magazines from which children may cut out pictures. Mail-order catalogs and color newspaper inserts also contain wonderful pictures which can be used for collages. If you do not want to let children loose with scissors in the library, you

can cut out pictures ahead of time for them to use. You will need to cut out a lot!

6. Several units contain group projects in which children are asked to write and/or illustrate materials to be compiled into a book. Publishing these creative writing efforts is an effective method of developing children's reading and writing interests and abilities. Make sure each child signs and dates his work. Attractively bind these compilations and store them in the reference section for children to read in the library. These homemade books are likely to become favorites with your patrons!

7. Try to encourage your community to support the summer reading program. Many public librarians visit schools in the spring to recruit participants. Some schools have their own awards ceremonies in the fall to honor reading club members.

Inviting local experts to speak is a good way to connect children to the world around them and encourage new interests. A local celebrity presenting awards at the closing ceremony really makes children feel important!

Perhaps you can get your local newspaper involved. Some papers may be willing to print activity sheets for the summer program. Or they may publish the names of super readers or pictures of children engaged in library activities.

Local businesses are also good resources to tap. Try to persuade fast food restaurants to donate food coupons as reading incentives. Some businesses may be willing to sponsor a theme-related unit, such as a pet store lending you gerbils for children to watch during the summer. Ask around – you never know what you might find!

8. Keep accurate participation and circulation statistics. Your ability to prove the importance of children's services and programs may come in handy at budget time and encourage more community support. Also, in these times of financial cuts, a good relationship with the community is a necessity to ensure your department's survival.

9. There are lots of great ideas available – you probably have several of them within reach! I have listed the titles of various craft books which may be helpful, but there are many, many more. The activities listed on the following pages represent a starting point. Feel free to expand, adapt, or add on to my suggestions with activities found in other sourcebooks or ones that you develop. Tailor your program to the needs of your patrons, and you will all enjoy a productive and fun-filled summer!

—WELCOME TO BOOKWORLD—

(Amusement and Theme Parks)

Attention fun-seekers! _____ Library's own amusement park will be operating this summer, and you can be a part of it! Create a merry-go-round. Make candy apples. Become a train, a carousel, and a fun house. Invent a new ride and design an amusement park. Play games and win prizes at the arcade. All are **Welcome to Bookworld** *for a summer full of fun!*

Promotional Items

1. Sign reading "Ticket Booth" for check-out area
2. "Season Passes" (membership cards)
3. Balloon cut-outs (for books read)
4. Reading logs entitled "List of Attractions"
5. "Welcome to Bookworld" bookmarks
6. Bookworld Fun-Seeker certificates (certificates of participation)
7. Helium balloons with library logo; pinwheels (game prizes)

Activities

1. Bulletin Board. Draw a large arch to indicate the entrance gate to an amusement park. Under the arch, draw a roller coaster, ferris wheel, balloons, people, etc. Above the arch, write, "WELCOME TO." On the arch, write, "BOOK-WORLD."

2. Reading Incentive Game: A Day at the Park. Draw the layout of an amusement park. (Use an actual park design or make one up.) Label all rides, the ticket booth, stands, etc. Label the ENTRANCE and EXIT points. Mark a path through the park, visiting all the rides. Place a child marker at ENTRANCE and advance it one space for every X books read by the group. Readers will win a prize if the child visits all the rides and reaches the EXIT by the closing ceremony.

3. Design a Park. Ask children what comes to their minds when they think of amusement parks. List all answers. Then tell children to design their own amusement or theme parks which include their favorite attractions. Let each child draw a poster advertising the park's name, rides and features, admission price, etc. Tell why it's the best park in the world.

4. Ferris Wheel. Give children plain paper plates. Draw six diagonal lines that cross at the center to form the spokes of a ferris wheel. Place stickers of cartoon characters at the outer ends of the spokes to look like twelve people are riding the wheel. Using a brass fastener, attach the wheel to a piece of oak tag so that the wheel turns. Draw an entrance to the ride and background details of an amusement park on the paper.

5. Ant Park. Supply Art Tape and a background paper for children to make an amusement park for ants. Strips of tape can be cut, spiraled, pleated, folded, etc., and glued to the paper. Then have children complete a crossword puzzle of amusement park attractions (bumper cars, midway, cotton candy, etc.)

6. Carousel Dance. Let children pretend they are carousel horses in a musical game. Have children stand in two circles, one inside the other, facing center. The two circles should have equal numbers of children. Children in the inner circle join hands; each child in the outer circle places his hands on the shoulders of a child in the inner circle. Play a typical carousel tune (preferably calliope music), such as "Have You Ever Seen a Lassie?" At the first downbeat, the children in the inner circle rise up on their toes, while their partners behind them bend their knees. Reverse action on the second downbeat, so that the children go up and down on alternate beats, like horses on a carousel. Let children practice this a few rounds. Then, have them move to the left in their circles as they go up and down to the music. Members of the outer circle will have to take bigger steps than their partners to stay even. Let children switch places in the circles, or speed up the music for more fun.

7. Carousels. Give children pictures of carousel horses to color. Then carefully cut out the horses. Glue each horse to the center of a popsicle stick, so that the stick protrudes above and below the horse. Stand horses up on a circular piece of styrofoam to look like a carousel. Add a pole in the center of the circle, and tie ribbons from the top of the pole to each horse to add to the effect. Several carousels may be made, depending upon the number of horses and the size of the styrofoam. Display in library.

8. Park Goodies. Make candy apples and popcorn with the children.

9. Roller Coasters. Show pictures of and discuss some famous roller coasters—how high or fast they go, whether they have wood or steel frames, etc. View film clips of roller coaster rides. Have children tell their favorites and complete a word search puzzle of roller coaster names (Cyclone, Python, Thunderbolt, etc.).

10. Coaster Car. Wash and dry several smooth, oval rocks. Give children paint to make faces and clothes on the rocks, and to paint the bumpy half of an egg carton. When everything is dry, sit the rock people in the egg carton to look like people in a roller coaster car. Display in library.

11. Fun House. Divide children into two groups. Tell each group that they should use their bodies to form a fun house maze/obstacle course for members of the other group to walk through. These fun houses can be a little scary, but not harmful. Give the groups several minutes to plan their attractions. Then let Group A pass through Group B's fun house, and vice versa.

12. Invent a Ride. Let children talk about their favorite amusement park rides. Give children drawing materials and let them create their own new rides. Name each ride and note its special features, as well as how old a person has to be to ride it.

13. Famous Parks. Give readers the names and locations of some amusement and theme parks in the United States. Have children find these places on a map.

14. Train Ride. Line up all the children in a row, front-to-back. Have them pretend they are riding an amusement park train. Let them chug around the library, stopping at various attractions along the way, such as the card catalog, the reference desk, the magazine area, the poetry section, etc. Take advantage of the opportunity to acquaint readers with many areas and features of the library.

15. Closing Ceremony: Arcade. Set up the library to look like an arcade, with a ticket booth and several games for children to play. Games might include penny pitch, knock down the pins, skee ball, ring toss, etc. Give children tickets to use for entry to each game. Extra tickets may be awarded to children who read a pre-set number of books during the summer. Present small prizes to winners. Play calliope music and make cotton candy.

Theme-Related Books

For Younger Readers

Barbato, Juli. *Mom's Night Out*. Macmillan, 1985.
Carlson, Nancy. *Harriet and the Roller Coaster*. Live Oak, 1985.
Kroll, Steven. *The Tyrannosaurus Game*. Holiday, 1976.
Lewis, Thomas P. *The Blue Rocket Fun Show: or Friends Forever*. Macmillan, 1986.
Lobel, Arnold. *A Holiday for Mister Muster*. Harper, 1963.
McCrady, Lady. *The Perfect Ride*. Parents, 1981.
Martin, Bill, Jr., and Archambault, John. *Up and Down on the Merry-Go-Round*. Holt, 1988.
Peek, Merle. *The Balancing Act*. Clarion, 1987.
Perero, Lydia. *Frisky*. Random, 1966.
Rey, Margaret, and Shalleck, Allen J. *Curious George Visits an Amusement Park*. Houghton, 1988.

Stevenson, James. *Wilfred the Rat.* Greenwillow, 1977.
Wildsmith, Brian. *Carousel.* Knopf, 1988.

For Older Readers

Adler, David A. *Jeffrey's Ghost and the Ziffel Fair Mystery.* Holt, 1987.
Blum, Lisa-Marie. *The Mysterious Merry-Go-Round.* Abelard-Schuman, 1962.
Bolton, Mimi D. *Merry-Go-Round Family.* Wisla, 1990.
Foster, Elizabeth. *Gigi in America: The Story of a Merry-Go-Round Horse.* North Atlantic.
Samstag, Nicholas. *Kay Kay Comes Home.* Astor-Honor, 1962.
Sharp, Margery. *Lost at the Fair.* Little, 1965.

Nonfiction

Anderson, Norman, and Brown, Walter. *Ferris Wheels.* Pantheon, 1983.
Hahn, Christine. *Amusement Park Machines.* Raintree, 1979.
Silverstein, Herma. *Scream Machines: Roller Coasters of Past, Present, and Future.* Walker, 1986.
Thomas, Art. *Merry-Go-Rounds.* Carolrhoda, 1981.
Van Steenwyk, Elizabeth. *Behind the Scenes at the Amusement Park.* Whitman, 1983.

Films and Videos

Carousel. NFBC, 8 mins.
A Penny Suite. PHX, 5 mins.
A Trip to the Amusement Park. CHUR, 14 mins.

—— READ A MASTERPIECE ——
(Art)

Some of the greatest art in the world awaits you at _____ Library: from the Ancient Greeks to twentieth century artists; from Michelangelo to Picasso. And don't forget the outstanding picture books that have won the Caldecott Medal! You can be an artist, too. Create clay art and a modern sculpture. Make a collage and draw cartoons. Experiment with an artist's palette and learn about different types of art. Contribute to our giant wall mural. Come to _____ Library this summer to create and **Read a Masterpiece**.

Promotional Items

1. Sign reading "Drawing Room" for check-out area
2. "Art Patron" cards (membership cards)
3. Artist's palette cut-outs (for books read)
4. Reading logs entitled "Portfolio"
5. "Read a Masterpiece" bookmark
6. Master Artist certificates (certificates of participation)
7. Watercolors paintboxes (game prizes)

Activities

1. Bulletin Board. Post pictures from Caldecott Medal and Honor books. Label each with the title, author, and illustrator. Post a full list of Caldecott books. Caption: READ A MASTERPIECE.

2. Reading Incentive Game: Masterpieces. Post cards with the name of several famous painters, sculptors, and other artists along one wall, leaving space for pictures to be added. For every X books read by the group, post a picture of a famous work of art above the artist's name. Also add the title and era of the piece. Readers will win a prize if all the masterpieces are posted by the closing ceremony.

3. Caldecott Books. Display Caldecott books on a separate shelf. Do book-talks on some of these, and encourage children to read them. Children may write short book reports or do art projects about these books to display in the library. Place a gold star on the artist's palette cut-out of every Caldecott book read to distinguish it from other books.

4. Shape Starters. Give each child a sheet of paper, divided in fourths. Each section will contain an outline of one shape: a circle, a triangle, a rectangle, and a square. A second sheet can contain an oval, a squiggly line, a triangle touching an oval, and a teardrop shape. Provide crayons and tell children to use each shape to make a picture.

5. Types of Art. Have children complete a word search puzzle of various art forms. Include types not mentioned elsewhere in this unit (weaving, papier-mâché, tie-dying, portraits, etc.)

6. Artist's Palette. Give each child a sheet of white oak tag cut into the shape of an artist's palette and a thin paint brush. Provide red, yellow, blue, and white watercolors and water. Let children place a dab of each color on their palettes. Then have them experiment with combining two colors to make a third. Supply extra paper for them to paint on. Remind children to rinse their brushes frequently.

7. What Color is This. Obtain a large box of Crayola Crayons. Read the names of some crayons and ask children to identify the colors (magenta is a purplish-red, etc.) Then let children make up their own funny names for colors (sky-blue pink, etc.) Take a poll of children's favorite colors.

8. Cartoons. Show children some single-frame cartoons without captions. Let children make up punchlines for them. Then supply punchlines and let children draw cartoons to go with them.

9. Tissue Paper Collage. Supply several colors of tissue paper for children to cut out snowflake designs or other shapes, crumple up into little balls, etc. Let them arrange these and glue onto a piece of oak tag.

10. Art Materials. Give children a fact sheet of art materials (sketch pad, tempera paints, easel, etc.) Have children complete a crossword puzzle with these terms.

11. Clay. Provide modeling clay and cookie-cutters in various shapes. Let children roll out the clay and use the cookie-cutters to make shapes. Use a stylus or the end of a paper clip to scratch designs and textures into the clay. Children may paint their clay art after it dries.

12. Modern Sculpture. Show children pictures of modern sculpture and three-dimensional art. Provide a variety of materials: spools, egg cartons, paper tubes, small stones and shells, buttons, etc. Let children glue any combination of these into a work of art. Provide paints so children may decorate their sculptures. Each child should write his name and the title of his sculpture on an index card. Display these in the library.

13. Art Museums. Have children locate cities where there are famous art museums on a world map.

14. Origami. Origami is the Japanese art of paper folding. Choose a simple activity from a book of origami projects to do with the children. Cut paper to the sizes needed ahead of time. Demonstrate each step and let children create their folded artwork along with you. You can also provide Art Tape and let children create their own paper sculptures.

15. Closing Ceremony: Group Mural. Post a huge roll of paper or canvas on a long wall. Supply various colors of paint, crayons and markers, brushes, water, plus a dropcloth or newspapers. Give each child a chance to contribute to the mural. The pictures may be focused on one theme, if desired. (This activity may also be done outdoors.)

Theme-Related Books

For Younger Readers

Agee, Jon. *The Incredible Painting of Felix Clousseau.* Farrar, 1988.
Cohen, Miriam. *No Good in Art.* Greenwillow, 1988.
Cooper, Jacqueline. *Angus and the Mona Lisa.* Lothrop, 1981.
Cummings, Pat. *C.L.O.U.D.S.* Lothrop, 1986.
Freeman, Don. *Norman the Doorman.* Viking, 1959.
Glass, Andrew. *Jackson Makes His Move.* Warne, 1982.
Johnson, Crockett. *Harold and the Purple Crayon.* Harper, 1955.
Lionni, Leo. *A Color of His Own.* Pantheon, 1975.

Rubin, Cynthia Elyce. *ABC Americana from the National Gallery of Art.* HBJ, 1989.
Schick, Eleanor. *Art Lessons.* Greenwillow, 1987.
Strand, Mark. *Rembrandt Takes a Walk.* Clarkson Potter, 1987.
Waddell, Martin. *Alice the Artist.* Dutton, 1988.

For Older Readers

Konigsberg, E. L. *The Second Mrs. Giaconda.* Atheneum, 1975.
Lessac, Frané. *Caribbean Canvas.* Harper, 1989.
Preston, L. E. *Chiang's Magic Brush.* Carolrhoda, 1973.
Raskin, Ellen. *The Tatooed Potato and Other Clues.* Avon, 1981.
Stolz, Mary. *Zekmet the Stone Carver: A Tale of Ancient Egypt.* HBJ, 1988.

Non-Fiction

Benjamin, Carol Lea. *Cartooning for Kids.* Crowell, 1982.
Cummings, Robert. *Just Look . . . A Book About Paintings.* Schribner's, 1980.
Goffstein, M.B. *An Artist.* Harper, 1980.
Keightley, Moy. *Investigating Art: A Practical Guide for Young People.* Facts on File, 1976.
Nakano, Dokuohtei. *Easy Origami.* Viking, 1985.
Payne, G. C. *Adventures with Sculpture.* Warne, 1971.
Peppin, Anthea. *The Usborne Story of Painting.* Usborne, 1980.
Sattler, Helen Ronex. *Recipes for Art and Craft Materials.* Lothrop, 1973.
Seidelman, James E., and Mintonye, Grace. *Creating with Clay.* Macmillan, 1967.
Warshaw, Jerry. *The I Can't Draw Book.* Whitman, 1971.
Weiss, Harvey. *Paint, Brush, and Palette.* Addison, 1966.
Witty, Ken. *A Day in the Life of an Illustrator.* Troll, 1981.

Films and Videos

Art for Beginners: Fun with Lines. COR, 11 mins.
A Boy Creates. BRIT, 10 mins.
Cat's Cradle. NFBC, 11 mins.
The Day the Colors Went Away. BRIT, 10 mins.
Liang and the Magic Paintbrush. RR, 30 mins.
Rainbow War. PYR, 20 mins.

READ THE STARS

(Astrology, Constellations)

Today's horoscope: It's a good time to sign up for _____ Library's summer reading club. Start by making a zodiac membership card. Compare personality traits with others who were born under the same astrological sign. Create a constellation and a zodiac chart. Learn about the mythological gods who supposedly rule the planets. Design an astrological sign banner. Participate in our Planetarium Light Show. We forecast a summer of fun as you **Read the Stars** *at _____ Library.*

Promotional Items

1. Sign Reading "What's Your Sign?" for check-out area
2. Zodiac ID cards (membership cards)
3. Sun cut-outs (for books read)
4. Reading logs entitled "Star Chart"
5. "Read The Stars" bookmarks
6. Astrologer Awards (certificates of participation)
7. Flashlights (game prizes)

Activities

1. Bulletin Board. Make a background of black construction paper. In the center, post a picture of one or more children sitting and reading. Post star cut-outs all around. Connect some of them with white chalk to form the Big Dipper and other constellations. Label stars with the titles and authors of popular books. Caption: READ THE STARS.

2. Reading Incentive Game: An Astrological Year. Post a cut-out of the earth. In a circle around it, place 365 dots to represent the days of the year. Draw lines from the earth through the outer circle to section the days into the sign of the zodiac. Starting with the first day of Aries, label the sections with the names and dates of the signs. For every X books read by the group, color in a consecutive dot along the circle. Readers will win a prize if all the dots are colored in by the closing ceremony.

3. Zodiac ID Cards. Show children the dates for the 12 zodiac signs and let them determine under which signs they were born. Then have them make their own zodiac membership cards. Take ID photos of the children, and glue them in the upper left corners of blank 3″ × 5″ index cards. Provide ink pads and stamps of the 12 signs. Let each child stamp his sign in the upper right corner and write his name below. Label or stamp the cards with the library's name and address.

4. Horoscope. Pass out paper. Have each child write his name and astrological sign at the top. Divide the paper into two columns, labeled "True" and "Not True." Read aloud the characteristics of people born under each sign. As you read their sign, have those children list each characteristic in the True or Not True column, as they think it pertains to themselves. When all the horoscopes have been read, have children review their papers. Did they think more characteristics were true or not true? Do they believe in astrology?

5. Banners. Let each child make a banner of his own astrological sign. Draw or glue cut-outs of the zodiac sign on construction paper. Write the name of the sign above the picture and the dates below it. Beneath the dates, draw the symbol for the sign.

6. Crossword. Hand out a fact sheet of astrological terms (house, elements, cast, planets, etc.) Have children complete a crossword puzzle with these terms.

7. Personality Traits. Divide children into 12 groups, according to their signs. Have them discuss their likes and dislikes. Do the children in each group share any common traits? Then have them look in almanacs to find the names of some famous people who were born under their signs. Do the children think they share any common traits with some of these celebrities?

8. Zodiacs. Paste a cut-out of the sun in the center of a large sheet of construction paper. Draw 12 lines radiating out of the sun at clock-position intervals. Let children trace stencils or paste cut-outs of the 12 zodiac signs in their proper positions to make zodiac charts.

9. Across the Globe. Astrology began thousands of years ago with the Babylonians. It eventually spread to Egypt, Greece, Rome, Arabia, and then the rest of Europe. Now it is known worldwide. Trace the spread of astrology on a world map with children. Name some important astronomers and have children locate the countries from which they came.

10. Planet Gods. Each sign of the zodiac has a ruling planet: Mars, Venus, Mercury, Saturn, Jupiter, or the sun and the moon, which early astrologers also considered to be planets. Draw the planet symbols for each of these, and explain a little about the corresponding Greek or Roman gods (Mars—god of war; Venus—goddess of love; etc.) Provide lots of old magazines. Let children cut out pictures of what they think the gods look like. On a large paper circle, glue all the Mars pictures. Glue Jupiter pictures on another circle, and so on for all seven planets. Display these planet gods collages in the library.

11. Star Search. Have children complete a word search puzzle with the names of stars.

12. Star Namesakes. Mention some phrases that have astrological references (Age of Aquarius, Scales of Justice, etc.) Explain how some days of the week are named after planets. Let children tell you other things with astrological names. What about brand names of cars and other products?

13. Constellations. Post a map of the sky and point out some constellations. Supply black construction paper and silver stick-on stars. Let each child choose a constellation and make a replica of it. Connect the stars with white chalk. Label each picture with the name of the constellation. Display in library.

14. Star Stories. List the 12 signs of the zodiac and their common names

(Gemini – the Twins; Taurus – the Bull, etc.) Other constellations may also be listed. Ask children to make up stories involving one or more of the star creatures.

15. Closing Ceremony: Planetarium Light Show. Show films or slides of the planets and stars. Then hand out flashlights to all children. Shut off the room lights and let them shine their flashlights on the ceiling to make their own planetarium light show. (Colored gels on the flashlights will produce multi-colored stars.) Play the record "Aquarius/Let the Sun Shine In" by the Fifth Dimension during the light show.

Theme-Related Books

For Younger Readers

Asch, Frank. *Mooncake*. Prentice, 1983.
Boon, Emilie. *Peterkin Meets a Star*. Random, 1984.
Cole, Joanna. *The Magic School Bus Lost in the Solar System*. Scholastic, 1990.
Elzbieta. *Dikou and the Baby Star*. Crowell, 1988.
Gerstein, Mordicai. *Where Does the Sun Go at Night?* Greenwillow, 1980.
Lee, Jeanne M., reteller. *Legend of the Milky Way*. Holt, 1982.
Obrist, Jurg. *The Miser Who Wanted the Sun*. Macmillan, 1984.
Ray, Deborah Kogan. *Stargazing Sky*. Crown, 1991.
Van Woerkom, Dorothy. *The Rat, the Ox, and the Zodiac: A Chinese Legend*. Crown, 1976.
Widman, Christine Barker. *The Star Gazers*. Harper, 1989.

For Older Readers

Cleaver, Vera, and Cleaver, Bill. *Delpha Green and Company*. Lippincott, 1972.
Hadley, Eric, and Hadley, Tessa. *Legends of the Sun and Moon*. Cambridge, 1983.
Jones, Diana Wynne. *Dogsbody*. Greenwillow, 1988.
Lurie, Alison, reteller. *The Heavenly Zoo: Legends and Tales of the Stars*. Farrar, 1980.

Nonfiction

Aylesworth, Thomas G. *Astrology and Foretelling the Future*. Watts, 1973.
Branley, Franklyn. *Age of Aquarius: You and Astrology*. Crowell, 1979.
_____. *Sun Dogs and Shooting Stars: A Skywatcher's Calendar*. Houghton, 1980.
Fisher, Leonard Everett. *Star Signs*. Holiday, 1983.
Gallant, Roy A. *The Constellations: How They Came to Be*. Four Winds, 1979.
Kettelkamp, Larry. *Astrology: Wisdom of the Stars*. Morrow, 1973.
Krupp, E. C. *The Big Dipper and You*. Greenwillow, 1989.
McLeisch, Kenneth. *The Shining Stars: Greek Legends of the Zodiac*. Cambridge, 1981.
Polgreen, John, and Polgreen, Cathleen. *The Stars Tonight*. Harper, 1967.
Simon, Seymour. *Look to the Night Sky: An Introduction to Star Watching*. Viking, 1977.

Films and Videos

A Beginner's Guide to the Constellations. BRIT, 12 mins.
Beyond Our Solar System. COR, 13 mins.
How Astronomers Study the Universe. COR, 13 mins.

—————— TAKE ME OUT ——————
TO THE LIBRARY

(Baseball)

Batter Up! This summer _____ Library is going to celebrate America's favorite summer pastime—baseball. Make a batting helmet and pennant for your favorite team. Learn about the minor leagues. Select your ideal All-Star teams. Get the scoop on collecting baseball cards and other souvenirs. Keep track of all the major league teams and predict who will win the World Series. Join us for a day at Baseball Camp. Don't strike out this summer. Tell your parents to **Take Me Out to the Library**!

Promotional Items

1. Sign reading "Home Base" for check-out area
2. "Dugout Passes" (membership cards)
3. Baseball cut-outs (for books read)
4. Reading logs entitled "Hall of Fame"
5. "Take Me Out to the Library" bookmarks
6. Big League Hitter certificates (certificates of participation)
7. Baseball caps and team patches (game prizes)

Activities

1. Bulletin Board. Post team emblems of all the major league teams along the sides. On cut-outs shaped like baseball gloves, write the titles and authors of fiction and nonfiction books about baseball. Post these cut-outs in the formation of a baseball diamond. In the center of the diamond place the caption: TAKE ME OUT TO THE LIBRARY.

2. Reading Incentive Game: Season Schedule. Use a real or made-up name of a baseball team. Make up a calendar for the team's season, modeled after the schedule of a major league team. Mark in days where home and away games will be played. For every X books read by the group, check off a game played from the schedule. (Perhaps flip a coin to decide if the team won or lost and mark the schedule accordingly.) Readers will get a prize if all the games have been marked played by the closing ceremony.

3. Pennants. Provide construction paper cut in pennant-size triangles, drawing materials, and dowels. Let children make baseball pennants of their own design, or they can copy a major league emblem.

4. Rules. Have children complete a word search puzzle of baseball terms used in scoring the game (inning, strike, run, safe, etc.).

5. The Ballpark. Ask children to list some foods that are sold at ballparks. Serve peanuts and Cracker Jack, and sing "Take Me Out to the Ball Game." Teach children how to do "the wave."

6. Equipment Mobile. Bend a metal clothes hanger into a diamond shape. Give children two each of the following contruction paper cut-outs: baseball, glove, bat, and cap. Staple fronts and backs together halfway around, stuff with newpaper, and staple closed. Hang these stuffed cut-outs from the four corners of the diamond. Display in library.

7. On and Off the Field. Have readers complete a crossword puzzle of baseball careers other than the players. Include jobs both on field (umpire, coach, manager, bat boy, etc.) and off field (owner, sports announcer, publicity, concessions, etc.).

8. Minor Leagues. Give children a list of farm teams, their rank (AAA, AA, or A), their location, and the major league team with which they are affiliated (AA-New Britain, CT, Red Sox, etc.). Have children locate these cities on a United States map.

9. Batting Helmets. For each helmet, place a white heavy paper soup bowl upside down on a table. Cut a visor of white poster board to fit around one-third of the bowl. Glue or staple the visor onto the rim of the bowl. Trim off the excess rim. Children can paint the batting helmets the colors of their favorite teams.

10. All-Star Teams. Draw or post a large picture of a baseball diamond. Have children help you label the nine field positions, plus other features (dugouts, bullpens, batter's circle, etc.). Then ask children to think of the perfect baseball team. Have them name their favorite players for the nine positions, plus back-up players, for both the American and National leagues.

11. Baseball Stories. Read "Casey at the Bat" or another baseball story. Have children write and illustrate their own stories or poems about a baseball player, game, team, or a day at the ballpark.

12. Uniforms. Show children pictures of baseball uniforms, past and present. Give children sheets of paper on which an outline of a baseball uniform has been drawn. Children can color the uniform to match any big league outfit, or make up their own design.

13. Cards and Other Collectibles. Invite a collector to display his baseball card collection and other baseball memorabilia. Talk to children about collecting baseball souvenirs as a hobby.

14. World Series. Set up a chart listing all the teams in the American and National leagues, East and West divisions. Every day, update the chart to show how many wins and losses each team has, and its division ranking. At the last meeting before the closing ceremony, determine the top two teams in each division (eight teams total). Let children vote to show which teams they think will win their divisions and league pennants. Then vote for the team they think will win the World Series.

15. Closing Ceremony: Baseball Camp. Encourage children to bring in their baseballs, bats, and gloves to the library. Invite Little League coaches and players (in uniform) to instruct children in holding and swinging a bat, pitching, catching, and fielding. If the party is indoors, children will not be able to hit the ball, but a demonstration of the basics can still be given. Little Leaguers can talk about their experiences to the group. Children can participate in a baseball quiz (Is the runner safe or out? etc.).

Theme-Related Books

For Younger Readers

Isadora, Rachel. *Max.* Macmillan, 1976.
Kessler, Leonard P. *Old Turtle's Baseball Stories.* Greenwillow, 1982.
Martin, Charles E. *Sam Saves the Day.* Harper, 1990.
Oechsli, Kelly. *Mice at Bat.* Harper, 1990.
Parish, Peggy. *Play Ball, Amelia Bedelia.* Harper, 1972.
Rey, Margaret. *Curious George Plays Baseball.* Houghton, 1990.
Sachs, Marilyn. *Fleet-Footed Florence.* Doubleday, 1981.
Stadler, John. *Hooray for Snail.* Crowell, 1984.`

For Older Readers

Adler, David A. *Jeffrey's Ghost and the Leftover Baseball Team.* Holt, 1984.
Baron, Nancy. *Tuesday's Child.* Atheneum, 1984.
Christopher, Matt. *The Fox Steals Home.* Little, 1978.
Cohen, Barbara. *Thank You, Jackie Robinson.* Lothrop, 1986.
Fisher, Leonard Everett. *Noonan: A Novel About Baseball, ESP and Time Warps.* Avon, 1978.
Giff, Patricia Reilly. *Left-Handed Shortstop.* Delacorte, 1980.
Konigsburg, E.L. *All About the B'Nai Bagels.* Atheneum, 1969.
Park, Barbara. *Skinnybones.* Knopf, 1982.
Slote, Alfred. *Hang Tough, Paul Mather.* Lippincott, 1973.
Tunis, John R. *World Series.* HBJ, 1990.

Nonfiction

Aaseng, Nathan. *Baseball: You Are the Manager.* Lerner, 1983.
Broekel, Ray. *Baseball.* Childrens, 1982.
Brondfield, Jerry. *Baseball's Hall of Fame.* Scholastic, 1983.
Dolan, Edward F., Jr. *Great Moments in the World Series.* Watts, 1982.
Jacobs, G., and McCrory, J.R. *Baseball Rules in Pictures.* Putnam, 1985.
Jaspersohn, William. *Ballpark: One Day Behind the Scenes at a Major League Game.* Little, 1980.

————. *Bat, Ball, Glove.* Little, 1989.
Jobe, Frank W., and Moynes, Diane Radovich. *The Official Little League Fitness Guide.* Simon and Schuster, 1984.
Ritter, Lawrence S. *The Story of Baseball.* Morrow, 1983.
Thorn, John, and Carroll, Bob, editors. *The Whole Baseball Catalogue.* Simon and Schuster, 1990.

Films and Videos

Babe Ruth and *Casey at the Bat.* DIS/COR, 9 mins.
The Bad News Bears. (Rated PG.) PAR, 102 mins.
Dinosaur Bob and His Adventures with the Family Lizardo. RR, 30 mins.
How to Play Baseball. DIS/COR, 8 mins.
Jose Canseco's Baseball Camp. FHE, 54 mins.

——— LET'S MAKE BOOKS! ———

(Book Publishing)

Have you ever wondered how a book got to be a book? Here's your chance to find out! This summer, ———— Library is going to help you write, illustrate, and publish your very own books. Find out what happens when a book goes to press. Experiment with block printing and stenciling. Meet author ———— in person and hear him/her read from his/her works. You'll find that books are as much fun to make as they are to read. So come along and ***Let's Make Books!***

Promotional Items

1. Sign reading "Make-Your-Own Books, Inc." for check-out area
2. "Press Passes" (membership cards)
3. Bookmark cut-outs (for books read)
4. Reading logs entitled "Book Contract"
5. "Let's Make Books!" bookmarks
6. Published Author Awards (certificates of participation)
7. Bookplates (stickers reading "This book belongs to ————") (game prizes)

Activities

1. Bulletin Board. Display books made by children in the past, plus an autograph book, along the four edges of the bulletin board. In the center, post some of the materials used in making the books (sheets of paper, crayons, a paint palette, etc.). Caption: LET'S MAKE BOOKS!

2. Reading Incentive Game: Book Production. Draw a large book standing upright, and a ladder leaning against it. Label the rungs of the ladder with the steps which occur in the production of a book. Start a cut-out of a person at the bottom of the ladder with "Author thinks of an idea." End on top with "Consumer reads the book." Advance the marker one rung for every X books read by the group. Readers will win a prize if the game is completed by the closing ceremony.

3. Newbery Medal Books. On a separate shelf, display Newbery Medal and Honor books. Give booktalks on some of them. Encourage children to read them by placing a gold star on the bookmark cut-out of every Newbery book that is read to distinguish it from the other books.

4. Book-Makers: Read *How a Book Is Made*, by Aliki; *The Puzzle of Books*, by Michael Kehoe; or another book about publishing. Assign children to play the various people who help make a book and let them act out their jobs. Have children complete a word search puzzle of publishing career terms.

5. Wordless Books. Supply several wordless books for children to examine. Have them "read" the stories aloud in their own words. Discuss different interpretations or "readings" of a particular book. Supply art materials or old magazines for children to cut up, and let them make their own wordless books.

6. Publishing Terms. Pass out a diagram of the different parts of a book and a fact sheet of publishing terms (proofs, color separator, film negatives, printing press, bindery, etc.). Have children complete a crossword puzzle with these terms.

7. Going to Press. Display actual film negatives, color proofs, and picture book sheets (before they are cut and bound). Show a film of what happens when a book goes to press (Reading Rainbow episode: *Simon's Book*).

8. Color Combinations. Use red, yellow, and blue transparencies and black outlining to show children how these four colors are combined to make all the colors in a picture book. Provide an assortment of stencils, white paper, red/yellow/blue pencils, and black markers, so that children can try it themselves. Outline a stencil with the black marker. Color it in with a pencil. Add a color over it and note the new color.

9. Block Printing. Cut several large potatoes in half. Let children etch designs in them with pointed popsicle sticks. Provide poster paint and paper and use the cut potatoes for block printing. Or, supply washable ink and several printing stamps for children to experiment with.

10. Critics. Discuss the role of a book reviewer. Then tell children to read a book of their choice and write a review of it. Would they recommend the book to anyone? Why or why not? Who would most likely want to read the book?

11. Print Media. Discuss print media with children (magazines, newspapers, hardcover and paperback books, etc.). How are they different or alike? What are their uses? Ask children to name different types of books (fiction, nonfiction, genres, etc.). Tell them each child is going to make his own book. Help them choose their topics and the type of book they want to write.

12. Make Your Own Book. Supply paper and drawing materials. Help children write and illustrate their own stories. Anyone who does not want to write a story may draw or block-print pages of pictures to combine into an art book. Make sure each book has a title page with the author's name. Use sheets of oak tag for front and back covers. Bind with looseleaf rings.

13. Dewey Numbers. Give an introduction to the Dewey Decimal System. Help children classify and label their own books with Dewey numbers.

14. Autograph Books. Supply sheets of colored paper. Let each child choose several to make an autograph book. Use sheets of oak tag for the front and back covers. Let children design front covers using their own names (Joey's Autograph Book). Tie with yarn to bind books. Save autograph books for children to sign at the closing ceremony.

15. Closing Ceremony: Meet an Author. Invite one or more local children's book authors to read their works and speak to the children. Have children read their own books aloud to the group. Let them sign each other's autograph books.

Theme-Related Books

For Younger Readers

Amoss, Berthe. *The Great Sea Monster: or, A Book by You.* Parents, 1975.
Bauer, Caroline Feller. *Too Many Books!* Warne, 1984.
Bonsall, Crosby. *Tell Me Some More.* Harper, 1961.
Bruna, Dick. *I Can Read.* Methuen, 1965.
Delton, Judy. *The Goose Who Wrote a Book.* Carolrhoda, 1985.
Duvoisin, Roger. *Petunia.* Knopf, 1950.
Hutchins, Pat. *The Tale of Thomas Mead.* Greenwillow, 1980.
Krauss, Ruth. *Is This You?* Scholastic, 1968.
Maris, Ron. *My Book.* Puffin, 1983.
Ormondroyd, Edward. *Broderick.* Houghton, 1969.

For Older Readers

Cleary, Beverly. *Dear Mr. Henshaw.* Morrow, 1983.
_____. *Emily's Runaway Imagination.* Morrow, 1961.
Conford, Ellen. *Jenny Archer, Author.* Little, 1989.
Greenwald, Sheila. *Give Us a Great Big Smile, Rosy Cole.* Little, 1981.
_____. *The Mariah Delany Lending Library Disaster.* Houghton, 1977.
Hahn, Mary Downing. *Daphne's Book.* Clarion, 1983.

Manes, Stephen. *Be a Perfect Person in Just Three Days!* Houghton, 1982.
Miles, Betty. *Maudie and Me and the Dirty Book.* Knopf, 1980.
Sachs, Marilyn. *A Summer's Lease.* Dutton, 1979.
Terris, Susan. *Author! Author!* Farrar, 1990.

Nonfiction

Aliki. *How a Book Is Made.* Harper, 1986.
Asher, Sandy. *Where Do You Get Your Ideas? Helping Young Writers Begin.* Walker, 1987.
Bernstein, Bonnie. *Writing Crafts Workshop.* Pitman, 1982.
Broekel, Ray. *I Can Be an Author.* Childrens, 1986.
Greenfield, Howard. *Books: From Writer to Reader.* Crown, 1976.
Harmon, Margaret, editor. *Working with Words: Careers for Writers.* Westminster, 1977.
Kehoe, Michael. *The Puzzle of Books.* Carolrhoda, 1982.
Tchudi, Susan. *The Young Writer's Handbook.* Scribner's, 1984.
Warren, Jean. *1-2-3 Books.* Warren, 1989.
Weiss, Harvey. *How to Make Your Own Books.* Harper, 1974.

Films and Videos

The Incredible Book Escape. CHUR, 16 mins.
Let's Make Up a Story. COR, 10 mins.
NeverEnding Story. WAR, 94 mins.
Simon's Book. RR, 30 mins.
Storymaker. CHUR, 14 mins.
Why We Need Reading: The Piemaker of Ignoramia. LCA/COR, 12 mins.

——— CAMP READSALOT ———

(Camping, Summer Camp)

It's time to register for summer camp at _____ Library. Become a Junior Trooper and set up a tent at our campsite. Make a compass and plot a hiking trail. Identify plants and animals in our nature exploration game. Sing campfire songs and make craft items. Collect merit stickers for each activity you do and book you read. Come to our Camp Jamboree and see live demonstrations of camping skills. So go on—take a hike! You're in for lots of fun at **Camp Readsalot!**

Promotional Items

1. Sign reading "Camp Readsalot Office" for check-out area
2. "Junior Trooper" cards (membership cards)
3. Tent cut-outs (for books read)
4. Reading logs entitled "Camping Manual" (Note: Reading logs should have two separate sections for stickers—one for books read and the other for activities completed)
5. "Camp Readsalot" bookmarks
6. Summer Survivor certificates (certificates of participation)
7. Whistles (game prizes)

Activities

1. Bulletin Board. Draw an enlarged copy of a "Camping Manual" reading log with all the reading and activity stickers filled in. Then post pictures to represent all the planned activities: a tent, a trail map, the various craft items to be made, the jamboree demonstrations, etc. Also post book cut-outs with names of theme-related books. Caption: CAMP READSALOT.

2. Reading Incentive Game: Pack the Backpack. Sketch the outline of a large backpack. Next to it, post cut-outs to represent necessary items to pack when going camping. (Cut-outs may be in the shape of the represented items, or just blocks labeled with the items' names.) For every X books read by the group, place one cut-out in the backpack. Readers will win a prize if all items are in the backpack by the closing ceremony.

3. Buddies. Encourage readers who have camping or scouting experience to discuss their experiences with the group. Campers may bring in some of their equipment and explain how it works, talk about where they have hiked, etc. Pair up experienced campers with children who are new to it. Award Buddy Merit Stickers to all participants.

4. Friendship. Gimp is a popular summer camp craft item. Teach children how to knot gimp into strands. These can be made into friendship bracelets when long enough. Friendship bracelets can also be made by braiding yarn or embroidery thread and tying the ends together. Award Friendship Merit Stickers.

5. Summer Camp. Have children complete a word search puzzle of summer camp activities (crafts, swimming, hiking, baseball, etc.). Award Summer Camp Merit Stickers.

6. Trail Blazers. Show children how to read a topographic map. Let them identify some hiking trails. Then map a good route to take. How far should you hike in one day? Where is a good place to set up camp? Award Trail Blazer Merit Stickers.

7. Compasses. Children can make pretend compasses out of plain paper plates. Mark N, S, E, and W and attach a black arrow with a brass fastener in the center. Let children practice orienting themselves with their compasses. Assign a definite place (such as the check-out desk) to be "North." Have children face in another direction, holding their compasses so that N and S are directly in front, E is at the right, and W is at the left. Tell them to point the arrow in the direction of the designated north point. Let children determine in which direction they are facing. Award Compass Merit Stickers.

8. Safe Campers. Ask readers to help you make a list of camping and hiking safety rules (stay on the trail, pick up your trash, etc.). Let them draw pictures to illustrate some of these rules. Display in library. Award Safe Camper Merit Stickers.

9. Tent Pitching. Display pictures of different types of tents and explain their uses. Let children set up a simple tent as a group project. Award Tent Pitching Merit Stickers.

10. Campfire Sing-Along. Sit children in a circle on the floor and sing camp songs. Share campfire stories. This may be done in a darkened room with a lantern in the middle to represent a campfire. Award Campfire Sing-Along Merit Stickers.

11. Survival. Tell children to imagine they have been shipwrecked and are stranded on a tropical island. What items would they need to have with them in order to survive? List all suggestions, then narrow the list to 12 items. Alter the scenario to being stranded in the desert, on a mountain in the winter, etc. Note how the list changes. Award Survival Merit Stickers.

12. Pouch Craft. Pre-cut leather or canvas pieces in two sizes: 4″ squares, and 4″ by 5″ rectangles. Punch holes along three edges of each square piece. Place it on a rectangle piece and punch holes to match. Let children sew the three edges together with gimp to make a pouch. Place stick-on velcro dots in the center of the open square edge and on the underside of the 1″ flap to close the pouch. Award Pouch Craft Merit Stickers.

13. Nature Exploration Game. Prepare by noting the Dewey Decimal numbers of several nonfiction books, each dealing with one type of plant, animal, or aspect of nature. List 15 numbers, in random order, on Nature Identification Sheets. Then divide children into teams. Give each team a Nature ID Sheet (make all sheets different to avoid confusion). The teams must look up the books which correspond to the Dewey numbers on their sheets, and list the book titles next to the proper numbers. Award Nature Exploration Merit Stickers.

14. Nature Craft. Nature materials, such as twigs, leaves, and pine cones, can be gathered when hiking and made into craft items. Have children draw pictures on white oak tag. Then cut four sticks slightly longer than the sides of the picture to make a frame. Lay the sticks on the picture edges and notch the twigs where they cross. Glue or tie the corners in place. Glue the frame to the picture. Award Nature Craft Merit Stickers.

15. Closing Ceremony: Camp Jamboree. Invite some Boy Scouts and

Girl Scouts to set up booths and demonstrate camping skills to the children. These may include arranging rocks or wood to make a campfire; rolling up a sleeping bag; first aid; tying knots; etc.

Theme-Related Books

For Younger Readers

Bach, Alice. *The Most Delicious Camping Trip*. Harper, 1976.
Brown, Marc. *Arthur Goes to Camp*. Little, 1982.
Carrick, Carol. *Sleep Out*. Houghton, 1979.
Cushman, Doug. *Camp Big Paw*. Harper, 1991.
Himmelman, John. *The Super Camper Caper*. Silver, 1991.
Marshall, James. *The Cut-Ups at Camp Custer*. Viking, 1989.
Parish, Peggy. *Amelia Bedelia Goes Camping*. Greenwillow, 1985.
Robins, Joan. *Addie Runs Away*. Harper, 1989.
Stock, Catherine. *Sophie's Knapsack*. Lothrop, 1988.
Weiss, Nicki. *Battle Day at Camp Belmont*. Greenwillow, 1985.

For Older Readers

Conford, Ellen. *Hail, Hail Camp Timberwood*. Little, 1978.
Gauch, Patricia Lee. *Night Talks*. Putnam, 1983.
Hallowell, Tommy. *Shot from Midfield*. Penguin, 1990.
Johnson, Annabel, and Johnson, Edgar. *The Grizzly*. Harper, 1964.
Levy, Elizabeth. *Dracula Is a Pain in the Neck*. Harper, 1983.
Norby, Lisa. *Crazy Campout*. Knopf, 1989.
Roy, Ron. *Nightmare Island*. Dutton, 1981.
Schwartz, Joel L. *Upchuck's Summer Revenge*. Doubleday, 1990.
Smith, Robert Kimmel. *Jelly Belly*. Delacorte, 1981.
Stolz, Mary. *A Wonderful, Terrible Time*. Harper, 1967.

Nonfiction

Arnold, Eric. *Lights Out! Kids Talk About Summer Camp*. Little, 1986.
Boy Scouts of America. *Camping*. BSA, 1984.
Cooke, Tom. *Hide and Seek Camping Trip: A Sesame Street Book*. McKay, 1990.
Foster, Lynne. *Take a Hike! The Sierra Club Beginner's Guide to Hiking and Backpacking*. Little, 1990.
Nagle, Avery, and Leeming, Joseph. *Fun with Naturecraft*. Lippincott, 1964.
Neimark, Paul. *Camping and Ecology*. Childrens, 1981.
Paul, Aileen. *Kids Camping*. Doubleday, 1973.
Randolph, John. *Backpacking Basics*. Prentice, 1982.
Winn, Marie, compiler. *The Fireside Book of Fun and Game Songs*. Simon and Schuster, 1974.
Zarchy, Harry. *Let's Go Camping: A Guide to Outdoor Living*. Knopf, 1964.

Films and Videos

Campfire Thrillers. WEST, 30 mins.
Old Lady's Camping Trip. NFBC, 9 mins.
The Parent Trap. DIS, 124 mins.
Solo. PYR, 16 mins.
Three Days on the River in a Red Canoe. RR, 30 mins.

——— TEST DRIVE A BOOK ———

(Cars)

Start your engines! It's time to rev up for another great summer at _____ Library. Pick up your Driver's Permit and learn about all types of cars and how they work. Race model cars, follow the Grand Prix, and help your team win the Bookrace 500. Design your own customized car and license plate. Create a car wash and join our automobile factory. View show cars and talk with their owners. All this plus lots of terrific books about cars are waiting for you right now in our showroom! So come on in and **Test Drive a Book** *today!*

Promotional Items

1. Sign reading "Showroom" for check-out area
2. "Driver's Permits" (membership cards)
3. Tire cut-outs (for books read)
4. Reading logs entitled "Track Record"
5. "Test Drive a Book" bookmarks
6. Licensed Reader certificates (certificates of participation)
7. Miniature cars (game prizes)

Activities

1. Bulletin Board. Post in an X formation at the left of the board two racing flags. Further right, draw a book with wheels on it, and a puff of smoke behind it to indicate motion. Draw a child riding on the book. Caption: TEST DRIVE A BOOK.

2. Reading Incentive Game: The Bookrace 500. Draw a race course with two identical tracks paced off in squares. Divide all the readers into two evenly matched groups, Team 1 and Team 2. Place race cars 1 and 2 at the starting line. For every X books read by a team, the appropriate car advances one square. All readers will win a prize if at least one car reaches the finish line by the closing ceremony. The members of the winning team may receive an additional prize.

3. Car Wash. Divide children into two or more groups. Tell each group to create a "car wash" by using their bodies as brushes, making water sounds, blowing air to dry cars, etc. Then, one at a time, let children from one group pretend to be cars, crawling on their hands and knees through the car wash. Then have groups switch places.

4. How They Work. Invite a mechanic to talk to children about how a car works, and the care and maintenance of a car. Display a model or show pictures of car parts. Let children label the parts on a diagram of a car. Pass out a fact sheet about cars and have children complete a crossword puzzle with these terms.

5. Wacky Cars. Discuss wacky (customized and show) cars with children. Let children draw and name their own wacky cars. Display in library.

6. Memory Game. Sit children in a circle. One person will start the game by saying, "I went on vacation, and in my car I packed (one item)." Let each person have a turn recalling the previous item(s) and adding one more to the list. See how many things the children can remember.

7. Safety. Invite a policeman to talk about car safety and traffic rules.

8. Types of Cars. Have children complete a word search puzzle of types of cars.

9. Model Cars. Supply an assortment of small boxes or cartons, spools, markers, paper, glue, etc. Cover the boxes with plain paper and let children create their own model cars. Use spools for wheels, draw or glue on doors and windows, etc.

10. Car Sales. Display pictures or models of old-fashioned and modern cars. Discuss how they differ. Tell children to pretend they are car dealers. Let each child pick a favorite car and invent a sales pitch for it.

11. Car Power. Tell children that early cars did not run on gasoline. Mention steam and electricity as short-lived energy sources for "the horseless carriage." Ask children to think of other energy sources which may be used to power a car. Encourage them to be creative, such as using shaken-up cans of soda or tightly wound rubber bands.

12. License Plates. Provide rectangles of poster board in various colors. Let children use stickers, stencils, and markers to create their own designer license plates. Display in library.

13. Grand Prix. Give each child a map of Europe and a list of cities. Tell children to locate these cities and connect them with a line in order to trace the route of the Grand Prix.

14. Automobile Factory. Ahead of time, cut a number of paper pieces to represent several car components (chassis, tires, body, bumpers, etc.). Assemble one car to show children how to put it together and what the finished product will look like. Then sit children down at a table, in a factory assembly line. Each child will have a pile of one item in front of him, which he will glue onto the picture at his turn. Onto a piece of oak tag, the first child will glue the chassis; then next child, one tire; the next, another tire; etc. Continue down the line until enough car pictures for all the children have been made.

15. Closing Ceremony: Car Show. For an outdoor show, invite members of the community who exhibit customized, historic, or sports cars to display and discuss them. For an indoor show, display a model automobile race track on a large table. Let children take turns racing the cars. Have children color and cut out paper people and buildings to make a community around the track.

Theme-Related Books

For Younger Readers

Brandenberg, Franz. *What's Wrong with a Van?* Greenwillow, 1987.
Burningham, John. *Mr. Gumpy's Motor Car.* Crowell, 1972.
Goor, Ron, and Goor, Nancy. *In the Driver's Seat.* Crowell, 1982.
Greenblat, Rodney A. *Uncle Wizzmo's New Used Car.* Harper, 1990.
Hillert, Margaret. *Birthday Car.* Follett, 1986.
Kraus, Robert. *Bumpy the Car.* Putnam, 1985.
Newton, Laura P. *William the Vehicle King.* Bradbury, 1987.
Oxenbury, Helen. *The Car Trip.* Dial, 1983.
Scarry, Richard. *Richard Scarry's Cars and Trucks and Things That Go.* Golden, 1983.
Stadler, John. *Rodney and Lucinda's Amazing Race.* Bradbury, 1981.

For Older Readers

Altman, Millys N. *Racing in Her Blood.* Harper, 1980.
Bumble, William. *Speedy Wheels.* Scholastic, 1988.
Christopher, Matt. *Drag Strip Racer.* Little, 1982.
Juster, Norton. *The Phantom Tollbooth.* Random, 1961.
Leoper, John. *Galloping Gertrude: By Motor Car in 1908.* Atheneum, 1980.
Robertson, Keith. *Henry Reed's Journey.* Viking, 1963.
Singer, Marilyn. *The Case of the Cackling Car.* Harper, 1985.
Spurr, Elizabeth. *Mrs. Minetta's Car Pool.* Macmillan, 1985.
Taylor, Mildred. *The Gold Cadillac.* Dial, 1987.

Nonfiction

Barrett, Norman. *Racing Cars.* Watts, 1985.
Cole, Joanna. *Cars and How They Go.* Harper, 1983.
Earl, Lawrence H. *The Usborne Guide to Model Cars.* Usborne, 1981.

Ford, Barbara. *The Automobile: Inventions That Changed Our Lives.* Walker, 1987.
Kanetzke, Howard. *The Story of Cars.* Raintree, 1987.
Lerner, Mark. *Careers in Auto Racing.* Lerner, 1980.
Lord, Harvey G. *Car Care for Kids . . . and Former Kids.* Atheneum, 1983.
Ready, Kirk L. *Custom Cars.* Lerner, 1982.
Sobol, Donald. *Encyclopedia Brown's Book of Wacky Cars.* Morrow, 1987.
Weiss, Harvey. *Model Cars and Trucks and How to Build Them.* Harper, 1989.

Films and Videos

Alexander and the Car with a Missing Headlight. WW, 14 mins.
The Car of Your Dreams. PYR, 18 mins.
Chitty Chitty Bang Bang. MGM/UA, 142 mins.
The Love Bug. DIS, 110 mins.
Tooth-Gnasher Superflash. RR, 30 mins.
What on Earth! NFBC, 10 mins.

— CHOCK FULL OF CHOCOLATE —

(Chocolate)

If you like chocolate (and who doesn't?), you won't want to miss a chocolate-filled day at _____ Library this summer. Experiment with new flavors of hot chocolate. Design your own chocolate bar and wrapper. Make chocolate-scented stationery. Participate in a chocolate poll. Create a chocollage. Build a cacao pod. Draw a poster for National Chocolate Day. Sample some chocolate and come to our Chocomania Party. No doubt about it, _____ Library will be **Chock Full of Chocolate** *this summer!*

Promotional Items

1. Sign reading "Chocolatier" for check-out area
2. "Choco-liker" cards (membership cards)
3. Chocolate kisses cut-outs (for books read)
4. Reading logs entitled "Chocolate Log"
5. "Chock Full of Chocolate" bookmarks

6. Chocolate Gourmet certificates (certificates of participation)
7. Gift certificates for a free chocolate item at a local store or restaurant (game prizes)

Activities

1. Bulletin Board. Post a large red construction-paper valentine, trimmed with white lace, to look like a box of Valentine's Day chocolates. Inside the box, post cut-outs of individual chocolates containing the names of the reading club members. All around, post pictures of chocolate bunnies, kisses, cakes, eclairs, and other foods. Caption: CHOCK FULL OF CHOCOLATE.

2. Reading Incentive Game: Chocolate Production. Post pictures to represent the stages involved in making chocolate. Start from the cacao tree, through processing the beans, to molding and packaging chocolate, to eating it (finish). Draw a conveyor belt trail from start to finish. Advance a cacao bean marker one space for every X books read by the group. Readers will win a prize if the trail is completed by the closing ceremony.

3. Sampler. Provide small samples of different types of chocolate: milk, semi-sweet, bittersweet, plus white chocolate and carob. Let children taste each type (it's a good idea to offer water in between tastes). Then have children list their preferences. Which type do they like best?

4. Cacao Pods. Help children understand how cacao beans grow by making cacao pods. Give each child a brown paper bag from which to cut out two football-shaped pods. (If there is writing on the bags, turn the cut-outs so that the plain sides face outward, one on top of the other.) Staple the two cut-outs together, leaving an opening at one end. Use almond-shaped pieces of cardboard or kidney beans as the cacao beans. Stuff 20 to 40 beans inside the pod. Then staple the opening closed. You may choose to build a cacao tree, making the trunk and leaves out of construction paper. Staple the pods onto the tree.

5. Chocolate Search. Have children complete a word search puzzle of chocolate foods.

6. Recipe Book. Have children write recipes which contain chocolate. They can make up a recipe or find one in a cookbook that they like. Collect these and compile them into a Chocolate-Lovers Recipe Book to keep in the library.

7. Create-Your-Own. Ask children to name some things that can be in a chocolate bar. List all answers. Then have each child create a new kind of chocolate bar, using any of the ingredients listed, or some others. They should describe the new chocolate bar in words and pictures.

8. Wrap It Up. Supply drawing materials. Have children design wrappers for the chocolate bars they created, or for a bar that already exists.

9. Hot Chocolate. Experiment with different flavors of hot chocolate. Help children mix cups of powdered hot chocolate. Then provide a variety of flavors to add to it (maraschino cherry juice, crushed peppermint candy, peanut butter chips, cinnamon candies, marshmallows, etc.). Each child can add one flavor per cup. Which is their favorite?

10. A World of Chocolate. Give children a list of countries that are producers of fine chocolates. Have children locate these countries on a world map. Also, have them find the countries in which cacao beans are grown.

11. Scented Stationery. Provide notepaper, some partially melted plain chocolate bars, and several stamps imprinted with a variety of designs. Using the chocolate bars as stamp pads, let children stamp pictures along the edges of the notepaper to make chocolate-scented stationery.

12. National Chocolate Day. Ask children to name some of the holidays at which chocolate is given. Then ask children to brainstorm ideas for a national holiday devoted to chocolate. When would it be? How would it be celebrated? Have children draw posters for National Chocolate Day.

13. Chocolate Poll. Throughout the summer, ask children to save the wrappers from the chocolate products they eat, and place them in a box in the library. After several weeks, empty the box, sort out and count the wrappers. List the results of this chocolate poll. Which type is the most popular? Save the wrappers for activity #14.

14. Chocollage. Provide lots of old magazines. Let children cut out pictures of chocolate or foods made from chocolate. Children may use these pictures plus the wrappers collected over the summer to create collages.

15. Closing Ceremony: Chocomania Party. Prepare a chocolate fondue and a buffet of items to dip in it. Include marshmallows, graham crackers, strawberries, bananas, melon slices, potato chips, unsalted pretzels, etc. After children sample the buffet, let them try to knock down a piñata shaped like a large cacao pod, which has been filled with wrapped chocolate candies.

Theme-Related Books

For Younger Readers

Catling, Patrick Skene. *The Chocolate Touch.* Morrow, 1979.
Douglas, Barbara. *The Chocolate Chip Cookie Contest.* Lothrop, 1985.
Wagner, Karen. *Chocolate Chip Cookies.* Holt, 1990.
Williams, Jay. *The Cookie Tree.* Parents, 1967.
Ziefert, Harriet. *Chocolate Mud Cake.* Harper, 1988.

For Older Readers

Dahl. Roald. *Charlie and the Chocolate Factory.* Knopf, 1964.
Manes, Stephen. *Chocolate-Covered Ants.* Scholastic, 1991.
Monsell, Mary Elise. *The Mysterious Cases of Mr. Pinn.* Atheneum, 1989.
Smith, Robert Kimmel. *Chocolate Fever.* Coward, 1972.

Nonfiction

Adoff, Arnold. *Chocolate Dreams.* Lothrop, 1989.
Ammon, Richard. *The Kid's Book of Chocolate.* Macmillan, 1987.
Black, Sonia, and Brigandi, Pat. *Chocolate, Chocolate, Chocolate: The Complete Book of Chocolate.* Scholastic, 1989.
Boynton, Sandra. *Chocolate: The Consuming Passion.* Workman, 1982.
Butts, David P., and Addison, E. Lee. *The Story of Chocolate.* Vaughn, 1967.
Mager, Marcy, and Mager, Michael. *The Chocolate Cookbook.* Scholastic, 1977.
Mitgutsch, Ali, et al. *From Cacao Bean to Chocolate.* Carolrhoda, 1981.
O'Neill, Catherine. *Let's Visit a Chocolate Factory.* Troll, 1988.
Sharfman, Amalie. *Papa's Secret Chocolate Desert.* Lothrop, 1972.
Smaridge, Norah. *The World of Chocolate.* Messner, 1969.

Films and Videos

The Chocolate Princess. AIMS, 4 mins.
Max's Chocolate Chicken. WW, 5 mins.
Willie Wonka and the Chocolate Factory. WAR, 100 mins.

—— COME JOIN THE CIRCUS! ——

(Circus)

Ladies and Gentlemen! The Greatest Show on Earth is now appearing at _____ Library! Enter the Big Top and create your own clown! Learn about people and animals who work at the circus! Watch live circus acts! Design a circus poster! Sample popcorn, play games, and perform in a circus yourself! For the most fun you can have this summer, **Come Join the Circus!**

Promotional Items

1. Sign reading "Center Ring" for check-out area
2. "Ticket—Good for All Attractions" (membership cards)
3. Reading logs entitled "Performance Schedule"
4. Balloon cut-outs (for books read)
5. "Come Join the Circus!" bookmarks

6. Main Attraction Awards (certificates of participation)
7. Balloons with library logo (game prizes)

Activities

1. Bulletin Board. Draw an outline of a circus Big Top which extends the length and height of the area. In the center, draw a picture of a ringmaster. Place three large brown circles in a triangular pattern around the ringmaster. Take head-shots of children and arrange them in circles. Caption: COME JOIN THE CIRCUS!

2. Reading Incentive Game: Build a Clown. Draw an outline of a clown. Post next to it various cut-outs needed to fill in the picture (clown head, body, legs, arms, facial features, clothes, polka-dots for costume, etc.). For every X books read by the group, add one piece to the outline. Readers will win a prize if the clown is completed by the closing ceremony.

3. Circus Posters. Ask children to tell you why they think the circus is called "The Greatest Show on Earth." Show them several circus posters. Provide art materials and let children design their own circus posters.

4. Big Tops. Provide strips of construction paper 4″ × 1″ in various colors, plus triangles 5″ × 5″ × 8″. On pieces of oak tag, let children paste eight strips side by side vertically to make a tent wall. Fold back the bottoms of the two center strips to make a triangular entrance. Paste a triangle atop the wall to be the tent roof. Children may embellish their pictures with crayons.

5. Circus Terms. Have children complete a word search puzzle of circus terms (sideshow, grandstand, ticket, trapeze, strong man, etc.).

6. Circus Jobs. Read a nonfiction book about circus people. Have a discussion about people who work at the circus—as performers, in sideshows, and behind the scenes. Ask children what circus jobs they would like to have. Let them draw pictures of themselves in their chosen roles.

7. Clown Faces. Prepare paper cut-out circles, ovals, triangles, and other shapes of various sizes and colors. Let children paste shapes on paper plates to create clown faces.

8. Circus Animals. Read a story about one or more circus animals. Let children name some animal acts, then draw pictures of their favorites.

9. Sideshow Games. Set up several games for children to play, such as a ring toss game, a bean-bag pitch, a fishing game, guess which cup the ball is under, knock down the pins, etc.

10. Ringmaster Doll. Using felt-tipped markers, have children draw hair, eyes, mouth, and a moustache on the rounded knob of slot-type clothespins. In black, color on boots to reach half-way up the legs. Color the area above the slot (coat front) red. Draw three yellow circles on the coat front for buttons. Twist a red pipe cleaner around the neck of the clothespin to make arms. Paste a black paper-cut top hat onto the head.

11. Circus Owners. Read *If I Ran the Circus*, by Dr. Seuss. Have children write stories of what they would do if they ran a circus. Collect and bind into a book called *If We Ran the Circus* to keep in the library.

12. The Circus Is Coming to Town. Give readers a state map and a list of towns. (Choose towns so that when they are connected in the order that they are listed, a picture of a Big Top will appear.) Tell children the circus is going to visit these places. Have them locate and mark each town. Then connect the marks to reveal the secret picture.

13. Popcorn. Make popcorn with the children and place a small amount in each of five bowls. Flavor each bowl differently, with parmesan cheese, taco seasoning, cinnamon, butter salt, and powdered fruit punch mix. Let children sample them. Give children their own paper cups of their favorite popcorn.

14. Backyard Circus. Assign children different roles, such as tight-rope walkers, a lion-tamer and lions, jugglers, trapeze artists, a person who is shot out of a cannon, etc. A librarian will be the ringmaster. Have children pantomime each circus act for the crowd. Simple costumes may be used.

15. Closing Ceremony: Circus Performance. Invite a clown, juggler, animal act, etc., to perform. Children may wear circus costumes and have a parade.

Theme-Related Books

For Younger Readers

Anno, Mitsumasa. *Dr. Anno's Magical Midnight Circus.* Weatherhill, 1972.
Cushman, Doug. *Mickey Takes a Bow.* Little, 1986.
Dr. Seuss. *If I Ran the Circus.* Random, 1980.
Freeman, Don. *Bearymore.* Viking, 1976.
Hill, Eric. *Spot Goes to the Circus.* Ventura, 1986.
Hoff, Syd. *Barkley.* Harper, 1975.
Lustig, Loretta, illustrator. *The Pop-Up Book of the Circus.* Random, 1979.
Modell, Frank. *Seen Any Cats?* Greenwillow, 1979.
Peet, Bill. *Pamela Camel.* Houghton, 1984.
Quackenbush, Robert. *Detective Mole and the Circus Mystery.* Lothrop, 1985.

For Older Readers

Ardizzone, Edward. *Paul, the Hero of the Fire.* Walck, 1962.
Beatty, Jerome, Jr. *Maria Looney and the Cosmic Circus.* Avon, 1978.
Hays, Wilma Pitchford. *Circus Girl Without a Name.* Washburn, 1970.
Lofting, Hugh. *Doctor Dolittle's Circus.* Delacorte, 1988.
Morris, Gilbert. *Barney Buck and the Phantom of the Circus.* Tyndale, 1985.
Potter, Beatrix. *The Fairy Caravan.* Penguin, 1986.
Powledge, Fred. *Born in the Circus.* HBJ, 1976.
Sutton, Jane. *Confessions of an Orange Octopus.* Dutton, 1983.
Wiese, Kurt. *Rabbit Bros. Circus: One Night Only.* Viking, 1963.

Nonfiction

Cassidy, Diane. *Circus People*. Little, 1985.
Fenten, D.X., and Fenton, Barbara. *Behind the Circus Scene*. Crestwood, 1980.
Harkonen, Helen B. *Circuses and Fairs in Art*. Lerner, 1965.
Harmer, Mabel. *The Circus*. Childrens, 1981.
Hintz, Martin. *Circus Workin's*. Messner, 1980.
Kirk, Rhina. *Circus Heroes and Heroines*. Hammond, 1972.
Klayer, Connie, and Kuhn, Joanna. *Circus Time! How to Put on Your Own Show*. Lothrop, 1979.
McGovern, Ann. *. . . If You Lived with the Circus*. Four Winds, 1972.
Prelutsky, Jack. *Circus*. Macmillan, 1974.
West, Robin. *Paper Circus: How to Create Your Own Circus*. Carolrhoda, 1984.

Films and Videos

Cannonball. PHX, 28 mins.
The Circus Baby. WW, 5 mins.
Circus Kids. BRIT, 16 mins.
Dumbo. DIS, 64 mins.
The Juggling Movie. BRIT, 10 mins.
Ringling Bros. Barnum & Bailey Circus. FHE, 110 mins.

—— CITY LOOKS AND BOOKS ——

(Cities, City Life)

It's summer in the city at _____ Library. Learn about the people who live and work in the city. Help create a model city. Find out about city transportation systems and build a bus. Decide how you would spend a fun day in the Big City. Design a city of the future. Go on a sightseeing tour of some of the great cities of the world. This summer, discover the many **City Looks and Books** at _____ Library.

Promotional Items

1. Sign reading "City Hall" for check-out area
2. "City Resident" cards (membership cards)

3. Parking meter cut-outs (for books read)
4. Reading logs entitled "Urban Development"
5. "City Looks and Books" bookmarks
6. Super Urbanite Awards (certificates of participation)
7. Pencil sharpeners or thermometers in the shape of a skyscraper (game prizes)

Activities

1. Bulletin Board. Along the edges, put up picture postcards of cities. If you live in or near a major city, use many postcard views of that city, past and present. Label each postcard to identify the scene shown. In the center area, sketch a background of high-rise buildings or another downtown scene. In the foreground, post a cut-out of an outdoor newsstand. On the newsstand, post magazine cut-outs with the titles and authors of fiction and nonfiction books about cities. Caption: CITY LOOKS AND BOOKS.

2. Reading Incentive Game: Skyscraper. Post a picture of the Empire State Building or another skyscraper. Clearly mark off the floors next to the building. Place an elevator cut-out (marker) on the ground floor. For every X books read by the group, move the elevator up one floor. Readers will win a prize if the elevator reaches the top floor by the closing ceremony.

3. Model City. Have the group create a model city. Provide cereal boxes and milk cartons of various shapes and sizes. Cover boxes with construction paper. Draw on features to make boxes look like apartment buildings, libraries, stores, movie theaters, and other city buildings. Boxes may be combined to make large structures, such as an office complex. Arrange the buildings on a table. Add roads, street signs, and toy cars. Adding on to the city can be an ongoing project throughout the summer.

4. Major Cities. Have children locate some modern major cities on a United States map, and on a world map. Ask them why they think many big cities are near the water.

5. Cities: Past, Present, and Future. Show children pictures of some early American cities. How did they differ from modern cities? How did people shop? Travel? Communicate? What did the buildings look like? Then ask children to imagine a city of the future. What would the buildings look like? How would people shop, travel, etc.? Divide children into small groups and have them draw their designs of a future city.

6. Transportation. Ask children to name some ways people get around in the city, or travel to and from the city. Show children a map of a city subway system. Then pass out half-gallon milk cartons and let children make buses. Unfold the pouring end of the carton and tape it down to make a flat side. Cover the carton with construction paper. Let children draw on windows, door, headlights, wheels, etc. Map out some bus routes on a city map.

7. 1-2-3 Red Light. Because cities are crowded places, traffic control is important. Let children play a traffic game called "1-2-3 Red Light." Line up all children but one at one end of a long room. The one child out is the caller, who stands at the opposite end, facing away from the other children. He can say "1-2-3 red light," "1-2-3 green light," or "1-2-3 yellow light." At "1-2-3" children walk quickly toward him. But as he calls out a color, he turns to face the walkers. If he says "red light," the children must freeze in place. If the caller catches anyone moving, that person must go back to the beginning and start again. If the caller says "green light," the children may continue walking. At "yellow light," children may hop forward on one foot. The caller can try to trick the walkers by quickly saying "1-2-3 green light, 1-2-3 red light." The first one to tag the caller gets to be the next caller.

8. Adopt a City. Let each child choose a major city, either in the United States or elsewhere in the world, to learn more about. Give children a form to fill in with certain facts about their cities (population, year founded, square miles, main industry, location, etc.). Teach children where to find this information. Post a large comparison chart on one wall and list the facts from everyone's papers. Provide children with the addresses of tourist information bureaus, so they can write away for more information on their cities. Help children figure out the distance in miles from your home town to their chosen cities. Construct a signpost indicating the cities and distances.

9. City Services. Ask children to name some city services and departments (education, sanitation, library, police, etc.). Have each child choose a city service and draw a poster about how important it is.

10. City Government. Show children a list of jobs in city government. Explain the duties of some of these positions. Have children complete a word search puzzle of city government jobs.

11. City Workers. Ask children to name some jobs in a city (other than government jobs). List all answers. Then have each child pantomime the action of one city worker, and let the others guess what it is.

12. City People. Ask children to name some types of people who live in the city. Include all ages, races, nationalities, economic and social situations, jobs, etc. Provide lots of old magazines. Have children cut out pictures of city people or street scenes. Glue them onto oak tag to make collages.

13. Entertainment. Show children the entertainment section of a city newspaper. List on a chalkboard the things city dwellers and visitors do for fun (go to movies, sports, discos; shop; etc.). Have children write a story or poem about how they would choose to spend a fun day in the Big City.

14. City vs. Country Life. Read a version of *The Country Mouse and the City Mouse*. Then show pictures of country and city scenes. Divide a chalkboard into two columns, labeled Country and City. Have children list the differences between the two.

15. Closing Ceremony: Sightseeing Tour. At various areas around the library, set up displays of the cities children adopted in activity #8 — one city per area. Displays should include posters and books of famous tourist attractions, appropriate music, and enough small souveniers for all the children (pins, postcards, little flags, tickets, etc.). Divide children into tour groups. With a librarian as a tour guide, visit each city and hear about its many features. Children should collect a souvenir from each city. After the tour, ask children which cities they would really like to visit some day.

Theme-Related Books

For Younger Readers

Gomi, Taro. *Bus Stops*. Chronicle, 1988.
Goodall, John S. *The Story of a Main Street*. Macmillan, 1987.
McCloskey, Robert. *Make Way for Ducklings*. Viking, 1941.
Maestro, Betsy. *Taxi: A Book of City Words*. Clarion, 1988.
Provensen, Alice, and Provensen, Martin. *Town and Country*. Crown, 1985.
Raskin, Ellen. *Nothing Ever Happens on My Block*. Atheneum, 1966.
Ringgold, Faith. *Tar Beach*. Dial, 1979.
Schick, Eleanor. *City in the Summer*. Macmillan, 1969.
_____. *City in the Winter*. Macmillan, 1970.
Stevenson, James. *Grandpa's Great City Tour: An Alphabet Book*. Greenwillow, 1983.

For Older Readers

Brooks, Jerome. *Make Me a Hero*. Dutton, 1980.
Corbett, Scott. *Cop's Kid*. Joy St., 1968.
Danzinger, Paula. *Remember Me to Harold Square*. Dell, 1989.
Hinton, S.E. *Rumble Fish*. Delacorte, 1975.
Hurwitz, Johanna. *Busybody Nora*. Morrow, 1976.
Myers, Walter Dean. *Fast Sam, Cool Clyde, and Stuff*. Viking, 1975.
Neville, Emily C. *The Seventeenth-Street Gang*. Harper, 1966.
Selden, George. *The Cricket in Times Square*. Farrar, 1960.
Stolz, Mary. *Noonday Friends*. Harper, 1965.

Nonfiction

Hirsch, S. Carl. *Cities Are People*. Viking, 1968.
Huff, Barbara A. *Greening the City Streets: The Story of Community Gardens*. Clarion, 1990.
Jupo, Frank. *Walls, Gates, and Avenues: The Story of the Town*. Prentice, 1964.
Kalman, Bobbie. *Early City Life*. Crabtree, 1983.
Lenski, Lois. *City Poems*. Walck, 1971.
Macaulay, David. *Underground*. Houghton, 1976.
Moorcraft, Colin. *Homes and Cities*. Watts, 1982.
Royston, Robert. *Cities*. Facts on File, 1985.
Unstead, R.J. *How They Lived in Cities Long Ago*. Arco, 1981.

Films and Videos

Animal Cafe. RR, 30 mins.
The Backstreet Six. PHX, 80 mins.
Communities and How They Work. BRIT, 12 mins.
Goggles! WW, 6 mins.
Plants and Animals in the City. NGEO, 2 films, 13 mins. each.
Tchiou Tchiou. BRIT, 15 mins.

—— READY-TO-WEAR BOOKS ——
(Clothes, Fashion)

> *Attention clothes-hounds, trendsetters, fashion plates, future models, designers, and everybody who likes clothes! The Library School of Fashion Design is now accepting applications for a summer of fun and creativity. Learn about historical and traditional costumes from many nations. Become a fashion critic and a fashion model. Find out what a tailor does and discover other careers in fashion. Design a hat and decorate a T-shirt. If you want to be in fashion this summer, come to _____ Library and check out our* **Ready-to-Wear Books.**

Promotional Items

1. Sign reading "Library School of Fashion Design" for check-out area
2. "Fashion Plate" cards (membership cards)
3. T-Shirt cut-outs (for books read)
4. Reading logs entitled "Patterns"
5. "Ready-to-Wear Books" bookmarks
6. Fashion Designer certificates (certificates of participation)
7. Plain T-shirts (game prizes)

Activities

1. Bulletin Board. Draw a large clothes rack with several clothes hangers, each holding a clothing item. On each item, write the title of a fiction or nonfiction book about some aspect of clothes or fashion. Above the rack, draw a shelf containing hatboxes which are also labeled with book titles. Caption: READY-TO-WEAR BOOKS.

2. Reading Incentive Game: Clothes of Many Lands. Post a large world map. Next to it, post labeled cut-outs representing types of traditional costume or dress from several countries (Scottish kilts, Indian saris, Dutch shoes, etc.). For every X books read by the group, post one cut-out in its proper country on the map. Readers will win a prize if all the cut-outs are on the map by the closing ceremony.

3. Weather Clothes. Give each child four sheets of paper with an identical sketch of a child. Label the pictures Spring, Summer, Fall, and Winter. Color in the pictures so that the child is wearing appropriate clothing for each season. Readers may add background details, such as weather and flowers, if desired.

4. Clothing Categories. Divide the children into five groups. Assign one category of clothing to each group: shoes, outerwear, hats, bottoms, and tops. Tell children to list as many types of their item as they can recall. For example, shoes: slippers, boots, sneakers, etc. Do not use brand names. Let the groups discuss their answers. Can some types be broken down further? (Boots: western, snow, etc.)

5. Work Clothes. Provide several types of hats, uniforms, and other work clothes. Let children try on different items and act out what a person who wears that outfit does. Can some items be worn by more than one type of worker? (Lab coat, overalls, etc.)

6. Shoe Prints. Have each child trace his shoes on a piece of construction paper. Cut out the shoe prints. Write the child's name on the underside of each print. Put all the right shoe prints in a pile and let children try to find their own without looking at the names. Then have children mount their prints on construction paper of a contrasting color. Note the child's name, age, shoe size, and date. Tell them to save their shoe prints and measure them against their shoe size next year.

7. Matching Socks. Children can play matching socks games as individuals or in teams. Place a huge pile of loose socks on the floor or in a box. Game A: Hold up one sock and have children find its mate. Game B: Tell children to find a particular type of sock (red knee socks, etc.). Game C: Tell children to find as many pairs of socks as they can within a certain time limit.

8. Historical Costumes. Invite someone from a local theater company or historical society to bring in some historical clothing items. Supplement with pictures and discuss the various styles of dress. What materials were used? How many layers of clothing were worn? How do they compare to today's styles?

9. Fashion Critics. Show pictures of children and teens in the 1950s, 1960s, and 1970s. Discuss their clothes. Are some styles coming back into fashion? Have children compile a list of what clothes and accessories are in fashion and out of fashion today. (Straight-leg jeans are "in," bell-bottoms are "out," etc.) Then let children make up a list of the "The Ten Best-Dressed People" and "The Ten Worst-Dressed People" today.

10. Fashion Model Books. Mount a headshot photo of each child on a sheet of construction paper, about one-third down the page. Cut holes in five sheets of white paper so that just the headshot will show through when the sheets are placed over the construction paper. Provide lots of old magazines. Let children cut out five similar-sized pictures of people wearing various outfits. Cut off the peoples' heads. Glue the pictures on the white papers, aligning the outfits directly under the holes. Make a cover sheet that says "Library Vogue, Featuring Superstar Model (Child's Name)." Bind the pages together, with the headshot page on the bottom, so that the child will appear to be wearing the different outfits as the pages are turned. Variation: Supply coloring-book pages of several outfits instead of using magazine pictures. Let children color the pictures and arrange books as before.

11. Sports Outfits. Show pictures of sports outfits and have children identify the sport in which they are worn. Ask children why they think the outfits look like they do. Note accessories, padding, and writing on clothing.

12. Tailor Shop. Explain that tailors and dressmakers must measure their clients in order to make their clothes fit properly. Pass out tape measures and show children how to measure height, chest, waist, hips, and inseam. Let girls measure girls and boys measure boys. Note their measurements. Then look at a chart of clothes sizes and have children find out what size shirts and pants they need. Display pattern pieces so children can see how clothes are cut and sewn.

13. Hat Boutique. Supply plain, inexpensive wide-brimmed costume hats. Provide glue and an assortment of colored feathers, toy whistles, stickers, buttons, glitter, lace, and other decorations. Let children assemble their own funny or fancy hats. They can wear these at the closing ceremony.

14. Careers. Give children a fact sheet on clothes-related careers (haberdasher, fashion designer, cobbler, model, sales, etc.). Have them complete a crossword puzzle with these terms.

15. Closing Ceremony: T-Shirt Factory. Children may wear their favorite T-shirts and fancy hats. Give children paper cut into the shape of a T-shirt and crayons with which to draw their own designs. Then give children white cloth T-shirts (the game prizes) and fabric crayons to decorate them with.

Theme-Related Books

For Younger Readers

Anderson, Leone Castell. *The Wonderful Shrinking Shirt.* Whitman, 1983.
Barrett, Judi. *Animals Should Definitely Not Wear Clothing.* Atheneum, 1970.
Carlstrom, Nancy White. *Jessie Bear, What Will You Wear?* Macmillan, 1986.
Daly, Niki. *Joseph's Other Red Sock.* Atheneum, 1982.
Estes, Eleanor. *The Hundred Dresses.* HBJ, 1944.
Hutchins, Pat. *You'll Soon Grow into Them, Titch.* Greenwillow, 1982.
Kellogg, Steven. *The Mystery of the Missing Red Mitten.*, Dial, 1974.
Maestro, Betsy. *On the Town: A Book of Clothing Words.* Crown, 1983.
Monsell, Mary. *Underwear!* Whitman, 1989.

Peek, Merle. *Mary Wore Her Red Dress and Henry Wore His Green Sneakers.* Clarion, 1985.
Rubel, Nicole. *I Can Get Dressed.* Macmillan, 1984.
Watanabe, Shigeo. *How Do I Put This On?* Philomel, 1980.
Wells, Rosemary. *Max's New Suit.* Dial, 1979.

For Older Readers

Bulla, Clyde Robert. *Shoeshine Girl.* Crowell, 1975.
Gaston, Susan. *New Boots for Salvador.* Ritchie, 1972.
Gibbons, Faye. *King Shoes and Clown Pockets.* Morrow, 1989.
Rinaldi, Ann. *The Last Silk Dress.* Holiday, 1988.
Roy, Ron. *Million Dollar Jeans.* Dutton, 1983.
Snyder, Carol. *Ike and Mama and the Once-a-Year Suit.* Coward, 1978.
Streatfield, Noel. *Traveling Shoes.* Dell, 1984.

Nonfiction

Beirne, Barbara. *Under the Lights: A Child Model at Work.* Carolrhoda, 1988.
Bozic, Patricia. *The Sweet Dreams Fashion Book: Looking Good Without Spending a Lot.* Bantam, 1983.
Buehr, Walter. *Cloth from Fiber to Fabric.* Morrow, 1965.
Cobb, Vicki. *Getting Dressed.* Lippincott, 1989.
———. *Supersuits.* Lippincott, 1975.
Cooke, Jean. *Costumes and Clothing.* Watts, 1987.
Hodgman, Ann. *A Day in the Life of a Fashion Designer.* Troll, 1987.
Sewell, Charlotte. *Clothes in History.* Wayland, 1983.
Thomas, Ruth. *Making Shoes.* Watts, 1987.
Wilcox, R. Turner. *Folk and Festival Costume of the World.* Scribner's, 1965.

Films and Videos

Charlie Needs a Cloak. WW, 8 mins.
Clothing. BRIT, 11 mins.
The Emperor's New Clothes. CBS/FOX, 60 mins.
The Purple Coat. RR, 30 mins.
A Three Hat Day. RR, 30 mins.

—— READING RODEO ——
(Cowboys, the Wild West)

Howdy, pardners! It's westward ho! at _____ Library this summer. Ride the range with us, and learn about life in the Old

West. Hear tales of outlaws and lawmen, of cattlemen and cowpokes. Watch the Pony Express rider carry mail across the country. Design a cattle brand. Pan for gold. Sing cowboy songs and join us in a square dance. Saddle up your horse and come on down for a rootin' tootin' time at the **Reading Rodeo!**

Promotional Items

1. Sign reading "Sheriff's Office" for check-out area
2. "Cowpoke" cards (membership cards)
3. Cowboy hat cut-outs (for books read)
4. Reading logs entitled "Reader's Roundup Roster"
5. "Reading Rodeo" bookmarks
6. Reading Rodeo Bronco-Buster Awards (certificates of participation)
7. Cowboy hats (game prizes)

Activities

1. Bulletin Board. Encircle the entire area with a length of thick rope. In the center, draw a picture of a cowboy to look like he is holding a lariat. Post cut-outs of horses on which the names of the reading club members have been written inside the lariat. Caption: READING RODEO.

2. Reading Incentive Game: The Pony Express. On a map of the United States, pace off the route of the Pony Express, with each step in the shape of a horseshoe. Start a cut-out of a Pony Express rider at Virginia. Advance the rider one horseshoe for every X books read by the group. Readers will win a prize if the rider reaches California by the closing ceremony.

3. Cowboy Legends. Ask children what they know about the Old West. Discuss cowboy legends (cowboy and Indian fights, saloons, covered wagons moving west, cattle stampedes, etc.). Read a cowboy story. Have children write their own stories.

4. Trail Drive. Read a nonfiction book about the life of a working cowboy. Discuss herding cattle and the trail drive. Locate on a map of the United States the Chisholm Trail and some famous boom towns.

5. Brand X. Show pictures of cattle brands. Let children draw their own brand designs. Cut the designs into potato halves and let children make prints with them.

6. Cowboy Terms. Give readers a fact sheet of various cowboy terms, such as ranch, lariat, roundup, branding, bronco, etc. Note the Spanish origins of many of these words and customs. Have readers compete a crossword puzzle with these terms.

7. Cowboy Clothing. Display or show pictures of cowboy clothing (bandana, chaps, boots, etc.). Explain the purpose of each item. Let each child trace and cut a pair of cowboy boots on brown paper bags. Provide crayons for children to draw designs on their boots.

8. Famous Cowboys. Ask children to name famous cowboys of whom they have heard. Were they "good guys" or "bad guys"? Read short biographies of a lawman and an outlaw. Give children a paper listing legendary lawmen in one column, and outlaws in another. Have children find these names in a word search puzzle.

9. Cowpoke Sing-Along. Play a record of cowboy songs. Teach some of the songs to the children.

10. Gold Rush. Hide several gold-colored rocks in a large sandbox ahead of time. Talk to children about the California Gold Rush. Give them sifters and let them pan for gold in the sandbox.

11. Western Ranch. Build a western ranch with Lincoln Logs. Have children play-act life on a ranch.

12. Horses. Show pictures of various types of horses, plus the saddles and other equipment that cowboys used for them. Discuss the importance of horses to cowboys. Give children pictures of horses to color.

13. Sheriff's Badges. Give children cut-outs of gold stars. Have each child write his name and the town of which he is the sheriff. Pin stars onto children's shirts with safety pins. Discuss the job of a sheriff.

14. Rodeo. Read a book about rodeos. Discuss the different rodeo events with children. Assign roles as bronco-riders, cattle-ropers, etc. Let them play-act rodeo events. Invite a guest to perform lasso tricks.

15. Closing Ceremony: Hoedown. Children can come in western attire. Play a square dance record and teach the children some dance steps. Play a game of horseshoes (make cardboard horseshoes for indoors).

Theme-Related Books

For Younger Readers

Anderson. L.W. *Blaze and Thunderbolt.* Macmillan, 1955.

Byars, Betsy. *The Golly Sisters Go West.* Harper, 1989.

Chandler, Edna Walker. *Cowboy Andy.* Random, 1959.

Hancock, Sibyl. *Old Blue.* Putnam, 1980.

Khalsa, Dayal Kaur. *Cowboy Dreams.* Crown, 1990.

Martin, Bill, Jr., and Archambault, John. *White Dynamite and Curly Kidd.* Holt, 1986.

Scott, Ann Herbert. *One Good Horse: A Cowpuncher's Counting Book.* Greenwillow, 1990.

Sewall, Marcia. *Riding That Strawberry Roan.* Viking, 1985.

For Older Readers

Benedict, Rex. *Last Stand at Goodbye Gulch.* Pantheon, 1974.
Brooks, Walter R. *Freddy the Cowboy.* Knopf, 1987.
Cohen, Peter. *Bee.* Atheneum, 1975.
Coren, Alan. *Arthur the Kid.* Little, 1977.
Deary, Terry. *The Custard Kid.* Carolrhoda, 1982.
Downing, Warwick. *Kid Curry's Last Ride.* Orchard, 1989.
Evans, Max. *My Pardner.* Houghton, 1972.
Fleischman, Sid. *By the Great Horn Spoon.* Little, 1963.
Greer, Gery. *Max and Me and the Wild West.* Crowell, 1972.
Kennedy, Richard. *The Rise and Fall of Ben Gizzard.* Little, 1978.

Nonfiction

Artman, John. *Cowboys: An Activity Book.* Good Apple, 1982.
Freedman, Russell. *Cowboys of the Wild West.* Clarion, 1985.
Keating, Bern. *Famous American Cowboys.* Random, 1977.
Malone, John Williams. *An Album of the American Cowboy.* Watts, 1971.
Martini, Teri. *Cowboys.* Childrens, 1981.
Patent, Dorothy Hinshaw. *Horses of America.* Holiday, 1981.
Stein, R. Conrad. *The Story of the Pony Express.* Childrens, 1981.
Surge, Frank. *Western Lawmen.* Lerner, 1969.
_____. *Western Outlaws.* Lerner, 1969.
Tinkleman, Murray. *Rodeo: The Great American Sport.* Greenwillow, 1982.
Zaidenberg, Arthur. *How to Draw the Wild West.* Crowell, 1972.

Films and Videos

Blaze Glory. PYR, 10 mins.
El Gaucho Goofy. DIS/COR, 8 mins.
The Great Toy Robbery. NFBC, 7 mins.
Meanwhile Back at the Ranch. RR, 30 mins.
Pecos Bill. CTI, 15 mins.
Rodeo Cowboy. BARR, 22 mins.

—— BONE UP ON DINOSAURS ——

(Dinosaurs, Fossils)

*Dinosaurs ruled the earth millions of years ago. But you can
have fun with them this summer at _____ Library. Find out where*

*and how dinosaurs lived. Hunt for bones and fossils. Construct
a dinosaur skeleton. Learn lots of fun facts and help your team
win the Dinosaur Game Show. If you really dig dinosaurs, this
is the place to be. Come to _____ Library and* **Bone Up on
Dinosaurs!**

Promotional Items

1. Sign reading "Dinosaur Museum" for check-out area
2. "Dinosaur Hunting Licenses" (membership cards)
3. Reading logs entitled "Dinosaur Diary"
4. Bone cut-outs (for each book read)
5. "Bone Up on Dinosaurs" bookmarks
6. Paleontologist Awards (certificates of participation)
7. Dinosaur stickers, plastic figures, or erasers (game prizes)

Activities

1. Bulletin Board. Post skeleton pictures of one or more large dinosaurs.
Write names of club members on the bones. Caption: BONE UP ON DINOSAURS!

2. Reading Incentive Game: The Dinosaur Eras. Draw a timeline and
list on it the names of some dinosaurs that lived during each era. For every X books
read by the group, post a dinosaur cut-out in its place along the timeline. Readers
will win a prize if all the dinosaurs are on the timeline by the closing ceremony.

3. Dino-Names. Give readers a fact sheet about various types of dinosaurs.
Include information for Activity #4. Have them complete a crossword puzzle with
these terms.

4. Categories. Have children list in separate columns which dinosaurs ate
plants and which ate meat. Then have children circle in green the dinosaurs that
lived in the water, circle in blue ones that could fly, and circle in red ones that lived
on land. (See fact sheet from Activity #3.) Which is the largest group?

5. Dino-Pets. Read *Danny and the Dinosaur*, by Syd Hoff. Let children
write and illustruate their own stories of what they would do if they had a dinosaur
as a pet.

6. Dino-Mobile. Give children two each of the following paper cut-outs:
stegosaurus, tyrannosaurus rex, pterodactyl, triceratops, and apatosaurus. Let
children decorate them with glitter and markers. Staple the two pieces together
halfway around, stuff with newspaper, and staple closed. Hang the dinosaurs on
metal coat hangers.

7. Dino-Life. Read a factual book about dinosaurs. Have children draw pictures of what they think the world was like when dinosaurs lived. Why do they think the dinosaurs died?

8. Models. Using modeling clay, let children mold dinosaurs and paint them when dry. Each child can name his dinosaur and tell you its special features.

9. Pantomime. Ask children to name their favorite dinosaurs. Have children act out how these dinosaurs lived.

10. Size-Wise. Explain that dinosaurs were various sizes. Give readers a fact sheet with the lengths and/or heights of several full-grown dinosaurs. Pass out a second sheet with measurements in the library (such as length of check-out desk, or distance from card catalog to picture book area, etc.). Have children compare the lengths and heights of dinosaurs to the library measurements to get an idea of the sizes of the animals.

11. Skeletons. Show children pictures or models of dinosaur skeletons. Provide an assortment of paper-cut dinosaur bones of various sizes. Let children paste onto contruction paper a dinosaur skeleton of their own design. Display in library.

12. Fossils. Tell how dinosaurs' footprints and bones are found in the ground. Let children make their own fossils and prints. Fill a long tray with wet plaster, about two inches deep. Children can make fingerprints, prints of toys, or press in small stones or leaves. After the plaster dries, let children identify their "fossils."

13. Bones. Locate on a world map where dinosaur bones have been discovered.

14. Scavenger Hunt. Let children pretend they are paleontologists hunting for dinosaur bones (popsicle sticks) and fossils (metal lids of frozen juice cans) which have been scattered about the library or outdoors. Prizes may be awarded for the most fossils and bones found.

15. Closing Ceremony: The Dinosaur Game Show. Divide group into teams of five or six children of varying ages. Acting as a game show host, ask questions (such as, "Which dinosaur had three horns?" or "What name was once given to 'apatosaurus'?") to one team at a time. If the first team misses the answer, the next team gets a chance. Give points for correct answers. Prizes can be awarded for the team that finishes with the most points.

Theme-Related Books

For Younger Readers

Blumenthal, Nancy. *Count-a-Saurus.* Four Winds, 1989.
Brown, Marc, and Krensky, Stephen. *Dinosaurs, Beware!* Little, 1982.
Carrick, Carol. *Patrick's Dinosaurs.* Clarion, 1983.
Cauley, Lorinda Bryan. *The Trouble with Tyrannosaurus Rex.* HBJ, 1990.
Joyce, William. *Dinosaur Bob and His Adventures with the Family Lizardo.* Harper, 1988.
Klein, Robin. *Thing.* Merrimak, 1983.
Kroll, Steven. *The Tyrannosaurus Game.* Holiday, 1976.
Lorenz, Lee. *Dinah's Egg.* Simon and Schuster, 1990.

Most, Bernard. *Whatever Happened to the Dinosaurs?* HBJ, 1984.
Thayer, Jane. *Quiet on Account of Dinosaur.* Morrow, 1964.

For Older Readers

Adrian, Mary. *The Mystery of the Dinosaur Graveyard.* Hastings, 1982.
Bates, Robin, and Bates, Simon. *The Dinosaurs and the Dark Star.* Macmillan, 1985.
Bograd, Larry. *The Fourth-Grade Dinosaur Club.* Delacorte, 1989.
Bonham, Frank. *The Friends of the Looney Lake Monster.* Dutton, 1972.
Butterworth, Oliver. *The Enormous Egg.* Little, 1956.
Lampman, Evelyn Sibley. *The Shy Stegosaurus of Indian Springs.* Doubleday, 1962.
Mannetti, William. *Dinosaurs in Your Back Yard.* Macmillan, 1982.
Richler, Mordecai. *Jacob Two-Two and the Dinosaur.* Knopf, 1987.
Senn, Steve. *The Double Disappearance of Walter Fozbeck.* Avon, 1983.

Nonfiction

Bolognese, Don. *Drawing Dinosaurs and Other Prehistoric Animals.* Watts, 1982.
Cobb, Vicki. *The Monsters Who Died: A Mystery About Dinosaurs.* Putnam, 1983.
Dixon, Dougal. *Be a Dinosaur Detective.* Lerner, 1988.
Freedman, Russell. *Dionosaurs and Their Young.* Holiday, 1983.
Hopkins, Lee Bennett. *Dinosaurs.* HBJ, 1990.
Kaufmann, John. *Flying Reptiles in the Age of Dinosaurs.* Morrow, 1971.
Parish, Peggy. *Dinosaur Time.* Harper, 1983.
Pringle, Laurence. *Dinosaurs and People: Fossils, Facts and Fantasies.* HBJ, 1978.
Rosenbloom, Joseph. *Dictionary of Dinosaurs.* Messner, 1983.
Sterne, Noelle. *Tyrannosaurus Wrecks: A Book of Dinosaur Riddles.* Harper, 1979.

Films and Videos

An Alphabet of Dinosaurs. COR, 15 mins.
Baby—Secret of the Lost Legend. DIS, 92 mins.
Digging Dinosaurs. CENT, 12 mins.
Digging Up Dinosaurs. RR, 30 mins.
Dinosaurs: Fun, Fact, and Fantasy. AIMS, 54 mins.
The Land Before Time. MCA, 70 mins.

— READING ON THE ROCKS —

(Earth Sciences)

You're going to rock on this summer at _____ Library!
Become a junior geologist and journey through the center of the

earth. Grow crystals and make fossils. Classify rocks and explore caves. Learn about earthquakes, volcanoes, and other geological wonders. Create a mountain range. Participate in our Earth Science Laboratory. You'll have a mountain of fun **Reading on the Rocks!**

Promotional Items

1. Sign reading "Earth Sciences Institute" for check-out area
2. "Junior Geologist" cards (membership cards)
3. Rock cut-outs (for books read)
4. Reading logs entitled "Geological Survey"
5. "Reading on the Rocks" bookmarks
6. Earth Sciences Specialist Degrees (certificates of participation)
7. Toy shovels and samples bags (game prizes)

Activities

1. Bulletin Board. Post pictures of various dynamic geological features of the earth (canyons, mountains, caves, stalactites, volcanoes, earthquake faults, geysers, etc.). Above each picture, write the title and author of a book on that subject. Caption: READING ON THE ROCKS.

2. Reading Incentive Game: Grand Canyon. Draw a picture representing a cross-section of the Grand Canyon. Label the layers of rock to represent the ages in millions of years. Also mark off steps at 1,000-foot intervals. Place a cut-out of a geologist at the top of the canyon. For every X books read by the group, move the man a step lower into the canyon. Readers will win a prize if the man reaches the canyon floor by the closing ceremony.

3. Dig. Read *How to Dig a Hole to the Other Side of the World*, by Faith McNulty. Ask children to design and draw their own "no-spaceships" in which they might dig through the earth.

4. Geological Word Search. Have children complete a word search puzzle with terms from *How to Dig a Hole to the Other Side of the World* and other geological terms.

5. Earth's Layers. Supply five different colors of Play-Doh. Let children make a small ball of one color to represent earth's inner core. Add a layer in another color around the ball for the outer core. Add layers in other colors to be the mantle, the asthenosphere (magma), and the lithosphere (earth's crust). Then carefully slice it in half to reveal the earth's layers.

6. Identify Rocks. Set up a display of different types of rocks and minerals.

Provide several loose rocks. Tell children they are geologists and have them identify these rocks by matching them to the ones in the display.

7. Mohs Hardness Scale. Display the Mohs Scale. Explain that geologists use this standard table to classify the hardness of rocks. Provide several identified rocks, pennies, and pieces of smooth glass. Let children scratch the rocks and glass to try to identify the hardness of the rocks.

8. Relief Maps. Make relief maps with children. Create mountain ranges, valleys, plains, rivers, etc. Invite a cartographer to talk to children about map-making.

9. Water Erosion. Show pictures of rain, waterfalls, glaciers, and other examples of water erosion which play a big part in changing the earth's features. Also display pictures of caves, canyons, mountains, and other places affected by water erosion. To help children understand how this happens, pile some cubes of sugar on a plate to represent a mountain. Slowly drip water on the cubes. The sugar will dissolve as the water "erodes" it.

10. Caves. Ask children if they have ever explored a cave. Discuss animals, rock formations, and other things that might be found in a cave. Tell them about some caves that are open to tourists (Polar Caves in New Hampshire, Carlsbad Caverns in New Mexico, etc.). Tell children to imagine they are exploring a cave. Write and illustrate a story about their adventures.

11. Careers. Pass out a fact sheet of careers in the earth sciences (geologist, seismologist, speleologist, paleontologist, etc.). Have children complete a crossword puzzle with these terms.

12. Growing Crystals. Show children how to make rock candy (this requires a stove or hot plate). In a pan, dissolve one cup of sugar in half a cup of water. Let it boil for one minute. Pour the syrupy solution into a jelly jar. Tie a clean weight to the end of a string and drop it into the jar. Hold the string in place by tying it to a pencil which rests atop the jar. Tell children to watch for crystals to form on the string as the water cools. (This will take several days.) Give children written directions so they can try this at home with adult supervision. The rock candy crystals can be eaten when they are large enough.

13. Map Skills. Show pictures of places which suffered damage from volcanoes and earthquakes. Give children a list of some active volcanoes and major fault lines around the world. Locate these on a world map.

14. Fossils. Pour a thick mixture of plaster of paris into a long, shallow box. Smooth the surface. Let children press shells, stones, and leaves onto the plaster, or make fingerprints. Allow the plaster to harden. Later, have children identify their fossils. These are similar to imprint and actual plant and animal fossils. Discuss another type: fossil fuels (oil, gas, and coal).

15. Closing Ceremony: Earth Sciences Laboratory. Invite an expert in earth sciences to perform lab experiments for children. These may include: demonstrating an erupting volcano, sorting soil, making a seismograph, weathering rocks, etc. Provide safety goggles and let children volunteer to be lab assistants.

Theme-Related Books

For Younger Readers

Baylor, Byrd. *Everybody Needs a Rock.* Scribner's, 1974.
Brown, Marcia. *Stone Soup.* Scribner's, 1947.
Chetwin, Grace. *Mr. Meredith and the Truly Remarkable Stone.* Bradbury, 1989.
Cole, Joanna. *The Magic School Bus Inside the Earth.* Scholastic, 1987.
Harshman, Marc et al. *Rocks in My Pockets.* Cobblehill, 1991.
McDermott, Gerald. *The Stonecutter.* Viking, 1975.
Steig, William. *Sylvester and the Magic Pebble.* Prentice, 1987.
Taylor, Mark. *Henry the Explorer.* Atheneum, 1966.

For Older Readers

Clifton, Lucille. *The Lucky Stone.* Dell, 1986.
Clymer, Eleanor. *Santiago's Silvermine.* Dell, 1989.
Drury, Roger W. *The Finches' Fabulous Furnace.* Little, 1971.
George, Jean Craighead. *One Day in the Alpine Tundra.* Crowell, 1984.
MacGregor, Ellen. *Miss Pickerell to the Earthquake Rescue.* McGraw, 1977.
Steiner, Barbara. *Ghost Cave.* HBJ, 1990.
Wallace, Bill. *Trapped in Death Cave.* Holiday, 1984.
Yolen, Jane. *The Boy Who Spoke Chimp.* Knopf, 1981.

Nonfiction

Beiser, Arthur. *The Earth.* Time-Life, 1979.
Bramwell, Martyn. *Volcanoes and Earthquakes.* Watts, 1986.
Burton, Virginia Lee. *Life Story.* Houghton, 1962.
Challand, Helen J. *Activities in the Earth Sciences.* Childrens, 1982.
Cobb, Vicki. *Chemically Active!* Harper, 1985.
Dixon, Dougal. *Geology.* Watts, 1982.
Fodor, R.V. *What Does a Geologist Do?* Dodd, 1977.
Gans, Roma. *Caves.* Crowell, 1976.
McNulty, Faith. *How to Dig a Hole to the Other Side of the World.* Harper, 1979.
Shedenhelm, W.R.C. *The Young Rockhound's Handbook.* Putnam, 1978.
Van Ryzin, Lani. *A Patch of Earth.* Messner, 1981.

Films and Videos

The Earth Beneath Your Feet. NGEO, 2 films, 15 mins. each.
Globes. COR, 10 mins.
Hill of Fire. RR, 30 mins.
A Journey to the Center of the Earth. CBS/FOX, 50 mins.
Treasures of the Earth. CHUR, 15 mins.
A World Is Born. DIS/COR, 20 mins.

WELCOME TO READABOOK FARM

(Farms)

We'll be down on the farm this summer at _____ Library. Be a farmhand: learn about raising animals and crops, and what it takes to run a farm. Plant a seed and watch it grow. Watch live chicks hatch. Design your own farm machinery, build a barn, and create food people. And there's always lots of fun and knowledge to harvest from our books. So join the new crop of readers at _____ Library. **Welcome to Readabook Farm!**

Promotional Items

1. Sign reading "Farmer's Dell" for check-out area
2. "Farmhand" cards (membership cards)
3. Barn cut-outs (for books read)
4. Reading logs entitled "Planting Schedule"
5. "Welcome to Readabook Farm" bookmarks
6. Harvester of Books Awards (certificates of participation)
7. Watering cans and spades (game prizes)

Activities

1. Bulletin Board. Post a large cut-out of the sun in the upper right corner, and a smiling scarecrow at the left. Use green and yellow construction paper to make several corn plants, filling the rest of the area. Write the names of reading club members on the ears of corn. Caption: WELCOME TO READABOOK FARM!

2. Reading Incentive Game: Sunflower. Draw an outline of a large sunflower. Mark off each individual petal, and pace off sections of the stem and leaves. Color in a section of the sunflower for every X books read by the group. Starting at the bottom of the stem, work up to the petals and end at the center of the flower. Readers will win a prize if the entire sunflower is colored in by the closing ceremony.

3. Planting Time. Provide materials and help children plant seeds in individual containers. Tell them to water their plants and watch them grow. Children can record their plants' progress on a growth chart in the library.

4. Growing Seasons. Use the *Old Farmer's Almanac* to tell children about growing seasons, or teach them how to read the instructions on seed packets. Pick a few crops and make a chart of planting and harvesting times.

5. Farm Crops. Discuss different types of plant farms (nurseries, tree farms, grain crops, truck farms, etc.). Have children complete a word search puzzle of farm crops.

6. Food People. Using paper-cut (or actual) fruits and vegetables, have children create food people. Use a large vegetable, such as a pumpkin or an eggplant, for the body. With glue (or toothpicks) stick on string beans as arms, peas for eyes, cherry tomatoes for the nose, etc.

7. Grains. Read *The Little Red Hen* as an introduction to grains. Make a list of various grains and their uses. Show pictures or models of a windmill and other machines used for processing grains. If possible, bake rolls or cookies with children to illustrate one use of wheat.

8. Puppet Show. Have children color and cut out pictures of farm animals. Tape onto popsicle sticks and present a puppet show to the song "Old MacDonald Had a Farm." Discuss various uses for different farm animals. Have children match the names of baby animals with their adult names.

9. Baby Chicks. Arrange with a local farmer to set up an incubator with fertilized chicken eggs. Try to program activities so children will be able to watch the chicks hatch. Discuss raising animals.

10. Farm Buildings. Show pictures of farm buildings (barns, chicken coops, milk houses, etc.) and discuss their uses. Supply clean milk cartons and cereal boxes. Cover with plain paper. Let children draw on features to make the boxes look like farm buildings.

11. Machines. Show pictures or models of various outdoor (tractors, etc.) and indoor (egg sorters, etc.) farm machines. Provide drawing materials and let children design and explain their own wacky or realistic farm machinery inventions. Display in library.

12. Agriculture Careers. Give children a fact sheet of farm-related jobs and chores. Have them complete a crossword puzzle with these terms.

13. Major Crops. Locate on a map of the United States where various crops are grown (potatoes in Maine and Idaho, etc.). Locate on a world map where other major crops are grown (coffee in Columbia, etc.).

14. Collages. Provide lots of old magazines. Have children cut out pictures of things that may be found on a farm. Then glue these pictures onto oak tag to make collages. Each collage should have a theme (farm animals, crops, etc.).

15. Closing Ceremony: Life on the Farm. Invite a member of the 4-H Club or Future Farmers of America to speak to children. Have a petting zoo with baby farm animals, and, if outdoors, offer pony or hay rides.

Theme-Related Books

For Younger Readers

Allen, Thomas B. *On Grandaddy's Farm.* Knopf, 1989.
Ipcar, Dahlov. *Hard Scrabble Harvest.* Doubleday, 1976.
The Little Red Hen. Macmillan, 1988.
Lloyd, Megan. *Chicken Tricks.* Harper, 1983.
Lobel, Arnold. *A Tree Full of Pigs.* Greenwillow, 1979.
Noble, Trinka Hakes. *The Day Jimmy's Boa Ate the Wash.* Dial, 1980.
Polushkin, Maria. *Morning.* Four Winds, 1983.
Provensen, Alice, and Provensen, Martin. *Our Animal Friends at Maple Hill Farm.* Random, 1974.
Schatell, Brian. *Sam's No Dummy, Farmer Goff.* Lippincott, 1984.
Steig, William. *Farmer Palmer's Wagon Ride.* Farrar, 1974.

For Older Readers

Byars, Betsy. *The Midnight Fox.* Viking, 1968.
Dahl, Roald. *Fantastic Mr. Fox.* Knopf, 1977.
Demuth, Patricia. *Joel: Growing Up on a Farm.* Putnam, 1982.
Farley, Carol. *Loosen Your Ears.* Atheneum, 1977.
Fleischman, Sid. *McBroom Tells the Truth.* Little, 1966.
Olsen, Violet. *View from the Pighouse Roof.* Macmillan, 1987.
Peck, Robert Newton. *Trig.* Dell, 1979.
Salassi, Otto R. *On the Ropes.* Greenwillow, 1981.
White, E.B. *Charlotte's Web.* Harper, 1952.
Wilder, Laura Ingalls. *Farmer Boy.* Harper, 1953.

Nonfiction

Anderson, George. *American Family Farm.* HBJ, 1989.
Arnow, Jan. *Hay from Seed to Feed.* Knopf, 1986.
Bushey, Jerry. *Farming the Land: Modern Farmers and Their Machines.* Carolrhoda, 1987.
Fradin, Dennis B. *Farming.* Childrens, 1983.
Gurney, Gene, and Gurney, Clare. *Agriculture Careers.* Watts, 1978.
Harkonen, Helen B. *Farms and Farmers in Art.* Lerner, 1965.
Henderson, Kathy. *I Can Be a Farmer.* Childrens, 1989.
Miller, Jane. *Farm Noises.* Simon and Schuster, 1989.
Roop, Peter, and Roop, Connie. *Hog Wild! Jokes for Down on the Farm.* Lerner, 1984.
Thomas, Robert B. *The Old Farmer's Almanac.* Yankee.

Films and Videos

Farm Animals in Rhyme. COR, 11 mins.
Farm Family series (*Summer, Autumn, Spring, Winter*). BRIT, 4 films, 15 mins. each.
The Little Rooster Who Made the Sun Rise. COR, 11 mins.

The Milk Makers. RR, 30 mins.
Old MacDonald Duck. DIS/COR, 8 mins.
Rosie's Walk. WW, 5 mins.

——— BLOSSOM WITH A BOOK ———

(Flower Gardens)

_____ *Library's summer reading club will be in full bloom soon, and we need you to help our garden grow. Learn about different types of flower gardens and plot one of your own. Make flower baskets and petal people. Plant a dish garden. Create a seed mosaic. Come to our Garden Party for more fun activities. You will discover that you can truly* **Blossom with a Book.**

Promotional Items

1. Sign reading "Garden Club" for check-out area
2. "Garden Club Member" cards (membership cards)
3. Watering can cut-outs (for books read)
4. Reading logs entitled "Growth Chart"
5. "Blossom with a Book" bookmarks
6. Green Thumb certificates (certificates of participation)
7. Plastic or miniature gardening tools (game prizes)

Activities

1. Bulletin Board. In the center, post a picture of a child reading a book. Draw a trellis around the child. Entwine a vine along the trellis and attach paper flowers throughout. Caption: BLOSSOM WITH A BOOK.

2. Reading Incentive Game: Floral Timeline. Mark off a timeline from spring to fall. Label along the line the names of flowers that bloom in your area around each time (tulips in mid–April, geraniums in May, etc.). For every X books read by the group, post a picture of a flower chronologically along the timeline. Readers will win a prize if all the flowers are in place by the closing ceremony.

3. Petal People. Take a headshot photo of each child. Carefully cut each photo into a circle. On construction paper, have children glue a green paper stem and leaves. Glue paper petals at the top of the stem in a daisy pattern. Glue the child's photo in the center of the flower. Display in library.

4. Memory Game. Sit children in a circle. Have the group chant, "(child's name), (child's name), what does your garden grow?" The child whose name is called answers, "It grows (name of a type of flower), all in a row." Go around the circle. Each child must recall all the previous flowers and then name a different one, ending with "all in a row." See how many flowers children can name and remember.

5. Gardening Terms. Pass out a fact sheet of gardening terms (weed, bud, cutting, transplant, etc.). Have children complete a crossword puzzle with these terms.

6. Play-Acting Exercise. Have children curl up on the floor to pretend they are seeds. Slowly, have them uncurl, stand, and stretch as tall as possible to represent flowers in full bloom. Strauss's "Also sprach Zarathustra" (theme from *2001: A Space Odyssey*) is particularly effective mood music for this exercise.

7. Picture Garden. Provide lots of old magazines and flower catalogs. Let each child cut out pictures of flowers, trees, shrubs, etc., and glue onto oak tag in a garden arrangement of his own design. The child may also wish to include a picture of a house, garden ornaments, a pond, etc. Display in library.

8. Planting Information. Pass out several seed and bulb packets. Teach children how to read them. Consider planting seasons and depth, type of soil, how far plant will spread, whether it is an annual/biennial/perennial, etc.

9. State Flowers. Every state has an official flower. Post a map of the United States. Cut out or draw pictures of each type of flower. Have children help you post the correct flower on each state. Make special note of your own state's flower. Is it a good choice for your state?

10. Outdoor Gardens. Show pictures of different types of outdoor flower gardens (Japanese, rock, rose, etc.). What are some characteristic plants and other features of each one? Ask each child to tell you his favorite type. Show pictures of some famous gardens (Cypress Gardens in South Carolina, Kew Gardens in London, etc.). Locate these places on a map.

11. Seed Mosaics. Provide several types of dried seeds. Let children glue these onto cardboard to make mosaic designs.

12. Gardening Tools. Show children pictures of gardening tools and explain their uses. Have children complete a word search puzzle of gardening tools (rake, hose, clippers, etc.).

13. Flower Baskets. Cut the top off a half-gallon rectangular milk carton. Draw a line 4″ from the bottom on all sides. On two opposite sides, from the top to the 4″ line, draw a 1″-wide strip down the center to serve as the handle. Cut the carton above the 4″ line, leaving the handle strips in place. Overlap the handle ends and staple together. Decorate the basket with paper doilies, gift wrap, glitter, or whatever. Fill with real or paper flowers. The basket will be waterproof.

14. Dish Gardens. For each garden, cut a plastic gallon milk jug in half. Help children plant three or four small plants in the bottom half. Decorate with colorful pebbles. Teach children how to care for their dish gardens.

15. Closing Ceremony: Garden Party. Let children participate in a Maypole dance, play croquet, and make dried flower arrangements or wreaths. Supply pink lemonade and dainty cookies.

Theme-Related Books

For Younger Readers

Carle, Eric. *The Tiny Seed.* Picture Book, 1987.
Carlson, Nancy. *Harriet and the Garden.* Carolrhoda, 1982.
Cooney, Barbara. *Miss Rumphius.* Viking, 1982.
Cristini, Ermanno, and Puricelli, Luigi. *In My Garden.* Picture Book, 1985.
Hutchins, Pat. *Titch.* Macmillan, 1971.
Lobel, Anita. *A Rose in My Garden.* Greenwillow, 1984.
Nakatani, Chiyoko. *The Zoo in My Garden.* Crowell, 1973.
Van Allsburg, Chris. *The Garden of Abdul Gasazi.* Houghton, 1979.

For Older Readers

Bjork, Christina. *Linnea in Monet's Garden.* Farrar, 1987.
Burnett, Frances Hodgson. *The Secret Garden.* Harper, 1962.
Cohen, Barbara. *Roses.* Lothrop, 1984.
Cresswell, Helen. *The Bongleweed.* Macmillan, 1973.
McCrea, James. *The Magic Tree.* Atheneum, 1965.
Nicolai, D. Miles. *The Summer the Flowers Had No Scent.* Coffee Break, 1977.
Pearce, Philippa. *Tom's Midnight Garden.* Lippincott, 1958.
Williams, Helen. *The Language of Flowers.* Dutton, 1988.

Nonfiction

Dowden, Anne Ophelia. *State Flowers.* Crowell, 1978.
Herda, D.J. *Making a Nature Plant Terrarium.* Messner, 1977.
Huff, Barbara A. *Greening the City Streets: The Story of Community Gardens.* Clarion, 1990.
Jobb, Jamie. *My Garden Companion.* Scribner's, 1977.
Lewis, Richard, editor. *In a Spring Garden.* Dial, 1965.
Paul, Aileen. *Kids Outdoor Gardening.* Doubleday, 1978.
Selsam, Millicent. *The Amazing Dandelion.* Morrow, 1978.
Sweningson, Sally. *Indoor Gardening.* Lerner, 1975.
Tarsky, Sue. *The Prickly Plant Book.* Little, 1980.

Films and Videos

Flower to Seed. CHUR, 9 mins.
Flowers and Bees: A Springtime Story. BRIT, 11 mins.

Harold and His Amazing Green Plants. DIS/COR, 8 mins.
The Selfish Giant. PYR, 27 mins.

—— FLY HIGH WITH A BOOK ——

(Things That Fly)

Look, up in the sky! It's a bird! It's a plane! Or maybe a balloon or kite! Whatever it is, it's flying. You'll see these and other things that fly this summer at _____ Library. You will also build a glider and a kite. Design your own flying machine and hot-air balloon. Come to the outdoor air show and see radio-controlled stunt planes in action. The sky's the limit! So come to the library and **Fly High with a Book!**

Promotional Items

1. Sign reading "Air Traffic Control" for check-out area
2. "Pilot's Permit" cards (membership cards)
3. Kite cut-outs (for books read)
4. Reading logs entitled "Flight Schedule"
5. "Fly High with a Book" bookmarks
6. Aviator Awards (certificates of participation)
7. Whirlycopter toys or bubble solution (game prizes)

Activities

1. Bulletin Board. Draw the curve of the earth at the bottom of the area, and a few clouds above it. Post cut-outs of several types of airplanes and jets above the clouds. Even higher, post a cut-out of a rocket ship and a space station. Write the name of a book on each aircraft. Caption: FLY HIGH WITH A BOOK.

2. Reading Incentive Game: Balloon Ride. Post a map of the world. Label your city or town "Home." Use dots to pace off a trail around the world, ending at home. For every X books read by the group, advance a balloon marker one dot. Readers will win a prize if the balloon reaches home by the closing ceremony.

3. Up, Up and Away. Hot air can make a balloon rise. So can hydrogen and helium, two light elements in the air. Have children blow up toy balloons, tie them closed, and let them go. What happens? Then inflate balloons with helium, tie closed and let go. What happens?

4. Balloon Pictures. Show children pictures of hot-air balloons, blimps, and zeppelins. Note how colorful they are. Let children paint or color designs on large white circles of paper to represent hot-air balloons. Paste each hot-air balloon on blue construction paper, near the top of the paper. Paste a brown square basket underneath it. Complete the scene by drawing people in the basket, clouds, the earth below, etc. Display in library.

5. 'Copters vs. Planes. Display models and pictures of helicopters and airplanes. How do they differ? Name some tasks and let children tell you which aircraft should be used (crop dusting—airplane; landing on a roof—helicopter; etc.).

6. Aviation Terms. Give children a fact sheet of aviation terms (air traffic controller, altitude, ballast, etc.). Have readers complete a crossword puzzle with these terms.

7. Jets. Show children diagrams and pictures of jet planes. Air forced out the back of a jet pushes it forward. Let children demonstrate this concept with toy balloons. Use markers to draw pictures of jets on balloons. Then blow them up and let go. The balloons will fly until the air runs out.

8. Space Flight. Display models or pictures of some rockets, satellites, and space stations. Show films of rockets blasting off and of space flight. Discuss how humans can float in space because of the lack of gravity there.

9. Space Crafts. Supply an assortment of plastic soda bottles, paper cups, paper towel tubes, and paper cones. Using duct or masking tape to connect these materials, let children design their own spaceships. Spray with a metallic-colored paint and allow to dry. Hang in library.

10. Gliders. Show pictures of hang gliders. How do they work? Let children use markers to draw designs on sheets of paper. Fold and tape the paper into gliders.

11. Flying Machines. Show children pictures and film clips of early man-made flying machines that didn't work. Let children design and draw their own flying machines. How would they work?

12. Animals in Flight. Ask children to tell you some animals that fly (birds, insects, bats, etc.). Do flying fish and flying squirrels really fly? Have children complete a word search puzzle of flying animals.

13. State Birds. Tell children that each state in the United States has an official bird mascot. Give each child a list of bird mascots and a map of the United States divided into states. Have children write the names of the official birds in (or near) their appropriate states. Use bird pictures or stickers if available.

14. Kites. Let children draw designs on large paper diamonds. Attach crepe paper tails. Display in library.

15. Closing Ceremony: Air Show. For an outdoor party, invite hobbyists to fly radio-controlled stunt planes for the crowd. For an indoor party, supply materials and follow instructions in a kite book to make real kites with children.

Theme-Related Books

For Younger Readers

Brenner, Barbara. *The Flying Patchwork Quilt.* Scott, 1965.
Coerr, Eleanor. *The Big Balloon Race.* Harper, 1981.
Florian, Douglas. *Airplane Ride.* Crowell, 1984.
Gerstein, Mordicai. *Arnold of the Ducks.* Harper, 1983.
Holl, Adelaide. *Too Fat to Fly.* Garrard, 1973.
Hughs, Shirley. *Up and Up.* Lothrop, 1986.
McPhail, David. *First Flight.* Little, 1987.
Oechsli, Helen, and Oechsli, Kelly. *Fly Away!* Macmillan, 1988.
Provensen, Alice, and Provensen, Martin. *The Glorious Flight: Across the Channel with Louis Bleriot.* Viking, 1978.
Scarry, Richard. *The Great Big Air Book.* Random, 1971.

For Older Readers

Brock, Betty. *No Flying in the House.* Harper, 1982.
Byars, Betsy. *The Winged Colt of Casa Mia.* Viking, 1973.
De Weese, Gene. *Major Colby and the Unidentified Flapping Object.* Doubleday, 1979.
Domke, Todd. *Grounded.* Knopf, 1982.
duBois, William Pené. *The Twenty-One Balloons.* Viking, 1947.
Gormley, Beatrice. *Mail-Order Wings.* Dutton, 1981.
Yep, Laurence. *Dragonwings.* Harper, 1975.

Nonfiction

Ardley, Neil. *Air and Flight.* Watts, 1984.
Build Your Own Airport. Watts, 1985.
Downer, Marion. *Kites: How to Make and Fly Them.* Lothrop, 1959.
Gibbons, Gail. *Catch the Wind!* Little, 1989.
Ireland, Karin. *Helicopters at Work.* Messner, 1983.
Kaufmann, John. *Birds Are Flying.* Harper, 1979.
Let's Discover Flying. Raintree, 1981.
Linsley, Leslie, and Aron, Jon. *Air Crafts.* Dutton, 1982.
Percefull, Aaron W. *Balloons, Zeppelins and Dirigibles.* Watts, 1983.
Rosenblum, Richard. *Wings: The Early Years of Aviation.* Four Winds, 1980.
Scarry, Huck. *Balloon Trip.* Prentice, 1983.

Films and Videos

Attic of the Wind. WW, 6 mins.
Birds: How We Identify Them. COR, 11 mins.
Bored—Nothing to Do! RR, 30 mins.
Hot-Air Henry. RR, 30 mins.
A Kite Story. CHUR, 16 mins.
Planes. DIS/COR, 15 mins.
The Red Balloon. FIV, 34 mins.

—— A BANQUET OF BOOKS ——

(Food)

*Something good is cooking at _____ Library! Our master chefs have concocted a menu of tempting activities to keep your appetite for fun well-fed this summer. Find out where different foods come from and what happens when you eat them. Become a taste-tester and rate your reactions to various foods. Play the "What's My Food?" game. Learn how to decode a recipe and whip up some fun foods. A tasty time and A **Banquet of Books** await you at the library.*

Promotional Items

1. Sign reading "Chez (name of library)" for check-out area
2. "Short-Order Cook" cards (membership cards)
3. Apple cut-outs (for books read)
4. Reading logs entitled "Menu"
5. "A Banquet of Books" bookmarks
6. Chef Supreme certificates (certificates of participation)
7. Chef's hats (game prizes)

Activities

1. Bulletin Board. Draw a picture of a chef at one side. Next to the chef, draw a long table. On it, post cut-outs of books labeled with the titles of various fiction and nonfiction books about food. Caption: A BANQUET OF BOOKS.

2. Reading Incentive Game: International Foods. Post a world map. Place colored push-pins in various countries. Prepare paper cut-outs to represent foods eaten in the United States which originated in these countries (pizza from Italy, etc.). For every X books read by the group, post a food cut-out in the appropriate country. Readers will win a prize if all the push-pins are used by the closing ceremony.

3. A Balanced Diet. Read *Gregory, the Terrible Eater*, by Mitchell Sharmat, as an introduction to junk food vs. nutritious food. Discuss the food pyramid and a healthy diet. Give children a fact sheet about vitamins and other nutrients. Have readers complete a word search puzzle with these terms.

4. Collages. Provide lots of old magazines. Let children cut pictures of food and paste them onto oak tag to make collages. Each collage should have a theme, such as: The Dairy Group, Foods That Are Baked, International Dishes, etc. Display in library.

5. Design-a-Pizza. Give each child a circular piece of cardboard. Supply paper, stickers, or art tape cut into the shapes of various pizza toppings. Let children create their own pizzas. They can also invent new, wacky toppings.

6. Taste Test. Prepare bite-size pieces of a variety of foods, divided into four categories: salty, bitter, sour, and sweet. Blindfold volunteers and have a taste-testing contest to see who can identify the most foods and their taste categories. Variation: have children hold their noses as they taste. What are some other factors that affect whether or not you like a food? (If it is spicy, crunchy, chewy, etc.)

7. Crazy Foods. Read *Green Eggs and Ham,* by Dr. Seuss. Ask children to tell you foods they refuse to eat. What happened when the character finally tasted the green eggs and ham? Let children make up some crazy food combinations and draw them to display in the library.

8. Food People. Using paper-cut (or real) fruits and vegetables, have children create food people. Use a large vegetable, such as a pumpkin or eggplant, for the body. With glue (or toothpicks), stick on string beans for arms, peas for eyes, cherry tomato for the nose, etc.

9. Special Delivery. Read *Night Markets,* by Joshua Horwitz. Locate on a map the points of origin for the foods mentioned. Note how foods are stored and transported to insure freshness. Read the ads from several supermarkets to see where their foods come from.

10. The Chef. Ask children to tell you what a chef does. Have children write about what they would do if they were chefs. What would their specialties be? In what type of restaurant would they work?

11. Recipes. Teach children how to read a recipe. Hand out fact sheets explaining measurements and other cooking terms (saute, simmer, etc.). Have children complete a crossword puzzle of these terms. Let them "decode" some recipes.

12. Favorite Foods. Take a poll of children's favorite foods. What is the most popular breakfast cereal? Sandwich? Desert? Ice cream flavor? Fast food? What is the overall most popular food?

13. Menus. Have children pretend they are restaurant owners. Let them make up menus of what they would serve.

14. "What's My Food?" Game. Define: herbivore, carnivore, omnivore, insectivore. Show one animal from each of the above types. Have children pick from a deck of cards on which there are pictures of food and guess which animal(s) eat the food picked. A point is given for each correct answer (some foods may be eaten by more than one animal, thus earning extra points). The winner(s) may be given a prize of something good to eat.

15. Closing Ceremony: Cooking Fun. Let children help make a variety of easy-to-make foods, such as homemade ice cream, hors d'oeuvres, trail mix, etc. Include these and samples of some international dishes for a banquet. Encourage children to taste all foods and rate them on a taste-testing sheet.

Theme-Related Books

For Younger Readers

Barrett, Judi. *Cloudy with a Chance of Meatballs.* Macmillan, 1978.
Burningham, John. *Avocado Baby.* Harper, 1982.
Degen, Bruce. *Jamberry.* Harper, 1983.
dePaola, Tomie. *Watch Out for Chicken Feet in Your Soup.* Prentice, 1974.
Dr. Seuss. *Green Eggs and Ham.* Random, 1960.
Friedman, Ina R. *How My Parents Learned to Eat.* Houghton, 1984.
Hoban, Russell. *Bread and Jam for Frances.* Harper, 1964.
Krasilovsky, Phyllis. *The Man Who Entered a Contest.* Doubleday, 1980.
McCloskey, Robert. *Blueberries for Sal.* Viking, 1948.
Sharmat, Mitchell. *Gregory, the Terrible Eater.* Four Winds, 1980.

For Older Readers

Birdseye, Tom. *I'm Going to Be Famous.* Holiday, 1986.
Conford, Ellen. *What's Cooking, Jenny Archer?* Little, 1989.
Corbalis, Judy. *The Ice Cream Heroes.* Little, 1989.
Dahl, Roald. *James and the Giant Peach.* Knopf, 1961.
Danziger, Paula. *The Pistachio Prescription.* Delacorte, 1978.
Heide, Florence Parry. *Banana Twist.* Holiday, 1978.
Hurwitz, Johanna. *Much Ado About Aldo.* Morrow, 1978.
Naylor, Phyllis Reynolds. *Beetles Lightly Toasted.* Atheneum, 1987.
Pinkwater, Daniel M. *Fat Men from Space.* Dodd, 1977.
Rockwell, Thomas. *How to Eat Fried Worms.* Watts, 1973.

Nonfiction

Adoff, Arnold. *Eats.* Lothrop, 1979.
Bourne, Miriam Anne. *A Day in the Life of a Chef.* Troll, 1988.
Cobb, Vicki. *Feeding Yourself.* Harper, 1989.
Horwitz, Joshua. *Night Markets.* Crowell, 1984.
Jones, Hettie. *How to Eat Your ABC's.* Four Winds, 1986.
Ontario Science Center. *Foodworks.* Addison, 1987.
Roop, Peter, and Roop, Connie. *Out to Lunch! Jokes About Food.* Lerner, 1984.
Seixas, Judith S. *Junk Food — What It Is, What It Does.* Greenwillow, 1984.
Warner, Margaret Brink, and Haywood, Ruth Ann. *What's Cooking? Recipes from Around the World.* Little, 1981.

Films and Videos

The Doughnuts. ww, 26 mins.
Food. cor, 10 mins.
The Junk Food Film. barr, 11 mins.
Lady Fishbourne's Complete Guide to Table Manners. nfbc, 6 mins.
The Robbery at the Diamond Dog Diner. rr, 30 mins.
What's Cooking? chur, 15 mins.

— FIND A FRIEND IN A BOOK —

(Friendship)

*Summer's here! Time to come to _____ Library and make
some new friends. Meet two hippos named George and Martha,
and an imaginary girl named Neesie. Write to pen pals. Make
friendship bracelets and necklaces. Try to guess the identity of
your own secret pal. Come to our Summer Valentine's Day Party.
Make an autograph book for all your friends to sign. At _____
Library, you will be sure to* **Find a Friend in a Book.**

Promotional Items

1. Sign reading "Find-a-Friend Agency" for check-out area
2. "Book Buddy" cards (membership cards)
3. Valentine cut-outs (for books read)
4. Reading logs entitled "New-Found Friends"
5. "Find a Friend in a Book" bookmarks
6. Secret Pal certificates (certificates of participation)
7. Friendship rings (game prizes)

Activities

1. Bulletin Board. Draw a picture of a child sitting with an open book. All
around him, post book cut-outs with titles of books about friends. Caption: FIND
A FRIEND IN A BOOK.

2. Reading Incentive Game: Friendship Tree. Post a large tree trunk,
and label it "Friendship Tree." Outline where the leaves will go, but keep the tree
bare. Place one leaf on the tree for every X books read by the group. On each leaf
should be a word associated with friendship (cooperation, love, peace, harmony,
etc.). Readers will win a prize if all the leaves are on the tree by the closing
ceremony.

3. Secret Pals. Place children in groups according to their ages. Give them
all name tags and let them introduce themselves. Have children write their names
on slips of paper. Put these in a hat and let each child draw one, making sure
children do not pick their own names. The names drawn are the children's secret
pals. Each child must then write a clue about himself and address it to the name
he selected. Clues are not to be signed. They will be placed in a box and delivered
by the librarian. You may want to have readers exchange clues once a week for

the duration of the program. At the closing ceremony, have each child guess the identity of his secret pal. Children may give simple presents (a candy bar, a pack of baseball cards, etc.) to their secret pals when their identities are revealed.

4. Paper Dolls. Show children how to fold paper and cut out a doll figure, so that there is a chain of paper dolls holding hands when the paper is unfolded. Let children mount their paper dolls on construction paper and color them in. Each child can write his own name plus the names of friends or family members under the dolls. You can also make a chain of paper dolls to post along a wall in the library. Write the name of a reading club member on each doll.

5. Book Friends. Read a book about friends, such as *George and Martha* by James Marshall. How do the characters demonstrate their friendship for each other? What happens when they disagree? Ask children if there are any book characters with whom they would like to be friends.

6. Friends Do/Friends Don't. Make two columns on a chalkboard. Label them "Friends Do" and "Friends Don't." Let children tell you what to list in both columns. (For example, "Friends do. . . cheer you up when you're sad. Friends don't. . . call you bad names.")

7. Leis. Hawaiians give lei necklaces to people as a sign of friendship. Let children thread pieces of crepe paper (in various colors) to make their own leis.

8. Qualities. Have children complete a word search puzzle of qualities that make a person a good friend (kind, helpful, honest, etc.).

9. Imaginary Friend. Read *Me and Neesie*, by Eloise Greenfield. Why do you think Janell sees Neesie? What do her parents think of it? Ask children if they were to make up a friend, what would he/she be like? Would it be a person, or an animal or toy that could talk? What adventures would they have together?

10. The Ideal Friend. Have children write and illustrate short poems or stories that start with "I want a friend who. . . ."

11. Friendship Bracelets. Show children how to braid yarn or embroidery floss to make friendship bracelets. They can make several and tie them onto each other's wrists.

12. Far-Away Friends. Ask children if they have friends in other cities, states, or countries. Have them locate these places on a map. How do they keep in touch with their friends?

13. Pen Pals. Pen pals are friends from different places who write to each other. Provide addresses of pen pal agencies. Let children who want pen pals request them. Children should give basic information about themselves, such as age, sex, and interests. They may want to request a boy or girl pen pal, and the state or country in which the person lives. Also, club members who go to different schools may wish to become pen pals and keep in touch when summer is over.

14. Autograph Books. Have children bind several sheets of colored paper into autograph books. Label the cover, "Find a Friend in a Book," and write the child's name. Children can pass their books around and write positive things about each other. They may also include their addresses or phone numbers.

15. Closing Ceremony: Summer Valentine's Day Party. Decorate the children's room with paper hearts and cupids. Serve "Friendship Potion Punch." Play songs about friends ("You've Got a Friend" by James Taylor, etc.). Let children guess who their secret pals are and exchange gifts.

Theme-Related Books

For Younger Readers

Aliki. *We Are Best Friends.* Greenwillow, 1982.
Brandenberg, Franz. *Nice New Neighbors.* Greenwillow, 1977.
Cohen, Miriam. *Will I Have a Friend?* Macmillan, 1967.
Freeman, Don. *Corduroy.* Viking, 1968.
Greenfield, Eloise. *Me and Neesie.* Crowell, 1975.
Hallinan, B.K. *We're Very Good Friends, My Brother and I.* Childrens, 1973.
Hoban, Russell. *Best Friends for Frances.* Harper, 1976.
Marshall, James. *George and Martha.* Houghton, 1972.
Steig, William. *Amos and Boris.* Farrar, 1971.
Zolotow, Charlotte. *The Hating Book.* Harper, 1969.

For Older Readers

Albright, Mollie. *Best Friends.* Troll, 1987.
Amdur, Nikki. *One of Us.* Dial, 1981.
Bunting, Eve. *Sixth Grade Sleepover.* HBJ, 1986.
Conford, Ellen. *Me and the Terrible Two.* Little, 1974.
Garrique, Sheila. *Between Friends.* Bradbury, 1978.
Gormley, Beatrice. *Best Friend Insurance.* Dutton, 1983.
Paterson, Katherine. *Bridge to Terabithia.* Harper, 1977.
Peck, Robert Newton. *Soup.* Knopf, 1974.
Stolz, Mary. *Noonday Friends.* Harper, 1965.
Taylor, Mildred. *The Friendship.* Dial, 1987.

Nonfiction

Anderson, Debby. *Being a Friend Means. . . .* Cook, 1986.
Berry, Joy. *Every Kid's Guide to Making Friends.* Childrens, 1987.
Glasscock, Paula, and Weber, Sally. *Castles, Pirates, Knights, and Other Learning Delights!* Good Appple, 1980.
Mahy, Margaret. *Making Friends.* Macmillan, 1988.
Naylor, Phyllis Reynolds. *Getting Along with Your Friends.* Abington, 1980.

Robison, Deborah. *Bye-Bye, Old Buddy.* Houghton, 1983.
Sachs, Marilyn. *Just Like a Friend.* Dutton, 1989.
Varebhorst, Barbara B. *Real Friends: Becoming the Friend You'd Like to Have.* Harper, 1983.
Warburg, Sandol S. *I Like You.* Houghton, 1965.

Films and Videos

Best Friends. RR, 30 mins.
The Crying Red Giant. AIMS, 18 mins.
Frog and Toad Are Friends and *Frog and Toad Together.* CHUR, 14 mins. each.
Making Friends. DIS/COR, 8 mins.
Tell Me About It: What Makes a Friend So Special? AIMS, 9 mins.

—— CHECK OUT A HERO ——

(Heroes, Heroines)

Everybody admires a hero or a heroine. At _____ Library this summer, you will learn about heroes in real life and in fiction. Help Hercules accomplish the Twelve Labors. Make a sports trophy and a poster for your favorite movie hero. Decorate a plaque for pacifist heroes. Create a carton superhero. Learn about heroes in mythology, American History, and everyday life. Design a medal for a hero. Vote for your #1 all-time favorite hero. Survive the Hero Trials and receive your reward from our special guest hero. A summer of excitement awaits you when you **Check Out a Hero.**

Promotional Items

1. Sign reading "Heroes Hall of Fame" for check-out area
2. "Visitor's Passes" to Heroes Hall of Fame (membership cards)
3. Hero sandwich cut-out (for books read)
4. Reading logs entitled "Heroic Deeds"
5. "Check Out a Hero" bookmarks
6. Hero Trials Survival Awards (certificates of participation)
7. Key chains shaped like the number 1 with library logo (game prizes)

Activities

1. Bulletin Board. Make a collage of bookcovers or book cut-outs with the titles of books about heroes. Include heroes from past and present, real and fictitious. Add pictures of these and other heroes. Caption: CHECK OUT A HERO.

2. Reading Incentive Game: The Twelve Labors of Hercules. Draw a gameboard, starting at the palace of Eurystheus. Pace off a trail which passes by 12 pictures representing the labors of Hercules and ends at Mount Olympus. Use a cut-out of Hercules as the marker. Advance Hercules one space for every X books read by the group. Readers will win a prize if Hercules reaches Mount Olympus by the closing ceremony.

3. Mythological Heroes. Many heroes in the mythology of their countries are famous for outwitting, conquering, or slaying a terrible foe. Give children a paper listing the names of heroes and their countries in one column, and names of foes in another column. Divide children in groups and let them look through books to match the heroes with their foes. Or, give children a fact sheet telling which hero fought which foe (Beowulf vs. Grendel, Perseus vs. Medusa, etc.) and have children complete a crossword puzzle with this information.

4. TV and Movie Heroes. Ask children to name some TV and movie heroes (Captain Kirk, Indiana Jones, etc.). Have each child draw a fan club poster for his favorite hero. Display in library. Children may also write adventure stories starring their heroes.

5. Picture Book Hero. Read a story about a classic children's book hero (*Peter Pan, Jack and the Beanstalk,* etc.). Assign roles and let children act out the story.

6. Animal Heroes. Ask children to name some real-life and fictitious animal heroes (the first space monkey, Lassie, Flipper, etc.). Recount some dangerous situations and have children tell you which animal could help and how. (A forest fire—Lassie gets the fire marshall; a boy falls off a boat—Flipper supports him until he is pulled onto the boat, etc.)

7. Sports Trophies. Star athletes and sports heroes sometimes get trophies for their winning performances. Children can make trophies in the sport of their choice. Glue the spout of an empty one quart milk container closed. Cover all sides with construction paper. Decorate with paint, markers, strips of colored paper, and glitter. Write the child's name and the nature of the award on a gummed sticker (Joe Doe, Star Pitcher for the Little League Baseball team). Place the sticker on one side of the trophy. Cut out two copies of a figure to represent the sport (baseball mitt, football, etc.). Glue these together onto the peak at the top of the milk carton.

8. Pacifist Heroes. Some people are heroes because they try to help people in a nonviolent manner. Ask children to name some pacifist heroes, past and present, from around the world (Rev. Martin Luther King, Jr.; Mahatma Gandhi; Mother Theresa, etc.). Cut out a large oval from construction paper. At the top, write, "Pacifist Honor Roll." List all the names under it. Provide stencils of olive leaves. Explain to children that these symbolize peace. Let children trace and cut green paper olive leaves. Glue the leaves along the edge of the oval. Display in library.

9. Everyday Heroes. A hero need not be somebody famous. Doctors, firemen, police and many other people save lives, stop crime, and perform other heroic acts every day just doing their jobs. There are also quiet heroes, who help people by doing volunteer work and other things that are not flashy. Ask children to think of everyday heroes they know or about whom they have heard. Have them write a headline and a short news article about their heroes. Bind these in a book called "Everyday Heroes" to keep in the library.

10. Local Hero. Every town has its local heroes. Invite someone who is a community leader, star athlete, war survivor, famous personality, or other type of hero to talk to children about his or her experiences.

11. Medals. Give children a choice of medals to make. Provide stencils of stars, circles, hearts, eagles, etc. Trace and cut out a shape on oak tag. Write a caption on the medal (True Blue Patriot, Valor, For Bravery Above and Beyond the Call of Duty, Purple Heart, Medal of Honor, etc.). Decorate the medal and tape a loop of ribbon onto the back. String a length of ribbon through the loop and tie ends together to make a necklace.

12. #1 All-Time Favorite Hero. Ask children to name their favorite heroes. Take down all names, past and present, real and fictitious, whether they have been mentioned before or not. Let each child vote for his three favorites. Tally the votes and narrow the list to the top ten vote-getters. Have children vote for one from this list. Determine the winner and have children decorate a banner for their #1 All-Time Favorite Hero. If possible, try to get someone to dress up like this hero to sign autographs and pose for pictures at the closing ceremony.

13. Historical American Heroes. Have children complete a word search puzzle of real American heroes (George Washington, Daniel Boone, Susan B. Anthony, etc.). What did these heroes do?

14. Cartoon Superheroes. Have children list some cartoon superheroes on a chart with three columns: hero's name, superpowers, and origin (Spiderman; climbs walls/makes webs/super strong; bit by a radioactive spider). What are some similar features of superheroes? Let each child create his own cartoon superhero. Draw a picture of him or her in costume, name the superpowers, and tell the origin. What enemies does the hero have?

15. Closing Ceremony: Hero Trials. Invite children to come dressed as their favorite heroes and heroines, or in a costume of their own design. Set up an obstacle course with 12 hero trials for children to complete: weight-lifting (fake weights); slaying monsters (beating a punching bag); jumping over tall buildings (a box with a picture of a skyscraper); rescuing people from drowning (plastic figures in a tub of water); etc. After the trials, have everyone march in a Heroes Victory Parade. An adult dressed as the #1 Hero or a popular cartoon superhero can sign autographs, pose for pictures, and hand out awards.

Theme-Related Books

For Younger Readers

Dr. Seuss. *The King's Stilts*. Random, 1939.
Hirsh, Marilyn. *The Rabbi and the Twenty-Nine Witches: A Talmudic Legend*. Holiday, 1976.
Hort, Lenny. *The Boy Who Held Back the Sea*. Dial, 1987.
Khalsa, Dayal Kaur. *Julian*. Crown, 1989.
Lauber, Patricia. *Clarence and the Burglar*. Coward, 1983.
Lewis, Marjorie. *The Boy Who Would Be a Hero*. Putnam, 1982.
Peet, Bill. *The Spooky Tale of Prewett Peacock*. Houghton, 1972.
Steig, William. *Brave Irene*. Farrar, 1986.
Ungerer, Tomi. *Crictor*. Harper, 1958.

For Older Readers

Bauer, Marion Dane. *Rain of Fire*. Clarion, 1983.
Brady, Esther Wood. *Toliver's Secret*. Crown, 1976.
Conford, Ellen. *The Revenge of the Incredible Dr. Rancid and His Youthful Assistant, Jeffrey*. Little, 1980.
Corcoran, Barbara. *The Long Journey*. Atheneum, 1974.
Evslin, Bernard. *Hercules*. Morrow, 1984.
Gardner, John R. *Stone Fox*. Crowell, 1980.
Kennedy, Richard. *Inside My Feet*. Harper, 1979.
Manes, Stephen. *Some of the Adventures of Rhode Island Red*. Harper, 1990.
Sharp, Margery. *The Rescuers*. Little, 1959.
Zei, Alki. *Petros' War*. Dutton, 1972.

Nonfiction

Baldwin, Margaret. *The Boys Who Saved the Children*. Messner, 1983.
Davis, Burke. *Heroes of the American Revolution*. Random, 1971.
Hazeltine, Alice. *Hero Tales from Many Lands*. Abington, 1961.
Phelps, Ethel Johnston. *The Maid of the North and Other Folk Tale Heroines*. Holt, 1981.
Reeder, Ed. *Medal of Honor Heroes*. Random, 1965.
Ross, Nancy Wilson. *Heroines of the Early West*. Random, 1960.
Rovin, Jeff. *The Encyclopedia of Super Heroes*. Facts on File, 1985.
Shapiro, Irwin. *Heroes in American Folklore*. Messner, 1962.

Films and Videos

American Tall Tale Heroes. COR, 15 mins.
The Brave Little Tailor. BNCH, 11 mins.
Cartoon All-Stars to the Rescue. BV, 30 mins.
The Puppy's Amazing Rescue. COR, 23 mins.
What Is a Hero? PHX, 17 mins.

—— CELEBRATE BOOKS ——
ALL SUMMER
(Holidays, Celebrations)

There are plenty of reasons to celebrate this summer at _____ Library, as we take a look at an entire year's worth of holidays. Join us for a Fourth of July picnic, a spring dance, and a day of thanks. Count down the New Year, march in a patriotic parade, and be a cheerleader. Exchange valentines, create a Halloween costume, and wish everybody a happy birthday. Then collect your diploma on Graduation Day. If you're looking for fun, come to _____ Library and help us **Celebrate Books All Summer!**

Promotional Items

1. Sign reading "Holiday Headquarters" for check-out area
2. "Party Person" cards (membership cards)
3. Balloon cut-outs (for books read)
4. Reading logs entitled "Books to Celebrate"
5. "Celebrate Books All Summer" bookmarks
6. Reading Club Diplomas (certificates of participation)
7. Noisemakers (game prizes)

Activities

1. Bulletin Board. Post pictures representing all the holidays and events celebrated in this unit. Post titles and authors of books on appropriate cut-outs (birthday books on birthday cake cut-outs, Halloween stories on jack-o-lanterns, etc.). Caption: CELEBRATE BOOKS ALL SUMMER.

2. Reading Incentive Game: Unusual Holidays. Post a large calendar. In an almanac, look up some unusual holidays and observances. Try to find something for every day of the year. For every X books read by the group, mark an unusual holiday on the calendar. Readers will win a prize if the calendar is complete by the closing ceremony.

3. Everybody's Birthday. Decorate with streamers and birthday balloons. Post a large calendar and write the names of all the children on their birthdates.

Let children decorate cone-shaped party hats and put them on. Serve a decorated cake or cupcakes and sing "Happy Birthday to Everybody."

4. Halloween Masquerade. Decorate with Halloween pictures. Provide art materials and let children make masks and costumes out of brown paper bags. Or, notify members ahead of time and have them come to the library in costume. Let children draw jack-o-lantern pictures. Pass out trick-or-treat bags.

5. Giving Thanks. Decorate with cornucopias and other Thanksgiving pictures. Ask children to tell you some things for which they are thankful. The Pilgrims came from England, but people from many other lands immigrated to America. Let children locate on a world map where they or their ancestors came from.

6. Yay, Team! Decorate with sports pictures and team pennants. Let children make pennants for their favorite teams. Teach children some sports cheers. Have them name some big sports events (Olympics, Superbowl, etc.).

7. Winter Holidays. Decorate with pictures of snowmen and holiday designs. Children can cut out paper snowflakes and mount them on colored construction paper. Sing winter holiday songs.

8. New Years Around the World. Decorate with symbols of New Year celebrations from different countries, and "Happy New Year" written in other languages. Have children write out New Year's resolutions. Pass out balloons. Designate a certain time to be midnight. Then count down the time and pop the balloons to celebrate the New Year.

9. Be My Valentine. Decorate with cupids and valentines. Supply art materials and let children create their own valentine cards, to be given to fellow club members or others.

10. Spring Is in the Air. Decorate with pictures of spring flowers. Have children complete a word search puzzle of spring flowers, items, and events. Teach children a Maypole dance. Play ring-around-the-rosy and other dancing games.

11. Fourth of July Picnic. Decorate with pictures of fireworks. Let children make American flags and wave them while singing "The Star Spangled Banner." Then give everyone a summer snack of watermelon and lemonade.

12. Patriots Parade. Decorate with pictures representing various patriotic holidays (Washington's Birthday, Veterans Day, etc.). Discuss why we celebrate these days. Pass out noisemakers and the children's flags from activity #11. Play marching music and let children march around the room in a parade.

13. Weddings and Anniversaries. Decorate with paper wedding bells and flower bouquets. Show children some wedding and anniversary cards. Have children make wedding or anniversary cards for people they know, or for make-believe people.

14. Make-Up-Your-Own Holiday. Discuss some of the unusual holidays listed on the game wall. Ask children to invent some holidays and celebrations they would like to see. They can draw pictures and write stories of their ideas.

15. Closing Ceremony: Graduation Day. Have children make graduation caps out of white poster board. Staple a two-inch wide strip of poster board into a circle to fit atop a child's head. Tape the circle to the center underside of a square piece of poster board, and tape a yarn tassel on top. Line up children and have them march to "Pomp and Circumstance." Pass out their diplomas and have a graduation party.

Theme-Related Books

For Younger Readers

Anno, Mitsumasa, editor. *All in a Day*. Philomel, 1986.
Cohen, Barbara. *Molly's Pilgrim*. Lothrop, 1983.
Hoff, Syd. *Henrietta's Fourth of July*. Garrard, 1981.
Kroll, Steven. *It's Groundhog Day!* Holiday, 1987.
Lee, Jeanne M. *Ba-Nam*. Holt, 1987.
Milhous, Katherine. *The Egg Tree*. Scribner's, 1950.
Modell, Frank. *One Zillion Valentines*. Greenwillow, 1981.
Rice, Eve. *Benny Bakes a Cake*. Greenwillow, 1981.
Stevenson, James. *That Terrible Halloween Night*. Greenwillow, 1980.

For Older Readers

Alcott, Louisa May. *An Old-Fashioned Thanksgiving*. Lippincott, 1974.
Alechem, Sholom. *Holiday Tales of Sholom Alechem*. Scribner's, 1979.
Dickens, Charles. *A Christmas Carol*. Holiday, 1983.
Holmes, Barbara Ware. *Charlotte Shakespeare and Annie the Great*. Harper, 1989.
Phelan, Terry Wolfe. *The S.S. Valentine*. Four Winds, 1979.
Singer, Isaac Bashevis. *The Power of Light: Eight Stories for Hanukkah*. Farrar, 1980.

Nonfiction

Adler, David. *A Picture Book of Jewish Holidays*. Holiday, 1981.
Barth, Edna. *Turkeys, Pilgrims, and Indian Corn: The Story of the Thanksgiving Symbols*. Clarion, 1975.
Bauer, Caroline Feller. *Celebrations: Read-Aloud Holiday and Theme Book Program*. Wilson, 1985.
Behrens, June. *Fiesta! Ethnic Traditional Holidays*. Childrens, 1978.
Bernstein, Joanne, and Cohen, Paul. *Happy Holiday Riddles to You*. Whitman, 1985.
Brown, Tricia. *Chinese New Year*. Holt, 1987.
Chaikin, Miriam. *Ask Another Question: The Story and the Meaning of Passover*. Clarion, 1985.
Cole, Ann, et al. *A Pumpkin in a Pear Tree: Creative Ideas for Twelve Months of Holiday Fun*. Little, 1976.
Hautzig, Esther. *Holiday Treats*. Macmillan, 1983.
_____. *Make It Special: Cards, Decorations, and Party Favors for Holidays and Other Celebrations*. Macmillan, 1983.
Ickis, Marguerite. *The Book of Festivals and Holidays the World Over*. Dodd, 1970.

Livingston, Myra Cohen. *Celebrations.* Holiday, 1985.
Quackenbush, Robert, editor. *The Holiday Songbook.* Lothrop, 1977.

Films and Videos

A Birthday in Japan, the U.S.A., and the U.S.S.R. BARR, 12 mins.
Disney Holiday Movies (several titles). DIS/COR, 10 mins. each.
Holidays and Celebrations Around the World. NGEO, 2 films, 16 mins. each.
The Pigs' Wedding. WW, 7 mins.
The Star-Spangled Banner. WW, 5 mins.

—— AT HOME WITH A BOOK ——

(Homes, Shelters, Houses)

*There's no place like home. But there are so many types of homes! At _____ Library this summer, you will learn about dwellings from many lands, past, present, and future. Build an Indian tepee and a log cabin. Help assemble a gingerbread house. Find out what goes into building a modern house and design your dream house. Plan a house of the future. Come to our Home Show and talk with some experts. _____ Library wants you to be **At Home with a Book!***

Promotional Items

1. Sign reading "Housing Authority" for check-out area
2. "Library Tenant" cards (membership cards)
3. House cut-out (for books read)
4. Reading log entitled "Housing Projects"
5. "At Home with a Book" bookmarks
6. Home Crafter certificates (certificates of participation)
7. Banks shaped like houses (game prizes)

Activities

1. Bulletin Board. Draw a large tree with a cut-away tree house in it. In the tree house, draw a child reading a book. Caption: AT HOME WITH A BOOK.

2. Reading Incentive Game: American Homes. Draw outlines of all types of modern American home styles. Include urban, suburban, and rural structures, and label underneath the outlines what they are (apartment building, split level, colonial, farmhouse, etc.). Prepare cut-outs of these buildings. For every X books read by the group, post a cut-out on the appropriate outline. Readers will win a prize if all the houses are in place by the closing ceremony.

3. Home Sweet Home. Tell children to draw pictures of their homes. Mount on oak tag frames. Under the pictures, write, "Home Sweet Home." Children may add designs along the frames.

4. Indian Homes. Display pictures or models of homes built by some American Indian tribes (wigwam, hogan, tepee, adobe hut, etc.). Explain that these are handmade with natural materials, such as palm fronds, clay, logs, animal skins, etc. Let children make pretend tepees. Cut a triangular opening on one side of a cone-shaped paper cup. Trim off the pointed tip. Arrange three toothpicks into the hole on top to look like tent poles and glue in place. Paint or color tepee with Indian designs.

5. Pioneer Homes. Early American settlers and pioneers built homes out of logs or sod. Let children use Lincoln Logs to build a log cabin. Or, supply popsicle sticks and let children glue them log cabin–style to build a house.

6. Building Materials. Give children a fact sheet of modern house-building materials (steel beams, glass, plaster, copper pipes, lumber, etc.). Pass out another sheet of primitive building materials and the types of houses in which they are used (tropical huts – grass, bamboo; tepees – animal skins; adobes – clay, straw; prehistoric – stones; etc.). Compare the lists. Have children complete word search puzzles of modern and primitive building materials.

7. Gingerbread House. Bake ahead of time the walls of a gingerbread house, or use corrugated cardboard. Supply white frosting, gumdrops, cookie wafers, candy hearts, and other goodies. Let children help put the house together and decorate it. Display the gingerbread house in the library.

8. House Builders. Tell children to pretend they are going to build a house. Ask them to name all the people that will be involved, from the owners, real estate developer, and architect to carpenters, interior decorators, and movers. List all answers. Have children decide the approximate order in which each person will do his job. Then assign children parts and have them briefly act out what the various people do, from planning to actual building to moving into the house.

9. House Plans. Show children some building blueprints and house plans that developers and architects use. Explain how to read them. Give each child a house plan for a one-level home. Supply various paper-cut appliances, kitchen and bathroom fixtures, furniture, etc. Let children arrange these in their house plans and glue them into place. Children may draw features instead of or in addition to the paper cut-outs.

10. Architectural Styles. Give children a fact sheet of architectural styles and types of houses (gothic, contemporary, bungalow, condominium, baroque, etc.). Have children complete a crossword puzzle with these terms.

11. Building Features. Many modern houses and other buildings employ architectural features developed centuries ago. Display pictures of ancient buildings and point to outstanding features (arch, dome, column, turret, gable, stained glass, etc.). Then show pictures of some modern homes and let children identify which features were used. Or let children look through books to find examples of the various architectural features.

12. Dream House. Provide lots of old magazines and catalogs. Tell children to cut out pictures of the type of house they would like to live in. Each child should choose an exterior picture and his own ideal bedroom, as well as any other rooms he would like to include. Glue the pictures onto construction paper and bind them into books titled "My Dream House."

13. Who Lives Here? Play a matching game with children. Post pictures of various houses and shelters throughout history and across the world (caves, igloos, medieval castles, sampans, tents, etc.). Then hold up pictures of people (caveman, Eskimo, king, Chinese fisherman, Bedouin, etc.) and ask children to tell you where these people live(d). Locate on a map where the houses may be found.

14. Homes of the Future. Show pictures of geodesic domes, solar homes, and other ultra-modern or experimental homes of today. Then show futuristic homes from science fiction. Divide children into small groups. Tell each one to design and draw a home of the future. What would some of its outstanding features be? What type of energy would it use? Where would it be built? Who would live in it? What would it be called?

15. Closing Ceremony: Home Show. Display the gingerbread house, tepees, log cabins and other houses made and drawn by children. Invite hobbyists and members of the community to set up doll houses, tents, and other models of houses. Have a carpenter, electrician, plumber, and other construction people talk to children about what they do. Provide various types of building blocks and let children build houses with them. If the party is outdoors, invite people with trailers and customized vans to give tours of their vehicles.

Theme-Related Books

For Younger Children

Asch, Frank. *Good-Bye House*. Prentice, 1986.
Beim, Lorraine, and Beim, Jerrold. *The Little Igloo*. HBJ, 1969.
Carle, Eric. *A House for Hermit Crab*. Picture Book, 1987.
Dupasquier, Phillipe. *Our House on the Hill*. Viking, 1987.
Grifalconi, Ann. *The Village of Round and Square Houses*. Little, 1986.
Krauss, Ruth. *A Very Special House*. Harper, 1990.
Pienkowski, Jan. *Homes*. Simon and Schuster, 1977.
Spier, Peter. *Oh, Were They Ever Happy!* Doubleday, 1978.

Stern, Simon. *Mrs. Vinegar.* Prentice, 1979.
Zelinsky, Paul O. *The Maid and the Mouse and the Odd-Shaped House.* Dodd, 1981.

For Older Readers

Boston, L.M. *The Children of Green Knowe.* HBJ, 1955.
Carris, Joan. *When the Boys Ran the House.* Harper, 1982.
Erwin, Betty K. *Go to the Room of the Eyes.* Little, 1969.
Hamilton, Virginia. *The House of Dies Drear.* Macmillan, 1968.
Klein, Norma. *A Honey of a Chimp.* Pantheon, 1980.
Krensky, Stephen. *A Ghostly Business.* Atheneum, 1984.
Lund, Doris. *You Ought to See Herbert's House.* Watts, 1973.

Nonfiction

Adkins, Jan. *How a House Happens.* Walker, 1972.
Carter, Katharine. *Houses.* Childrens, 1982.
Fisher, Timothy. *Huts, Hovels and Houses.* Addison, 1977.
Floethe, Louise, and Floethe, Richard. *Houses Around the World.* Scribner's, 1973.
Hindley, Judy. *Once There Was a House, and You Can Make It!* Random, 1987.
Robbin, Irving. *The How and Why Book of Caves and Skyscrapers.* Grosset, 1963.
Rosenbloom, Joseph. *Ridiculous Nicholas Haunted House Riddles.* Sterling, 1984.
Schaaf, Peter. *An Apartment House Close Up.* Scholastic, 1980.
Walker, Les. *Housebuilding for Children.* Overlook, 1977.
Weiss, Harvey. *Model Buildings and How to Make Them.* Harper, 1989.
_____. *Shelters: From Tepee to Igloo.* Crowell, 1988.
Williams, Vera B. *It's a Gingerbread House: Bake It! Build It! Eat It!* Greenwillow, 1978.

Films and Videos

Apt. 3. ww, 8 mins.
How to Build an Igloo. nfbc, 11 mins.
The Little House. dis/cor, 8 mins.
People and Places Where They Live. ngeo, 3 films, 11–15 mins. each.
Shelter. cor, 11 mins.

—— CHIEF BIG READER AND —— THE INDIANS OF NORTH AMERICA
(Indians)

Chief Big Reader and the Indians of North America are at
_____ Library with a summer full of activities for you. Create

an Indian village. *Learn about Indian legends, sign language, and culture. Make your own totem pole and Indian costume. Come to the Indian Pow-wow for more fun and games. Become a member of the tribe! Join **CHIEF BIG READER AND THE INDIANS OF NORTH AMERICA.***

Promotional Items

1. Sign reading "Chief Big Reader's Tepee" for check-out area
2. "Tribe Member" cards (membership cards)
3. Tomtom cut-outs (for books read)
4. Reading logs entitled "Indian Guide"
5. Bookmarks in the form of Indian headdress feathers
6. Indian Brave certificates (certificates of participation)
7. Toy tomtoms and rattles (game prizes)

Activities

1. Bulletin Board. Sketch an outline of North America in the center area. Post a large picture of a costumed Indian chief and three smaller Indians to the right of the map. On the left, post pictures of a totem pole and a tepee. Caption: CHIEF BIG READER AND THE INDIANS OF NORTH AMERICA.

2. Reading Incentive Game: Mosaic. Draw an outline of a mosaic design. For tiles, have ready several sheets of square stickers in the colors needed to fill in the design. Add a tile to the mosaic for every X books read by the group. Readers will win a prize if the mosaic is completed by the closing ceremony.

3. Indian Village. Use cone-shaped paper cups to make tepees. Cut a triangular opening on one side. Trim off the pointed tip. Arrange three toothpicks into the hole on top to look like tentpoles and glue in place. Paint or color designs on tepees. Then color pictures of Indians and glue them to cardboard backings to make them sturdy. Tape cardboard props to the backings and stand pictures up. Arrange pebbles and sticks to make a campfire. Add paper or toy trees, animals, etc., to complete the village. This can be an ongoing project throughout the summer.

4. Folklore. Read some Indian legends from different tribes. Do these stories sound like other stories the children have heard? Help readers to find books of Indian folklore to read on their own.

5. Communication. Ask children if they know some ways, other than speaking, by which Indians communicate. Discuss sign language, smoke signals, trail signs, etc., as communication methods. Find a book on Indian communication and pick a few simple words to teach children in sign language.

6. Tribal Regions. Give children maps of North America and have them locate where some of the major Indian tribes originally lived. Divide the map into regions (California, Southwest, Plains, etc.) and have children color them in.

7. Tribe Names. Have children complete a word search puzzle of tribe names.

8. Culture. Display or show pictures of various Indian artwork and crafts. Discuss how Indian culture has influenced our jewelry (beads), clothing (fringe), shoes (moccasins), home decorations (woven rugs, baskets), etc. Ask children if they own anything that was inspired by Indian culture. Have them write a story or draw a picture about Indian arts and crafts.

9. War Paint. Show pictures of Indians in war paint. Explain that this is another type of communication. Supply crayons and give each child a picture of a face on which to draw a war paint design. You can also supply costume makeup and let children paint their own faces.

10. Indian Terms. Give children a fact sheet of Indian terms, (papoose, tomahawk, peace pipe, brave, etc.). Have them complete a crossword puzzle with these terms.

11. Totem Poles. Show children pictures of totem poles. Give them various-sized wooden spools or clean stones to make their own totem poles. Glue three spools or stones together, the largest on the bottom and the smallest on the top. Let children paint faces or designs on the spools or stones.

12. Place Names. Ask children to look at a United States map and name the states which have Indian names. Point out the cities and towns in your state which have Indian names. Are any local buildings, rivers, streets, parks, etc., named after Indians or tribes?

13. Indian Names. Read some names of actual and fictitious Indians. Note how animals and descriptive words are often used. Let children invent Indian names for themselves. Give them sheets of fringed construction paper and drawing materials. Let children design plaques with their Indian names.

14. Indian Costumes. Staple paper or real feathers to strips of oak tag and fit around child's head to make a headdress. Let children string together colorful beads or macaroni to make necklaces. Cut fringed vests out of brown paper bags and decorate with crayon, bits of yarn, and feathers.

15. Closing Ceremony: Indian Pow-Wow. Have children wear their Indian costumes. Give them tomtoms and rattles. Let them dance in a circle to a record of Indian music. Children can play games that were first played by Indians, such as dodge ball, archery (use rubber-tipped arrows), ring-toss, and guessing games.

Theme-Related Books

For Younger Readers

Baylor, Byrd. *Hawk, I'm Your Brother.* Scribner's, 1976.

Benchley, Nathanial. *Small Wolf.* Harper, 1972.
dePaola, Tomie. *The Legend of the Indian Paintbrush.* Putnam, 1988.
Fritz, Jean. *The Good Giants and the Bad Pukwudgies.* Putnam, 1982.
Goble, Paul. *The Girl Who Loved Wild Horses.* Bradbury, 1978.
Haller, Danita. *Not Just Any Ring.* Knopf, 1982.
McDermott, Gerald. *Arrow to the Sun.* Viking, 1974.
Martin, Bill, Jr., and Archambault, John. *Knots on a Counting Rope.* Holt, 1987.
Waterton, Betty. *A Salmon for Simon.* Atheneum, 1980.
Wheeler, M.J. *Fox Tales.* Carolrhoda, 1984.

For Older Readers

Baker, Olaf. *Where the Buffaloes Begin.* Puffin, 1981.
Banks, Lynne Reid. *The Indian in the Cupboard.* Doubleday, 1981.
George, Jean Craighead. *The Talking Earth.* Harper, 1987.
Kittleman, Laurence R. *Canyons Beyond the Sky.* Macmillan, 1985.
Mayne, William. *Drift.* Delacorte, 1986.
Moore, Ruth N. *Peace Treaty.* Herald, 1977.
O'Dell, Scott. *Sing Down the Moon.* Houghton, 1970.
Ortiz, Simon J., and Graves, Sharol. *The People Shall Continue.* Childrens, 1977.
Speare, Elizabeth George. *The Sign of the Beaver.* Houghton, 1983.

Nonfiction

Brandt, Keith. *Indian Festivals.* Troll, 1985.
DeAngulo, Jaime. *Indian Tales.* Farrar, 1962.
Fronval, George, and Dubois, Daniel. *Indian Signals and Sign Language.* Sterling, 1979.
Gates, Frieda. *North American Indian Masks.* Walker, 1982.
Hofsinde, Robert. *Indian Costumes.* Morrow, 1968.
Lyon, Nancy. *Totem Poles and Tribes.* Raintree, 1977.
Marrin, Albert. *War Clouds in the West: Indians and Cavalrymen, 1860–1890.* Macmillan, 1984.
Payne, Elizabeth. *Meet the North American Indians.* Random, 1965.
Red Hawk, Richard. *A Trip to a Pow Wow.* Sierra Oaks, 1988.
Whitney, Alex. *Sports and Games the Indians Gave Us.* McKay, 1977.

Films and Videos

Annie and the Old One. PHX, 15 mins.
Hiawatha. FHE, 52 mins.
The Legend of the Boy and the Eagle. DIS/COR, 21 mins.
Native American Myths. BRIT, 21 mins.
Paddle-to-the-Sea. NFBC, 28 mins.
Pow-Wow! COR, 16 mins.

—— THERE'S MAGIC IN BOOKS ——

(Magic)

*Hocus pocus! Shazam! Abracadabra and Prestidigidoo! You're in for a summer of magic at _____ Library. Learn about all types of magic, here and around the world. Wave your wand and make a rabbit jump out of a hat. See invisible coins and messages appear before your eyes. Create your own mystical spells and potions. Make a magic carpet. See a live magician perform. Don't let the summer disappear without coming in to _____ Library, because **There's Magic in Books!***

Promotional Items

1. Sign reading "Den of Mystery" for check-out area
2. "Conjurer's Cards" (membership cards)
3. Yellow lightning bolts (for books read)
4. Reading logs entitled "Magician's Handbook"
5. "There's Magic in Books" bookmarks
6. Apprentice Magician Awards (certificates of participation)
7. Store-bought magic tricks (game prizes)

Activities

1. Bulletin Board. Draw clouds across the top. At the bottom, draw a large open book. Paste several star cut-outs of various colors to look like they are rising out of the book. On each star, write the title of a fiction or nonfiction book about magic. At either side of the book and stars, paste cut-outs of yellow lightning bolts. Spatter glitter over the display. Caption: THERE'S MAGIC IN BOOKS.

2. Reading Incentive Game: Card Magic. Post several rows of papers drawn to resemble playing cards. For every X books read by the group, flip over one card to reveal a letter of a secret message. (Cards need not be turned in order.) Individual readers will receive one clue for every book they read, and can try to guess the message. All readers will win a prize if all the cards are flipped over by the closing ceremony. Children who guess the message before then may also receive a prize (but must keep the secret!). Suggested secret message: "Coming next summer at _____ Library – Ride the Reading Railroad!" Suggested Clues: "All aboard!" "You're on track." "What comes after spring?" "Not going, but _____."

3. Magic Wands. Give each child a wooden or cardboard dowel, about

½ inch in diameter and about 11 inches long. Paint all but one inch at the tip black or another dark color. Paint the tip white and sprinkle with glitter.

4. Magic Terms. Have children complete a word search puzzle of magic terms (potion, magic lamp, witch, spell, levitate, etc.).

5. Types of Magicians. Discuss different types of magicians, such as genie, witch, fortune teller, sorcerer, alchemist, wizard, and the top-hat-and-cape type. Ask children to name some real or fictitious magicians. Tell children to imagine themselves as magicians (any type). They can invent names and draw pictures of themselves in costume. Display in library.

6. Three Wishes. Read a story in which a magic person grants somebody three wishes. Then let children write or discuss what they would ask for if they had three wishes.

7. Chants. Read some popular magic words and chants ("Mirror, mirror on the wall," "Hocus pocus," "Double double, toil and trouble," "A la peanut butter sandwich," etc.). Have readers make up their own magic chants or magic phrases. Collect and publish in a book to keep in the library.

8. Appearing Objects. Provide several real or fake coins. Show children how to place a coin under a sheet of paper, then rub over the paper with a pencil or crayon so that an impression of the coin will appear. Experiment with other items that have raised surfaces, such as a piece of cardboard on which a design has been punched out.

9. Magic Trick. Perform a simple trick from a book of magic tricks. Then teach the children how to do it.

10. Rabbit Trick. Give each child a heavy paper cup. Tape a circular rim made of oak tag to the open edge of the cup, so it looks like an upside-down top hat. Then insert a straw into a Styrofoam ball which is small enough to fit inside the cup. Paste paper rabbit ears onto the top of the ball. Use a felt-tip marker to draw eyes, nose, and mouth. Poke a hole in the bottom of the cup and push the straw up and down to look like a rabbit jumping out of a magician's top hat.

11. Potion Recipes. Ask readers to pretend they are sorcerers or witches. Tell them to write down the ingredients and instructions for making a magic potion. What would the potion do? Who would they give it to? Collect recipes to publish along with the book of magic spells (activity #7).

12. Disappearing Messages. Prepare ahead of time: On white paper, write the following with an artist's brush dipped in lemon juice: "Science magic— Writing and revealing hidden messages." The message will be invisible when dry. Later, show children the paper. To reveal the message, hold the paper near a hot light bulb (be careful!). The message will magically appear. Reason: The acid in the lemon juice you used reacted to the heat from the bulb by turning the paper brown. Provide paper, brushes, and lemon juice so children can write their own magic messages. Send them home with an instruction sheet for parents.

13. Magic Around the World. Give readers a fact sheet about magic tales from different parts of the world (such as India—magic carpets, Arabia—genies,

Russia—gypsies, etc.) to use in completing a crossword puzzle. Locate these countries on a map.

14. Magic Carpet. Give each child a rectangle of burlap material, about 8 inches by 12 inches. With scissors, cut ½ inch fringe around all four edges. Provide yarn and bits of felt so children can glue designs on the cloth.

15. Closing Ceremony: Magic Show. Invite one or more magicians to perform. Serve "Magic Potion Punch" (punch in a large bowl with dry ice in it). Children may come dressed as magicians, witches, etc., if desired.

Theme-Related Books

For Younger Readers

Alexander, Sue. *Marc the Magnificent.* Pantheon, 1978.
Allen, Sue. *Farley, Are You for Real?* Coward, 1976.
Cole, Babette. *The Trouble with Mom.* Coward, 1984.
Coville, Bruce, and Coville, Katherine. *The Foolish Giant.* Harper, 1978.
Galdone, Paul. *The Magic Porridge Pot.* Houghton, 1976.
Graves, Robert. *The Big Green Book.* Macmillan, 1962.
Himmelman, John. *Amanda and the Witch Switch.* Viking, 1985.
Lester, Helen. *The Wizard, the Fairy and the Magic Chicken.* Houghton, 1983.
Nixon, Joan Lowery. *Magnolia's Mixed-Up Magic.* Putnam, 1983.
Nozaki, Akihiro, and Anno, Mitsumasa. *Anno's Hat Tricks.* Putnam, 1985.
Steig, William. *The Amazing Bone.* Farrar, 1976.

For Older Readers

Alexander, Lloyd. *The Cat Who Wished to Be a Man.* Dutton, 1973.
Bellairs, John. *The House with a Clock in Its Walls.* Dell, 1973.
Berenstain, Michael. *The Sorcerer's Scrapbook.* Random, 1981.
Chapman, Vera. *Miranty and the Alchemist.* Avon, 1983.
Fleischman, Sid. *Mr. Mysterious and Company.* Little, 1962.
Gaskin, Carol. *The War of the Wizards.* Troll, 1985.
Gormley, Beatrice. *Fifth Grade Magic.* Dutton, 1982.
Lewis, C.S. *The Lion, the Witch, and the Wardrobe.* Macmillan, 1950.
McGraw, Elios Jarvis. *Joel and the Great Merlini.* Pantheon, 1979.
Selden, George. *The Genie of Sutton Place.* Farrar, 1973.

Nonfiction

Beisner, Monika. *Secret Spells and Curious Charms.* Farrar, 1985.
Broekel, Ray, and White, Laurence B., Jr. *Now You See It: Easy Magic for Beginners.* Little, 1979.
Eldin, Peter. *The Magic Handbook.* Messner, 1985.
Fulves, Karl. *Self-Working Table Magic: Ninety-Seven Foolproof Tricks with Everyday Objects.* Dover, 1981.
Miller, Marvin. *Your Own Super Magic Show.* Scholastic, 1984.

Reisberg, Ken. *Card Tricks.* Watts, 1980.
Shalit, Nathan. *Science Magic Tricks: Over 50 Fun Tricks That Mystify and Dazzle.* Holt, 1981.
Van der Meer, Ron. *The Pop-Up Book of Magic Tricks.* Viking, 1983.
Walter, Marion. *Another Magic Mirror Book.* Scholastic, 1978.

Films and Videos

Aladdin and His Wonderful Lamp. PHX, 10 mins.
Bedknobs and Broomsticks. DIS, 117 mins.
The Sorcerer's Apprentice. PYR, 28 mins.
Strega Nona. WW, 9 mins.
A Trip to a Magic Show. CHUR, 14 mins.
The Wizard's Son. PHX, 10 mins.

—— KING ARTHUR ——
AND THE READERS
OF THE ROUND TABLE
(Medieval Times)

Hear ye! Hear ye! Good King Arthur hereby invites all noble boys and girls to become Readers of the Round Table. Journey back in time to sixth century England and see young Arthur pull the sword from the stone to become king. Explore magic with the wizard Merlin. Rescue fair damsels from fire-breathing dragons. Join Lady Guinevere, Sir Lancelot, and other citizens of Camelot at the Medieval Fair. Sign up now for a summer of fun and adventure. **King Arthur and the Readers of the Round Table** *await!*

Promotional Items

1. Sign reading "Camelot" for check-out area
2. "Loyal Subject of King Arthur's Court" cards (membership cards)

3. Shield cut-outs for books read
4. Reading logs entitled "King Arthur's Quest"
5. "Reader of the Round Table" bookmarks
6. "Noble Reader of the Round Table" scrolls (certificates of participation)
7. Dragon figures (game prizes)

Activities

1. **Bulletin Board.** At the center, place a large open scroll, flanked on both sides with pictures of knights in armor. On the scroll (in calligraphy) write: "Hear ye! Hear ye! Let it be known that at _____ Library, in the summer of _____, these good dames and knights have joined King Arthur as loyal READERS OF THE ROUND TABLE!" List the names of all reading club members, preceded by "Sir" or "Dame."

2. **Reading Incentive Game: Build a Castle.** Sketch a medieval castle made of several white bricks. For every X books read by club members, color in one of the bricks. Readers will win a prize if the entire castle is colored in by the closing ceremony.

3. **Round Table.** Explain that King Arthur had his knights sit at a round table to show they were all equal. Have children sit in a circle. Go around the circle and let each child make up a medieval-type name for himself. Using a toy sword, have a librarian dub each child by his chosen name.

4. **Legendary Folk.** Give each reader a fact sheet with the names of famous Arthurian characters (Lancelot, Merlin, Excalibur, etc.). Have readers complete a word search puzzle containing these names. Name some famous characters from later medieval times (Robin Hood, Richard the Lion-Hearted, etc.).

5. **Castle Project.** Use paper towel rolls, shoe boxes, packing crates, and other materials to build a model medieval castle. This can be an ongoing project, with children adding figures and decorating the castle throughout the summer.

6. **The Sword in the Stone.** Prepare a toy sword stuck in a papier-mâché stone. Relate the story of *The Sword in the Stone*. Tell the children they are knights and have them act out the story. Let them use their dubbed names and brag about their strength as characters in the legend did. Select a small child to play Arthur. How do the others react when Arthur pulls out the sword?

7. **Crowns.** Cut out construction paper crowns. Let children decorate them with markers, glitter, and crumpled tissue paper.

8. **Coat-of-Arms.** Explain to the children about coat-of-arms designs which were displayed on medieval shields and flags. Give each child a paper shield and let him draw his own coat-of-arms to display in the library.

9. **Dragons.** Read a medieval dragon story. Have children write and illustrate their own dragon stories.

10. Medieval Terms. Have children complete a crossword puzzle containing various medieval terms (armor, castle, squire, moat, dragon, etc.).

11. The Medieval Times. Ask children to draw a picture or write a story or news article about a medieval event, book, or character. Bind these in a book called "The Medieval Times" to be kept in the library.

12 Merlin. Discuss the role of Merlin in the Arthurian legend. Let children name other real or fictitious magicians of whom they have heard. Invite a magician to perform at the library.

13. Puppets. Have children color paper cut-outs of medieval characters (knights, kings, ladies, dragons, etc.). Glue the figures onto popsicle sticks to make stick puppets. Let children create their own puppet shows of a jousting match, a knight rescuing a maiden from a fire-breathing dragon, an audience with the king, etc.

14. Clothing. Show children pictures of the types of clothing various people wore in medieval times. Include garb of royalty, servants, knights, etc. Then have children make costume armor. Cut two breastplates from cardboard or a brown paper bag for each child. Draw on scales. Tie front and back together at the child's shoulders and under the arms with string.

15. Closing Ceremony: Medieval Fair. Children can dress as members of King Arthur's court. Entertainment may include jugglers, minstrels, games of chance, magic show, dancing, and a costume parade.

Theme-Related Books

For Younger Readers

Aliki. *A Medieval Feast.* Crowell, 1983.
Anno, Mitsumasa. *Anno's Medieval World.* Collins, 1980.
dePaola, Tomie. *The Knight and the Dragon.* Putnam, 1980.
Garrick, Liz. *Quest for King Arthur.* Bantam, 1988.
Gerrard, Roy. *Sir Cedric.* Farrar, 1984.
Hodges, Margaret. *Saint George and the Dragon.* Little, 1984.
Hunter, Mollie. *Knight of the Golden Plain.* Harper, 1983.
Lasker, Joe. *Merry Ever After: A Story of Two Medieval Weddings.* Viking, 1976.
Peet, Bill. *Cowardly Clyde.* Houghton, 1979.
Pyle, Howard. *The Story of the Champions of the Round Table.* Macmillan, 1984.
Tripp, Wallace. *Sir Toby Jingle's Beastly Journey.* Coward, 1976.

For Older Readers

Bulla, Clyde Robert. *Sword in the Tree.* Crowell, 1956.
Curry, Ann. *The Book of Brendan.* Holiday, 1990.
deAngeli, Marguerite. *The Door in the Wall.* Doubleday, 1949.
Eager, Edward. *Knight's Castle.* HBJ, 1956.
Fleischman, Sid. *The Whipping Boy.* Greenwillow, 1986.

Greer, Gery, and Ruddick, Bob. *Max and Me and the Time Machine.* HBJ, 1983.
Sancha, Sheila. *Walter Dragun's Town: Crafts and Trade in the Middle Ages.* Harper, 1989.
Storr, Catherine. *The Sword in the Stone.* Raintree, 1985.
Twain, Mark. *A Connecticut Yankee in King Arthur's Court.* Morrow, 1988.

Nonfiction

Bishop, Ann. *Riddle Ages.* Whitman, 1977.
Cosman, Madeline Pelner. *Medieval Holidays and Festivals.* Scribner's, 1981.
Cummings, Richard. *Make Your Own Model Forts and Castles.* McKay, 1977.
Martin, Sidney, and McMillan, Dana. *Puppets and Costumes.* Monday Morning, 1986.
Norvell, Flo Ann Hedley. *The Great Big Box Book.* Crowell, 1979.
Schnurberger, Lynn. *Kings, Queens, Knights and Jesters: Making Medieval Costumes.* Harper, 1978.
Suskind, Richard. *Men in Armor: The Story of Knights and Knighthood.* Norton, 1968.

Films and Videos

The Middle Ages. NGEO, 3 films, 20 mins. each.
The Sword in the Stone. DIS, 79 mins.
The Table Round. CTI, 15 mins.
Tom Thumb in King Arthur's Court. COR, 20 mins.

—— DR. BOOKENSTEIN'S —— MONSTER MARATHON

(Monsters)

Dr. Bookenstein, the infamous mad scientist, welcomes you to his laboratory this summer at _____ Library. Help him build his latest creature. Learn about storybook monsters, legendary and mythological monsters, and movie monsters. Create your own monster friends and meet some nice monsters, too. Then gather together for the big Monster Mash at Dr. Bookenstein's Haunted House Party. So sign up now. You'll have a howling good time at **Dr. Bookenstein's Monster Marathon!**

Promotional Items

1. Sign reading "Dr. Bookenstein's Laboratory" for check-out area
2. "Lab Passes" (membership cards)
3. Bat cut-outs (for books read)
4. Reading logs entitled "Laboratory Journal"
5. "Dr. Bookenstein's Monster Marathon" bookmarks
6. Monsterpiece Awards (certificates of participation)
7. Monster makeup kits (game prizes)

Activities

1. Bulletin Board. In the bottom right corner, post a picture of a mad scientist holding a laboratory beaker. Draw the outline of a huge cloud of smoke rising out of the beaker and encircling the remaining area. Inside the cloud, post pictures of various movie, folklore, picture book, etc., monsters. Caption: DR. BOOKENSTEIN'S MONSTER MARATHON.

2. Reading Incentive Game: Dr. Bookenstein's Monster. Draw the mad scientist at one side. Next to him, draw a long operating table standing upright, on which the monster will be built. Above, in random order, post cut-outs of various monster parts. A part of the monster will go on the table for every X books read by the group. Readers will win a prize if the monster is built by the closing ceremony. (The monster need not look like Frankenstein's monster.)

3. Folklore Monsters. Read a story about Bigfoot or another folklore monster. Ask children to name any other monsters that are supposed to be real. Have children draw pictures of what they think these monsters may look like. Display in library.

4. Literary Monsters. Give readers a fact sheet of monsters from mythology and literature. Have children complete a crossword puzzle of these terms.

5. Monster Friends. Look at some friendly monsters in picture books, such as the *Little Monster* books by Mercer Mayer. Let children draw and name their own monster friends. Display in library.

6. Rock Monsters. Supply lots of clean, smooth stones in various sizes. Let children glue stones together and paint them to make rock monsters.

7. Monster Movies. Show children pictures of some famous movie monsters. Let children name other movie monsters and complete a word search puzzle of these terms.

8. Monster Homes. Hand out a list of places where various monsters supposedly lived (Dracula—Transylvania, etc.). Have children locate these places on a world map.

9. Creature Features. Have children name some characteristics of monsters (ugly, big, evil, scary, etc.). Then show them puppets or pictures of the Sesame

Street monsters (Cookie Monster, etc.) to show that there are also friendly monsters. Can they think of any other good monsters? (This can be made into a lesson on stereotypes.)

10. Hungry Monsters. Read *There's a Monster Eating My House*, by Art Cumings. Compare this with other monsters who eat things (Cookie Monster, The Blob, etc.). Let children make up their own funny or scary stories about monsters that eat things. Collect and print in two books, "Funny Monster Stories" and "Scary Monster Stories," to keep in the library.

11. Dealing with Fears. Read some books about childhood fears, such as *Harry and the Terrible Whatzit*, by Dick Gackenbush. Discuss how the children in the books overcame their fears. Let readers suggest additional ways to deal with fear.

12. Monster School. Tell children to pretend they are young monsters going to monster school. What subjects would they take to learn to be scary? (Growling, rattling chains, etc.) Have children act out some of these "lessons."

13. Make-Your-Own Monster Movie. Divide children into groups and have them think of plots for monster movies. Let each group perform a 5- to 10-minute movie. These may be videotaped and shown at the closing ceremony.

14. Masks. Let children draw scary monster faces on paper bags to make monster masks. Pipe cleaners, yarn, etc., may be added.

15. Closing Ceremony: Haunted House Party. Children may wear monster costumes or masks. Provide various Halloween-type activities (squishy things in a box to feel, haunted house tour, spooky music, etc.). Play novelty songs ("Monster Mash," "Purple People Eater," etc.) and let children sing along.

Theme-Related Books

For Younger Readers

Bang, Molly. *Wiley and the Hairy Man.* Macmillan, 1976.
Cumings, Art. *There's a Monster Eating My House.* Parents, 1981.
Dillon, Barbara. *The Beast in the Bed.* Morrow, 1981.
Gackenbush, Dick. *Harry and the Terrible Whatzit.* Clarion, 1978.
Mayer, Mercer. *Little Monster at School.* Golden, 1978.
Pinkwater, Daniel M. *I Was a Second Grade Werewolf.* Dutton, 1983.
Sesame Street. *Grover's Monster Album.* Random, 1980.
Steig, William. *Rotten Island.* Godine, 1969.
Turkle, Brinton. *Do Not Open.* Dutton, 1981.
Viorst, Judith. *My Momma Says There Aren't Any Zombies, Ghosts, Vampires, Creatures, Demons, Monsters, Fiends, Goblins or Things.* Atheneum, 1973.

For Older Readers

Bridwell, Norman. *How to Care for Your Monster.* Scholastic, 1988.
Coville, Bruce. *The Monster's Ring.* Pantheon, 1982.
Dahl, Roald. *The BFG.* Farrar, 1982.

Giff, Patricia Reilly. *The Beast in Ms. Rooney's Room.* Dell, 1984.
Hitchcock, Alfred, editor. *Alfred Hitchcock's Monster Museum.* Random, 1982.
Koltz, Tony. *Vampire Express.* Bantam, 1984.
Leach, Maria. *Thing at the Foot of the Bed.* Philomel, 1987.
Shelley, Mary. *Frankenstein.* Raintree, 1981.
Williams, Jay, and Abrashkin, Raymond. *Danny Dunn and the Swamp Monster.*
McGraw, 1971.

Nonfiction

Ames, Lee J. *Draw 50 Beasties: And Yugglies and Turnover Uglies and Things That Go Bump in the Night.* Doubleday, 1988.
Aylesworth, Thomas G. *Monsters from the Movies.* Harper, 1972.
Berenstain, Michael. *The Creature Catalog: A Monster Watcher's Guide.* Random, 1982.
Cole, William. *Monster Knock Knocks.* Simon and Schuster, 1988.
Gates, Frieda. *Easy to Make Monster Masks and Disguises.* Prentice, 1981.
Lindsay, Barbara. *Monsters of the Sea.* Four Winds, 1966.
Manning-Sanders, Ruth. *A Book of Ogres and Trolls.* Dutton, 1973.
Ross, Dave. *How to Prevent Monster Attacks.* Morrow, 1984.
Simon, Seymour. *Creatures from Lost Worlds.* Harper, 1979.
Wise, William. *Monsters from Outer Space?* Putnam, 1978.

Films and Videos

The Island of the Skog. ww, 13 mins.
The Making of Michael Jackson's Thriller. ves, 59 mins.
Misunderstood Monsters. chur, 44 mins.
Monster Hits! rh, 30 mins.
Where the Wild Things Are. ww, 8 mins.

— BOOKS ON THE BIG SCREEN —

(Movies)

Lights! Camera! Action! You're in for a blockbuster summer at _____ Library as we explore the art of motion pictures. Learn about filmmaking equipment and what goes into shooting a movie. Make a storyboard and a flipbook. Watch some great clips and be a movie critic. Join Hollywood's famed "Walk of Stars." Play the Movie Trivia Game. Come to our own movie premiere and Library Oscar Awards Ceremony. Come to _____ Library this summer and see **Books on the Big Screen!**

Promotional Items

1. Sign reading "Casting Office" for check-out area
2. "Studio Passes" (membership cards)
3. Clapboard cut-outs (for books read)
4. Reading logs entitled "Screenplay"
5. "Books on the Big Screen" bookmarks
6. Oscar Awards (certificates of participation)
7. Library Oscar statuettes, movie trivia books (game prizes)

Activities

1. Bulletin Board. Cover the area with black construction paper. Make a movie screen with white paper in the center of the top half. On the screen, write the caption: BOOKS ON THE BIG SCREEN. Fill the bottom half with orange circles to represent heads of audience members looking at the screen. Write the names of reading club members on these heads.

2. Reading Incentive Game: Stars on Film. At one end of a wall, draw a movie camera (START). Pace off and number squares to look like frames of blank film along the wall, with END at a movie theater. For every X books read by the group, post a picture of a famous movie actor, actress, or scene in one of the frames. Readers will receive a prize if every frame is filled by the closing ceremony. (The pictures will also be used in a film trivia game, activity #14.)

3. Movie Careers. Ask children to name the types of people needed to make a movie (producer, actors, gaffers, etc.). List all jobs. Then read *Lights! Camera! Action!* by Gail Gibbons and add to the list. Have children complete a word search puzzle of these terms.

4. Flipbooks. Give each child a small white notepad. Position it with the binding on the left. On the first page, draw a line about one-third from the bottom of the page. Color the lower part tan (for sand) and the upper part blue (for water). Repeat this scene on all the pages. On the second page, add a sailboat just entering the water from the left. Draw the boat on each page, moving it slightly to the right each time, until it sails off the last page. When the drawings are completed, hold the notepad in the left hand and flip through the pages with the right. Explain to children that this illustrates how motion pictures work. Artistic children can add other details, such as a sunset, to their movie books if desired.

5. Book vs. Movie Versions. Books are often changed when they are made into movies. Read a picture book, then show the movie of the story. What is different in the film? Why do the children think the changes were made? Which version do they prefer? Suggest that they read another book from which a movie was made. Have them write a film review comparing the book to its movie.

6. Filmmaking. Invite an expert to speak to the children about filmmaking.

Display motion picture and video cameras, projectors, and other equipment and explain how they work. Give readers a fact sheet of film terms (soundtrack, studio, credits, screenplay, etc.) and have children complete a crossword puzzle with these terms.

7. Storyboards. Provide two copies of a coloring book which tells a story. Rip out all the pages and assign a page to each child to color. Make sure they use the same colors throughout for the characters' clothes, etc., to assure continuity. When done, have children arrange the pictures on the wall in correct sequence, just as an editor would edit scenes in a movie. The completed display illustrates the concept of a film storyboard. Children can make their own storyboards by folding a large piece of paper in half three times and drawing sequential pictures in each box.

8. Make-Your-Own Movie. If video or film equipment is available, film a movie based on the storyboard or another popular children's story. Provide simple costumes and assign roles. Filming may be done in or out of sequence, depending upon the availability of editing equipment. Show the film as a movie premiere at the closing ceremony.

9. Special Effects. Explain that filmmakers use a variety of special effects and stunt people to create realistic or fantastic scenes. Show a film of how a popular movie was made. List the types of special effects used (matte paintings, miniatures, makeup, etc.). Discuss a current movie with the children. How do they think the special effects were created?

10. Video Book Reports. Film or videotape children giving oral book reports on books read this summer (as on "Reading Rainbow"). Show at the closing ceremony.

11. Silent Movies. Explain that early motion pictures had no soundtracks. Show some old silent movies (Charlie Chaplin, Keystone Kops, etc.) to the group. How has the quality of filmmaking improved since then? Why are those oldies considered classics?

12. Star Prints. Discuss Hollywood's famed "Walk of Stars." Let children make their own star handprints with poster paint on construction paper. Write on each "square" what that child is famous for (acting, directing, etc.) and display in library.

13. Star Names. Tell children that many famous actors and actresses changed their names. Play a game in which children try to match some movie stars' real names to their star names. Ask children to tell you what name they would use as a star name.

14. Movie Trivia Game. Have children guess (individually or in teams) the famous people or movies depicted in the reading incentive game frames.

15. Closing Ceremony: Hollywood and the Oscars. Hold a Hollywood movie premiere: Show all films taken of the group during the summer. Then present the Library Oscar Awards: Invent awards (Best Scene-Stealer, Best Scream, etc.) and note these on the Oscar Awards. Read each "winner's" name and award, and have children accept their prizes as in the real Oscar ceremony.

Theme-Related Books

For Younger Readers

Adler, David A. *Cam Jansen and the Mystery of the Monster Movie.* Dell, 1989.
Bradman, Tony. *Dilly and the Horror Movie.* Viking, 1989.
Bridwell, Norman. *Clifford Goes to Hollywood.* Scholastic, 1980.
Chatalbash, Ron. *A Perfect Day for the Movies.* Godine, 1983.
Chorao, Kay. *Ida Makes a Movie.* Houghton, 1974.
Lobel, Arnold. *Martha the Movie Mouse.* Harper, 1966.
Nixon, Joan Lowry. *Big Foot Makes a Movie.* Scholastic, 1983.

For Older Readers

Bond, Michael. *Paddington on Screen.* Houghton, 1982.
Byars, Betsy. *The Two-Thousand Pound Goldfish.* Harper, 1982.
Greene, Constance C. *Star Shine.* Dell, 1987.
Hughs, Dean. *Nutty, the Movie Star.* Macmillan, 1989.
Kassil, Lev. *Once in a Lifetime.* Doubleday, 1970.
Pfeffer, Susan Beth. *Take Two and Rolling.* Putnam, 1985.
Pinkwater, Daniel M. *Return of the Moose.* Dodd, 1979.
Snyder, Carol. *Ike and Mama and the Once-in-a-Lifetime Movie.* Coward, 1981.
Streatfield, Noel. *Movie Shoes.* Random, 1949.
Weber, Judith E. *Lights, Camera, Cats!* Lothrop, 1978.

Also: Suggest books from which movies have been made.

Nonfiction

Clemens, Virginia P. *Behind the Filmmaking Scene.* Westminster, 1982.
Edelson, Edward. *Great Movie Spectaculars.* Doubleday, 1976.
Fradin, Dennis B. *Movies.* Childrens, 1983.
Gibbons, Gail. *Lights! Camera! Action! How a Movie Is Made.* Crowell, 1985.
Gleasner, Diana C. *The Movies: Inventions That Changed Our Lives.* Walker, 1983.
Goldreich, Gloria, and Goldreich, Esther. *What Can She Be? A Film Producer.* Lothrop, 1977.
Horvath, Joan. *Filmmaking for Beginners.* Nelson, 1974.
Ireland, Karin. *Hollywood Stunt People.* Messner, 1980.
Meyer, Nicholas E. *Magic in the Dark: A Young Viewer's History of the Movies.* Facts on File, 1985.
O'Connor, Jane, and Hall, Katy. *Magic in the Movies: The Story of Special Effects.* Doubleday, 1980.
Thurman, Judith, and David, Jonathan. *The Magic Lantern: How Movies Got to Move.* Atheneum, 1978.

Films and Videos

Bambi Meets Godzilla. PYR, 2 mins.
From Star Wars to Jedi: The Making of a Saga. FIV, 65 mins.

History of Animation. DIS/COR, 21 mins.
The Muppet Movie. CBS, 94 mins.
Really Rosie. WW, 26 mins.

—— SEE 'EM IN A MUSEUM ——

(Museums)

What do wax figures, baseball bats, dinosaur skeletons, arrowheads, the Mona Lisa, and the Hope Diamond have in common? They can all be found in museums! This summer, _____ Library will introduce you to all kinds of museums. Create a work of art to hang in our Art Gallery. Add to our Transportation Museum. Discover some famous homes and museums in (name of state). Be part of a science museum exhibit. Make a clay artificat. Start your own special collection. Design an entry for a Hall of Fame museum. Talk to a museum curator and find out what it's like to work in a museum. Come to _____ Library and **See 'em in a Museum.**

Promotional Items

1. Sign reading "(Name of Library) Museum of Books" for check-out area
2. "Friend of (Name of Library) Museum" cards (membership cards)
3. Picture frame cut-outs (for books read)
4. Reading logs entitled "Exhibits"
5. "See 'em in a Museum" bookmarks
6. Exhibitor's Awards (certificates of participation)
7. Frames for certificates (game prizes)

Activities

1. Bulletin Board. Post pictures of famous artwork and exhibits from all types of museums around the world. Label each item with its name and where it can be found. (Example: "Mona Lisa," painting by Leonardo DaVinci, Louvre, Paris, France.) Caption: SEE 'EM IN A MUSEUM.

2. Reading Incentive Game: Historical Costumes. Label one wall, "Museum of Historical Costumes." Draw a timeline for the period of history you wish to cover (such as America from colonial times to present). For every X books read by the group, post a picture on the timeline, in chronological order, of a costume worn during that era. Readers will win a prize if the timeline is completed by the closing ceremony.

3. Transportation Museum. Some museums feature cars, trolleys, airplanes, or other modes of transportation. Ask children to bring in miniature vehicles of any type. Set up a Transportation Museum display. Make sure each item is labeled with the owner's name.

4. Special Collections. Museums display collections of things. Ask each child to select a different item to collect. Be specific; instead of "toys," pick dolls or bicycles or teddy bears. Throughout the summer, children should collect pictures of their chosen item. (These can be saved at home or in the library, as you see fit.) Later in the summer, have children glue their pictures onto oak tag to make collages. Display in the Special Collections Gallery (see activity #12).

5. Natural History Museums. Read *Dinosaurs, Dragonflies and Diamonds*, by Gail Gibbons. Ask children if they have ever been to a natural history museum. Which one? What did they see there? What were their favorite exhibits?

6. Art Gallery. Provide several types of drawing and painting materials. Tell children that an area in the library will be set up as an art gallery. Let each child create a work of art for the gallery. Mount these pictures on oak tag. Display in the art gallery, with the title of the work and the artist's name.

7. Famous Homes. The homes of many famous people have been preserved as museums. Give children a list of museum homes. Have children locate these homes on a United States map.

8. Artifacts. Archaeologists find many interesting artifacts of past cultures which go on display in history museums. Show pictures of some artifacts to children. Then provide modeling clay. Let children mold replicas of various artifacts (arrowheads, coins, vases, bowls, etc.).

9. State Museums. Have children complete a word search puzzle of museums and galleries located in your state.

10. Science Exhibit. Many science museums have "hands-on" or participatory exhibits. Have ten children create their own participatory "Perpetual Motion Exhibit." Child #1 starts one motion that affects child #2, such as tapping his head. Child #2, in turn, does another motion that affects child #3, and so on. Other groups of children may form motion exhibits. Have each child use a sound effect along with his motion.

11. Halls of Fame. There are several "Hall of Fame" museums in the United States, from Baseball to Rock and Roll. Give children a list of these museums. Divide children in groups and assign each one a different Hall of Fame. Ask groups to think about what their hall does or should contain. Then have each group make a poster, mobile, or other art project to advertise or add to the collection of their hall.

12. Display Plates. Help children find four books (fiction and nonfiction) in the library that are related to their special collections (see activity #4). Then children may make display plates for their collages. On each plate, print the name of the collection and the child's name: "Special Collection: HATS, by (name)." Underneath, write, "For more information, read: (list of books)." Children may add decorative borders to their display plates. Post each plate beneath its collage in the Special Collections Gallery.

13. Museum People. Give children a fact sheet about people who work in museums. Have children complete a crossword puzzle with these terms.

14. Parchments. Many museums contain original historical documents. Let children write their own special documents. Give each child a piece of a brown paper bag and have him write a message or draw a treasure map on it. Then wrinkle the paper by crumpling it up into a ball and opening it several times. This will give a weathered, parchment effect to the documents.

15. Closing Ceremony: Guest Speaker. Invite a curator from a nearby museum to speak to the children. Perhaps the curator can bring one or more exhibits along and explain how they were acquired or set up. The curator and a librarian can discuss the similarities between a museum and a library. Let children ask the speaker questions about working in a museum. Make sure parents and other guests look at the various galleries and exhibits on which the children have worked during the summer.

Theme-Related Books

For Younger Readers

Bjork, Christina. *Linnea in Monet's Garden.* Farrar, 1987.
Cohen, Miriam. *Lost in the Museum.* Greenwillow, 1979.
Fradon, Dana. *Sir Dana—A Knight: As Told by His Trusty Armor.* Dutton, 1988.
Freeman, Don. *Norman the Doorman.* Viking, 1959.
Gramatky, Hardie. *Hercules.* Putnam, 1940.
Hoff, Syd. *Danny and the Dinosaur.* Harper, 1958.
Mayhew, James. *Katie's Picture Show.* Bantam. 1989.
Ross, Pat. *M and M and the Mummy Mess.* Viking, 1985.
Rubin, Cynthia Elyce. *ABC Americana from the National Gallery of Art.* HBJ, 1989.
Simmonds, Posy. *Lulu and the Flying Babies.* Knopf, 1988.

For Older Readers

Cameron, Eleanor. *The Court of the Stone Children.* Dutton, 1973.
Carey, M.V. *The Three Investigators in the Mystery of the Wandering Caveman.* Random, 1982.

Christian, Mary Blount. *The Undercover Kids and the Museum Mystery.* Whitman, 1983.
Estes, Eleanor. *The Moffat Museum.* HBJ, 1983.
Gilson, Jamie. *Harvey the Beer Can King.* Lothrop, 1978.
Konigsburg, E.L. *From the Mixed-Up Files of Mrs. Basil E. Frankweiler.* Atheneum, 1967.
McHargue, Georgess. *Funny Bananas: The Mystery in the Museum.* Holt, 1975.
Selden, George. *The Genie of Sutton Place.* Farrar, 1973.
Wandelmaier, Roy. *Secret of the Old Museum.* Troll, 1985.
Winn, Chris, and Beadle, Jeremy. *Rodney Rootle's Grow-Up Grappler and Other Treasures from the Museum of Outlawed Inventions.* Little, 1983.

Nonfiction

Althea. *Visiting a Museum.* Cambridge, 1983.
Anderson, Joan. *From Map to Museum.* Morrow, 1988.
Cutchins, Judy, and Johnston, Ginny. *Are Those Animals Real? How Museums Prepare Wildlife Exhibits.* Morrow, 1984.
Doda, Margaret B. *Collections for Kids.* Oak Tree, 1982.
Gibbons, Gail. *Dinosaurs, Dragonflies and Diamonds.* Four Winds, 1988.
Papajani, Janet. *Museums.* Childrens, 1983.
Stan, Susan. *Careers in an Art Museum.* Lerner, 1983.
Thomson, Peggy. *Museum People.* Prentice, 1977.
Watts, J.F. *The Smithsonian.* Chelsea, 1987.
Weil, Lisl. *Let's Go to the Museum.* Holiday, 1989.
Zubrowski, Bernie. *Bubbles: A Children's Museum Activity Book.* Little, 1979.

Films and Videos

Don't Eat the Pictures: Sesame Street at the Metropolitan Museum of Art. RH, 60 mins.
Fossils: From Site to Museum. COR, 11 mins.
Mummies Made in Egypt. RR, 30 mins.
Ox-Cart Man. RR, 30 mins.
This Is Your Museum Speaking. FIV, 13 mins.

— TUNE IN TO THE LIBRARY —

(Music)

There's a lot to sing about this summer at _____ Library.
Music is everywhere! Sing rounds and play musical games. Listen
to all kinds of music. Make musical instruments. Find out about

*life in the recording industry. Design an album cover. Vote for
your favorite Top 40 songs and create a collage of your favorite
musicians. You can even see a live band perform. Don't miss the
fun! Make plans to* **Tune In to the Library!**

Promotional Items

1. Sign reading "Recording Studio" for check-out area
2. "Music-Maker" cards (membership cards)
3. Music note cut-outs (for books read)
4. Reading logs entitled "Recording Contract"
5. "Tune in to the Library" bookmarks
6. Grammy Award certificates (certificates of participation)
7. Toy musical instruments (game prizes)

Activities

1. Bulletin Board. At the center, draw a stave with a G clef. On it, write the caption: TUNE IN TO THE LIBRARY. Around the stave, post cut-outs of various musical instruments and notes. Write the name of a reading club member on each note or instrument.

2. Reading Incentive Game: Grammy Awards. Post a list of Grammy Award categories. For every X books read by the group, write in the name of a Grammy Award winner. (You can look up actual winners, or have the children pick them.) Readers will win a prize if all the categories are filled in by the closing ceremony.

3. Musical Games. Teach children some rounds to sing and some musical games to play.

4. Musicians. Ask children who play musical instruments to bring them in. Have them show the group how their instruments work and how to take care of them. Why did they choose their particular instruments? How long have they been playing them? Invite children to play short selections at the closing ceremony.

5. Homemade Instruments. Make simple musical instruments with children, such as water glass chimes, comb harmonicas, or paper plate tambourines.

6. Identifying Instruments. Explain the four types of musical instruments in a symphony orchestra: strings, woodwinds, brass, and percussion. Show pictures and play recordings of some of these, and let children guess what they are. List each instrument under its proper category.

7. Music Terms. Give children a fact sheet of basic music terms (stave, G clef, pitch, melody, etc.). Have them complete a crossword puzzle with these terms.

8. Sheet Music. Ask children to sing the music scale. Then play "Do Re Mi" from *The Sound of Music*. Show children sheet music and identify staves, types of notes, clefs, sharps, etc. Play recordings for which you have sheet music and let children follow along.

9. Collages. Provide lots of teen and music magazines. Let children cut out pictures and glue them onto oak tag to make collages or concert scenes. Have them label their art work: "My Favorite Groups," "Backstage with _____," etc. Display in library.

10. Types of Music. Give readers a fact sheet and play recordings of different types of music (baroque, opera, pop, sea shanties, R&B, etc.). Have children complete a word search puzzle with these terms.

11. Top 40 Countdown. Ask children to tell you their favorite songs— children's, pop, any type. List all answers and let them vote for their three favorites. Total the votes and list the top vote-getter as #1, and so on to #40. Do the same for favorite musicians. Print lists and distribute at the closing ceremony.

12. Album Covers. Supply paper, drawing materials, and old magazines to cut. Let children design album covers for a real or made-up musician or group.

13. Concert Tour. Give readers a list of international cities. Tell them to imagine that their favorite musician is going on a tour to these cities. Have children locate the places on a world map.

14. Boom Boxes. Have children list some electronic equipment used for listening to music (CD player, radio, etc.). Use cereal or shoe boxes to make pretend boom boxes. Cover the boxes with plain paper. Cut out cardboard circles for speakers. Number a rectangular strip of cardboard with AM and FM frequencies. Use buttons for on/off and volume dials. Glue on all pieces and use markers to add a brand name and label the dials. Attach a sturdy cardboard handle, and a pipe cleaner for an antenna.

15. Closing Ceremony: Music Recital. Let volunteers play short pieces on their musical instruments for the group. Invite a local band or orchestra to perform.

Theme-Related Books

For Younger Readers

Andersen, Hans Christian. *The Nightingale.* HBJ, 1985.
Elwell, Peter. *The King of the Pipers.* Macmillan, 1984.
Hurd, Thacher. *Mama Don't Allow.* Harper, 1984.
Isadora, Rachel. *Ben's Trumpet.* Greenwillow, 1979.
Komaiko, Leah. *I Like the Music.* Harper, 1987.
Kuskin, Karla. *The Philharmonic Gets Dressed.* Harper, 1982.
McCloskey, Robert. *Lentil.* Macmillan, 1940.
Seeger, Pete. *Abiyoyo.* Macmillan, 1986.
Stevenson, James. *Clams Can't Sing.* Greenwillow, 1980.
Williams, Vera B. *Music for Everyone.* Greenwillow, 1984.

For Older Readers

Angell, Judie. *The Buffalo Nickel Blues Band.* Bradbury, 1982.
Bond, Nancy. *A String in the Harp.* McElderry, 1976.
Clymer, Eleanor. *The Horse in the Attic.* Dell, 1985.
Fox, Paula. *The Slave Dancer.* Bradbury, 1973.
Green, Melinda. *Rachel's Recital.* Little, 1979.
Kidd, Ronald. *Sizzle and Splat.* Dell, 1986.
MacLachlan, Patricia. *The Facts and Fictions of Minna Pratt.* Harper, 1988.
Pringle, Laurence. *Popcorn.* Bradbury, 1985.

Nonfiction

Berger, Melvin. *The Photo Dictionary of the Orchestra.* Methuen, 1980.
Collier, James C. *Which Musical Instrument Shall I Play?* Norton, 1969.
Davis, Marilyn K. *Music Dictionary.* Doubleday, 1956.
Evans, Roger. *How to Read Music.* Crown, 1979.
Hankin, Rebecca. *I Can Be a Musician.* Childrens, 1984.
Hayes, Phyllis. *Musical Instruments You Can Make.* Watts, 1981.
Mundy, Simon. *The Usborne Story of Music.* Usborne, 1980.
Nelson, Esther L. *Musical Games for Children of All Ages.* Sterling, 1977.
Yolen, Jane, editor. *Rounds About Rounds.* Watts, 1977.

Films and Videos

Barn Dance! RR, 30 mins.
The Concert. PYR, 12 mins.
The Hoffnung Palm Court Orchestra. PHX, 8 mins.
Melody. AIMS, 8 mins.
A Symposium on Popular Songs. DIS/COR, 16 mins.
Ty's One Man Band. RR, 30 mins.
Who's Afraid of the Opera? MGM/UA, 57 mins.

——— EXTRA! EXTRA! ———
READ ALL ABOUT IT!
(Newspapers, Journalism)

Extra! Extra! Read All About It! Get the scoop on _____
Library's summer reading club! If you have a nose for news, you

will want to join up and explore the world of newspaper publishing. Get your press pass and write a headline for a real news article. Conduct an opinion poll for the editorial page. Write your own feature stories and amusements for our newspaper, The Reading Times. *Have fun with newspaper art projects. Be a roving reporter at our Press Conference. Check out some great books and* **Read All About It!**

Promotional Items

1. Sign reading "Managing Editor" for check-out area
2. "Press Passes" (membership cards; see activity #3)
3. Papers to represent newspaper pages, with headline "Read All About It!" (for books read)
4. Reading logs entitled "The Chronicle"
5. "Extra! Extra! Read All About It!" bookmarks
6. Journalism certificates (certificates of participation)
7. Spiral notepads, pencils, visors (game prizes)

Activities

1. Bulletin Board. Post pictures from popular fiction books. Caption them with newspaper-type headlines, such as: "Miracle in Garden – Invalid Boy Walks! Read *The Secret Garden*, by Frances Hodgson Burnett"; or "Monkey Saves Circus Baby! Read *Curious George Rides a Bike*, by H.A. Rey." Short articles may be written for each book. Caption: EXTRA! EXTRA! READ ALL ABOUT IT!

2. Reading Incentive Game: Layouts. Draw four large rectangles to represent four newspaper page layouts. Section off areas into which headlines, articles, ads, puzzles, photos, and other news copy will later be inserted. In addition to a front page, you may want to include features, amusements, sports, weather, editorials, classifieds, etc. Name the newspaper *The Reading Times* and include library-related articles. Children's contributions may be used, as suggested later on. For every X books read by the group, drop one piece of copy into its pre-set area in the layouts. Children will win a prize if the entire newspaper is pasted up by the closing ceremony.

3. Press Passes. Take ID photos of children. Have them glue photos in the upper right corners of blank 3″ × 5″ index cards. Next to the photos, print, "Press Pass." Stamp passes with the library's name and address, and have children sign their names below. These will serve as the reader's membership cards.

4. Publishing Terms. Give children a fact sheet of newspaper publishing terms (headline, deadline, paste-up, copy edit, etc.). Have children complete a crossword puzzle with these terms.

5. News Copy. Bring in several sheets of news copy. (These can be obtained from a newspaper publisher or a radio station.) Display them so children can see how news items come in over the wire services (AP, UPI). Have children cut up the copy and separate the stories into types of news (national, foreign, sports, political, etc.). Assign children to small groups representing various news departments. Have each group decide on a lead story and make up a headline for it.

6. Paper Boats. Read *Curious George Rides a Bike,* by H.A. Rey. Follow directions in the book to make newspaper boats (or hats) with children. Discuss: Was George a good paper carrier? Let children who are paper carriers talk about their routes.

7. Editorial Page. Opinions are given on the editorial page. Have each child think of one opinion poll topic and phrase it in a question that can be answered simply ("What is your favorite comic strip?" "Do you think the price of movie admission is fair?"). Let children ask each other their questions and note the answers with slash lines on notepaper. Tabulate answers and publish the results of these opinion polls in *The Reading Times.*

8. Hot Off the Press. Display pictures of or actual newspaper printing materials from the past and present. Explain their uses to children. Try to find an old hand-operated duplicating machine or printing press. Let children help you run off printed pages (such as the opinion polls results) with this equipment.

9. Amusements. Ask children to name some things that are amusements in newspapers (crossword puzzles, TV and movie listings, comics, horoscopes, etc.). Let children create their own amusements. Make copies of puzzles to distribute to club members. Comics, etc., may be included in the *The Reading Times.*

10. Features. Look at the features sections of several newspapers. Feature articles present news, but they also entertain. Note the types of articles included there (hobbies, fashion, food, reviews, etc.). Ask children to write and illustrate articles on any features subject of interest. Include some in *The Reading Times.*

11. Newshounds. Provide lots of old newspapers. Ask children to choose a newspaper theme (sports, comics, movie reviews, local news, etc.). Let children cut out headlines, pictures, and parts of articles on their themes. Glue these on sheets of oak tag that have been cut into the shape of a hound dog, to make newshound collages.

12. Classifieds. Show children the classified section of a newspaper. What types of ads are listed? Use some ads in a role-playing game. One child can pretend to call up another about an ad (to buy a car, apply for a job, look at a house, etc.). What questions would he ask? How would the person who placed the ad answer? Ask children if they have anything they would like to sell. How would they write an ad for it?

13. Great Papers. Give readers a fact sheet of some important newspapers, past and present, nationwide and from around the world. List each paper's name, place of publication, year founded, and daily circulation. Discuss why some of these papers are important. Have children locate on a map the cities in which these papers are published.

14. Paper Boys. Trace gingerbread-boy patterns onto sheets of newspaper. Cut out these paper boys and mount them on oak tag. Experiment with different paper sections for different looks.

15. Closing Ceremony: Press Conference. Invite some people who work for a local newspaper to talk to children about their jobs. Hold a mock press conference, with children as reporters asking questions of the speakers. Have the news staff bring actual pasted-up pages, printing plates, and other items of interest.

Theme-Related Books

For Younger Readers

Brennan, Mimi. *The Golden Egg: A Comic Adventure.* Holiday, 1990.
Hall, Malcolm. *Caricatures.* Coward, 1978.
————. *Headlines.* Coward, 1973.
Kroll, Steven. *Newsman Ned and the Broken Rules.* Scholastic, 1989.
Rey, H.A. *Curious George Rides a Bike.* Houghton, 1973.
Waber, Bernard. *Dear Hildegarde.* Houghton, 1980.

For Older Readers

Angell, Judie. *First the Good News.* Bradbury, 1983.
Christian, Mary Blount. *Deadline for Danger.* Whitman, 1985.
Conford, Ellen. *Dear Lovey Hart: I Am Desperate.* Little, 1975.
Greenwald, Sheila. *Write On, Rosy!* Joy St., 1988.
Lowry, Lois. *Anastasia Has the Answers.* Houghton, 1986.
Norby, Lisa. *Star Reporter.* Knopf, 1989.
Roos, Stephen. *Twelve-Year-Old Vows Revenge After Being Dumped by Extra-Terrestrial on First Date.* Doubleday, 1990.
Ruckman, Ivy. *Who Invited the Undertaker?* Harper, 1989.
Wolkoff, Judie. *In a Pig's Eye.* Bradbury, 1986.

Nonfiction

Arnold, Caroline, and Silverstein, Herma. *Hoaxes That Made Headlines.* Messner, 1986.
Carey, Helen H. *How to Read a Newspaper.* Watts, 1983.
Debnam, Betty, and Avery, Lois. *The Mini Page and Your Newspaper Activity Book.* Andrews, 1980.
Fenton, D.X., and Fenton, Barbara. *Behind the Newspaper Scene.* Crestwood, 1980.
Fisher, Leonard Everett. *The Newspapers.* Holiday, 1981.
Gibbons, Gail. *Deadline! From News to Newspaper.* Crowell, 1987.
Koral, April. *Headlines and Deadlines.* Messner, 1981.
Leedy, Lorean. *The Furry News: How to Make a Newspaper.* Holiday, 1990.
Miller, Margaret. *Hot Off the Press!* Crown, 1985.

Striker, Susan. *The Newspaper Anti-Coloring Book.* Holt, 1992.
Walters, Sarah. *How Newspapers Are Made.* Facts on File, 1989.
Weekly Reader: 60 Years of News for Kids 1928–1988. Field, 1988.

Films and Videos

The Great Muppet Caper. CBS, 98 mins.

—— READING ON THE JOB ——

(Occupations)

> You should make it your job to come to _____ Library this summer and learn about all types of occupations and careers. Pick up your worker ID tag at our Employment Agency. Join a factory assembly line. Contribute to our Illustrated Occupations Dictionary. Create a job application and take part in a job interview. Attend our Job Fair and set your career goals. At _____ Library, everybody is **Reading on the Job.**

Promotional Items

1. Sign reading "Employment Agency" for check-out area
2. "Worker ID" tags (membership cards; see activity #3)
3. Dollar bill cut-outs (for books read)
4. Reading logs entitled "Employment Record"
5. "Reading on the Job" bookmarks
6. "Graduate of _____ Library's Job Training Program" certificates (certificates of participation)
7. Play money (game prizes)

Activities

1. Bulletin Board. Post pictures of various people at work. Represent as wide a variety of jobs as possible. Near or on each worker, place a tiny book cut-out. Caption: READING ON THE JOB.

2. Reading Incentive Game: Shopping Center. Caption one area, "Shopping Center." Post pictures to represent various shops. Label pictures with the type of shop and the occupation of a person who works there (florist, waitress, post office clerk, banker, etc.). Pace off a trail through the shopping center. Move a shopping cart marker one square for every X books read by the group. Readers will win a prize if all the shops have been visited by the closing ceremony.

3. Worker ID Tags. Take headshot photos of each child and glue them in the upper left corner of blank $3'' \times 5''$ index cards. List the child's name, age, and library ID number. Ask each child what he wants to be when he grows up. Write this on the ID as Future Occupation. These ID cards will serve as children's membership cards.

4. Illustrated Occupations Dictionary. Each child should choose one or more different occupations. Make sure there is at least one job chosen for each letter of the alphabet. Children will draw and label pictures of their chosen occupations. Have them sign their names on the backs of the pictures. Arrange pictures in alphabetical order. Bind in a looseleaf notebook so more pictures can be added throughout the summer. Keep the dictionary in the library.

5. Land/Sea/Air. Divide children into three groups. Assign them "On Land," "On Sea," and "In the Air." Have each group compile a list of outdoor jobs for their category. Include transportation, military, farming, construction, public service, etc. Let groups share their lists and add on to them. These jobs may be added to the occupations dictionary (activity #4).

6. Pencil Holders. Wrap clean, empty tin cans with gift wrap or construction paper to make pencil holders. Ask children to list some people who might use a pencil holder at work (secretary, teacher, the president, etc.).

7. Work Hats. Supply several types of hats. Name some occupations and let children find the hats to match. Or, let each child choose a hat to wear and play-act the person at work.

8. Cash Registers. Cut the bottom half of an egg carton to fit inside a shoe box. This will hold change. Cut a slit near one end of the box lid as wide as adding machine tape. Place a roll of tape in the box and pull the end through the slit in the lid. Turn the box so that the tape end of the lid is away from you. Label stick-on dots with the numbers 0 through 9, +, −, "tax," and "total." Arrange on box lid. Jingle bells may be glued inside the lid so the register will ring up sales. Children can take turns playing cashier of different types of shops. Have them write each sale total on the tape, tear it off, and give the customer his receipt.

9. Tools of the Trade. Post numbered pictures of several job-related tools (hammer, garden hose, broom, microscope, computer, etc.). Hand out sheets of lined paper and have children number them. To the right of each number, they will write one occupation that uses the item shown. Have children compare and discuss their answers.

10. Arts Collage. Provide lots of old magazines. Let children pick a theme involving careers in the arts, entertainment, or media (dancers, reporters, television stars, etc.). Children can cut out pictures and words that fit their theme to glue onto a collage. Label each collage with its theme. Display in library.

11. Lab Coats. Use white 13-gallon plastic trash bags to make lab coats. Slit up one side and along the top of the bag to get a rectangle. Put it up to each child and cut holes for the arms and neck. Ask children to act out different jobs done by people who wear lab coats (doctor, chemist, dental assistant, etc.). [Note: Do not do this activity with young children who cannot work safely with plastic bags.]

12. Unusual Jobs. Give children a fact sheet of unusual jobs or careers (taxidermist, calligrapher, lion tamer, etc.). Have children complete a crossword puzzle with these terms.

13. Assembly Line. Supply paper-cut pieces of several components of a boom box (plain box, speakers, many dials, antenna, etc.). Assemble one boom box picture to show children how to put it together, and what the final product will look like. Then sit children at a table, in a factory assembly line. Each child will have a pile of one item in front of him, which he will glue onto the picture. The first child will glue the plain box onto a piece of oak tag; the next child one speaker; the next child another speaker; etc. Continue down the line until enough pictures for all the children have been made. Ask children to list some other items that are made in a factory assembly line.

14. Job Applications. Working in small groups, ask children to design a job application. It may be for a specific company or occupation, or an all-purpose application. Afterwards, show children some actual job applications. Explain terms they don't understand and discuss which information is always necessary and what is optional. Using these forms, let children conduct mock job interviews with each other.

15. Closing Ceremony: Job Fair. Invite people in the community with various occupations. Guests can wear their work clothes and set up booths with displays, samples, information, and hands-on activities regarding their jobs. Children can visit the booths to learn what each occupation entails. Let them note on separate job sheets which occupations interest them most.

Theme-Related Books

For Younger Readers

Allen, Jeffrey. *Mary Alice, Operator Number Nine.* Little, 1978.
Berenstain, Stan, and Berenstain, Jan. *He Bear, She Bear.* Random, 1974.
Blacker, Terence. *If I Could Work.* Lippincott, 1988.
Cummings, Pat. *C.L.O.U.D.S.* Lothrop, 1987.
Foote, Patricia. *Girls Can Be Anything They Want.* Messner, 1980.
Goffstein, M.B. *Goldie the Dollmaker.* Farrar, 1969.
Johnston, Tony. *Odd Jobs.* Putnam, 1977.
Merriam, Eve. *Daddies at Work.* Simon and Schuster, 1989.

_____. *Mommies at Work*. Simon and Schuster, 1989.
Scarry, Richard. *Richard Scarry's What Do People Do All Day?* Random, 1968.

For Older Readers

Bridges, Sue Ellen. *Home Before Dark*. Knopf, 1977.
Cleary, Beverly. *Henry and the Paper Route*. Morrow, 1957.
Krantz, Hazel. *100 Pounds of Popcorn*. Vanguard, 1961.
Levine, Betty K. *The Great Burgerland Disaster*. Atheneum, 1981.
Pfeffer, Susan Beth. *Kid Power*. Watts, 1977.
Robertson, Keith. *Henry Reed's Baby-Sitting Service*. Viking, 1966.
Rounds, Glenn. *Mr. Yowder, the Peripatetic Sign Painter*. Holiday, 1980.
Smith, Alison. *There's a Cat Washing in Here!* Dutton, 1981.
Walsh, Jill Paton. *A Chance Child*. Avon, 1978.

Nonfiction

Alexander, Sue. *Finding Your First Job*. Dutton, 1980.
Ancona, George. *And What Do You Do? A Book About People and Their Work*. Dutton, 1976.
Barkin, Carol, and James, Elizabeth. *Jobs for Kids*. Lothrop, 1990.
Fisher, Leonard Everett. *The Factories*. Holiday, 1979.
Florian, Douglas. *People Working*. Crowell, 1983.
Heyman, Abigail, and Saul, Wendy. *Butcher, Baker, Cabinetmaker: Photographs of Women at Work*. Crowell, 1978.
Johnston, Neil. *All in a Day's Work: Twelve Americans Talk About Their Jobs*. Joy St., 1989.
Let's Discover What People Do. Raintree, 1981.

Also: There are several series about careers and jobs from various publishers.

Films and Videos

Bea and Mr. Jones. RR, 30 mins.
Dad's Job Is Cool! BARR, 15 mins.
Get a Job. NFBC, 19 mins.
People Serving Your Community. NGEO, 4 films, 11–13 mins each.
Why People Have Special Jobs: The Man Who Made Spinning Tops. LCA/COR, 7 mins.

——— READOLYMPICS ———

(Olympics – Summer)

*The Games are about to begin at _____ Library, as we
celebrate the Summer Olympics. Learn about the events played*

and some of the heroic athletes who competed in past Olympics. Collect gold medals for books read. Invent a new Olympic event. Make an Olympic torch and flag. Compete in the decathlon and other events. Represent a country in the Parade of Nations. Sign up now to be in _____ Library's **Readolympics.**

Promotional Items

1. Sign reading "Olympic Committee" for check-out area
2. "Readolympic Athlete" cards (membership cards)
3. Gold medal cut-outs (for books read)
4. Reading logs entitled "Schedule of Events"
5. "Readolympics" bookmarks
6. Olympic Achievement Awards (certificates of participation)
7. T-shirt transfers: "Readolympic Athlete" (game prizes)

Activities

1. Bulletin Board. Post the Olympic rings in the center. They should be arranged in the following formation: top from left to right—blue, black, and red; bottom—yellow and green. Under the rings, post the Olympic oath, "We swear that we will take part in these Olympic games in the true spirit of sportsmanship, and that we will respect and abide by the rules that govern them, for the glory of the sport and the honor of our country." Post two large cut-outs of the Olympic torch, one on either side of the rings and oath. List the names of reading club members on the torches. Caption: READOLYMPICS.

2. Reading Incentive Game: Great Race. Choose a racing event (marathon, rowing, equestrian, bicycling, etc.) and draw a track to represent it. Use an appropriate cut-out (runner, boat, horse, bicycle, etc.) as the marker. Advance it one space for every X books read by the group. Readers will win a prize if the marker has crossed the finish line by the closing ceremony.

3. Olympic Torch. Glue one section of an egg crate into one end of a paper towel tube. Crumple up some red tissue paper to be the flame. Make sure there is enough so that it will stick out of the egg section. Glue the flame in place and glue on some red glitter. Let children carry their torches as they jog around a pretend track.

4. Olympic Stars. Encourage children to read books about Olympic athletes. Post the child's name and Olympic book read on a star cut-out, rather than a medal cut-out. For each book read about the Olympics, or any athlete or sport, award the reader a gold medal (see activity #11). Invite children to tell the group about an athlete or Olympic achievement they consider particularly memorable.

5. Olympic Events. Have children complete a word search puzzle of Summer Olympics events.

6. Wreaths. The Olympic games began in ancient Greece. Each winner was crowned with a wreath of olive leaves. Use long vines to make wreaths with children. Wind the vine into a circle to fit the child's head. Dried flowers can be tied on with florist ribbon.

7. Olympic Terms. Give children a fact sheet of Olympic terms (Olympiad, gold medal, demonstration sport, amateur athlete, etc.). Have children complete a crossword puzzle with these terms.

8. Olympic Rings. Cut out rings in the five colors given earlier. Glue them onto white construction paper in the Olympic formation. Tape the paper onto a dowel to make a flag.

9. Decathlon. The man who wins the decathlon is considered the best athlete in the world. Set up games to represent the ten events. The races (100-meter dash, 400-meter run, 110-meter high hurdles, and 1,500-meter run) can be board games designed as race tracks, using dice to move the markers. The jumps (long jump, high jump, pole vault) can be represented by tiddly-winks. For the throwing events, have children throw a cardboard circle (discus), a crumpled-up ball (shot put), and a rolled-up tube of newspaper (javelin). Children may compete in all events individually or in teams, as space and time permit. Score points giving the highest number to first place, etc. See which child or team is the greatest athlete in the world.

10. Judging. Explain to children that there are different ways to judge the winners, depending upon the type of event that is being played. Divide a chalkboard into three areas. Label them "Fastest," "Farthest or Highest," and "Most Points." Name some events and have children place them in correct category of how they are judged (Fastest—marathon; Farthest/Highest—pole vault; Most Points—gymnastics, etc.). Explain that the gold, silver, and bronze medals are awarded to the first, second, and third place winners in each event.

11. Olympic Medals. Cut out circles of cardboard and silver foil. Give each child one cardboard and two foil circles. Glue the foil onto both sides of the cardboard to make a silver medal. Poke a hole near an edge, string yarn through it, and tie ends together to make a necklace. Children who read sports books (see activity #4) may additionally receive a medal of gold foil for each book read.

12. New Events. Show children a list of current Summer Olympics events, demonstration sports, and some old ones that are no longer played. Explain a bit about each one. Divide children into small groups. Each group must decide on one new event to add to the Summer Olympics. It may be a sport that already exists but is not in the Olympics, or it can be something that children invent themselves. Consider: Would it be a men's or women's event? What equipment would be needed? Is it a team or individual sport? How would it be judged? What would the event be called? Children may draw pictures of their new events. Have the groups tell everybody about their new events.

13. Host Countries. Give children a list of cities and countries that have hosted past Summer Olympics. Have children locate these on a world map.

14. Flags of Olympic Countries. Show children a list of countries that participate in the Summer Olympics. Let each child choose a different country and draw a replica of that country's flag. Attach flags to dowels. Children can march with their flags in the Parade of Nations at the closing ceremony.

15. Closing Ceremony: The (year) Summer Library Olympics. If an outside party is possible, let children participate in several track and field events. Children can walk fast while making swimming motions with their arms to represent swimming races. Soccer, baseball, and volleyball can also be played. If the party is indoors, let children participate in simulated gymnastics events: balance beam (walking in a straight line on the floor), rhythmic gymnastics, floor exercises (tumbling and cartwheels), and the vaulting horse (leap frog). Pretend weightlifting and rowing races (children slide backwards on the floor while making rowing motions) can also be done. After awards are handed out, children may march with their flags in the Parade of Nations.

Theme-Related Books

For Younger Readers

Brown, Marc. *D. W. Flips!* Joy St., 1988.
Eagle, Mike. *The Marathon Rabbit.* Holt, 1985.
Isenberg, Barbara, and Jaffe, Marjorie. *Albert the Running Bear's Exercise Book.* Clarion, 1984.
Kessler, Leonard P. *On Your Mark, Get Set, Go! The First All-Animal Olympics.* Harper, 1972.
Patience, John. *Sports Day.* Crown, 1983.
Schultz, Charles M. *You're the Greatest, Charlie Brown.* Random, 1979.

For Older Readers

Birenbaum, Barbara. *The Olympic Glow.* Peartree, 1990.
Duder, Tessa. *In Lane Three, Alex Archer.* Houghton, 1990.
Gault, William Campbell. *In the Back Court.* Dutton, 1976.
Herman, Spring. *Flip City.* Orchard, 1988.
Higdon, Hall. *The Electric Olympics.* Holt, 1971.
Knudson, R.R. *Rinehart Lifts.* Farrar, 1980.
Robison, Nancy. *On the Balance Beam.* Whitman, 1978.
Schulman, Janet. *Jenny and the Tennis Nut.* Greenwillow, 1978.
Teague, Sam. *The King of Heart's Heart.* Little, 1987.

Nonfiction

Allen, Anne. *Sports for the Handicapped.* Walker, 1981.
Arnold, Caroline. *The Summer Olympics.* Watts, 1988.

Bortstein, Larry. *After Olympic Glory: The Lives of Ten Outstanding Medalists.* Warne, 1978.

Durant, John. *Highlights of the Summer Olympics from Ancient Times to the Present.* Hastings, 1977.

Fradin, Dennis B. *Olympics.* Childrens, 1983.

Glubok, Shirley, and Tamarin, Alfred. *Olympic Games in Ancient Greece.* Harper, 1976.

Laklan, Carli. *Golden Girls.* McGraw, 1980.

Morrison, Lillian, editor. *Sprints and Distances: Sports in Poetry and the Poetry of Sports.* Harper, 1965.

Rosenbloom, Joseph. *Sports Riddles.* HBJ, 1982.

Walt Disney Productions. *Goofy Presents the Olympics.* Random, 1979.

Films and Videos

Animalympics. FHE, 79 mins.
The Hare and the Tortoise. BRIT, 10 mins.
The Olympic Champ. DIS/COR, 8 mins.
SportsPages. RR, 30 mins.
Tumbles, Mumbles and Bumbles. PYR, 13 mins.

—— SPACE OUT —— AT THE LIBRARY

(Outer Space)

This is Mission Control at _____ Library, preparing to launch our summer reading club. Join the Space Cadets and learn fascinating facts about our solar system, the stars, and space exploration. Build a starscope and a spacecraft. Create a space creature and a new planet. See a NASA *display and rockets blasting off. Don't countdown the summer with nothing to do. You'll have a blast right here when you* **Space Out at the Library!**

Promotional Items

1. Sign reading "Space Station" for check-out area
2. "Space Cadet" cards (membership cards)

3. Spacecraft cut-outs (for books read)
4. Reading logs entitled "Starship Log"
5. "Space Out at the Library" bookmarks
6. Intergalactic Space Explorer Awards (certificates of participation)
7. Frisbees (spaceships) with library logo (game prizes)

Activities

1. Bulletin Board. In the bottom right corner, post a small cut-out of the sun. On the left, post a large orbiting rocket ship with the names or headshots of reading club members. Add a few planets of various shapes and colors. Caption: SPACE OUT AT THE LIBRARY.

2. Reading Incentive Game: Voyager's Voyage. Post a picture of the sun. Place pictures of the planets in our solar system at their relative distances from the sun. (You may wish to label the distances and planet sizes.) Position the Voyager rocket on Earth. Pace off squares from Earth to Pluto. The Voyager will advance one square for every X books read by the group. Readers will win a prize if the Voyager reaches Pluto by the closing ceremony.

3. Astronomy Terms. Give readers a fact sheet of astronomy terms (asteroid, galaxy, universe, etc.) and planet names. Have them complete a crossword puzzle with these terms.

4. Solar System Spin. Read a nonfiction book about the solar system. Pick children to be the sun and the planets, and have them stand in correct order in a large, open space. Have children spin around to indicate planets rotating on their axes. Then tell planets to move in orbit around the sun.

5. Sun and Planets Mobile. Bend a wire coat hanger into a circle. Give each child two each of paper cut-outs for a yellow sun and four different size planets. Let children color the planets. For each shape, staple the fronts and backs together, stuff with newspaper, and staple closed. Tape one end of a length of string or fishing wire to the sun. Hang it from the hook so that the sun is in the center of the circle. Tape strings to the planets and hang them at various points along the circle, so that the planets are situated around the sun.

6. Lunar Features. Show a map of the moon's surface and discuss its terrain (seas and craters) and their approximate sizes. Give children modeling clay to form into moon balls. They can press their fingers into the balls to make craters.

7. Space Inventions. Many scientific advancements came about as a result of space exploration. Discuss some of these (dehydrated foods, computer technology, lasers, etc.). Ask children what they think is the most important space-related discovery or invention. Have them draw a poster about it.

8. Spacecrafts. Supply an assortment of plastic soda bottles, paper cups, paper towel tubes, and paper cones. Using duct or masking tape to connect these materials, let children design their own spaceships. Spray with metallic-colored paint and allow to dry. Hang in library.

9. Space Creatures. Have children list some physical features of space creatures, as seen in science fiction shows. Then let them draw their own pictures of space creatures, using any combination of these or other features. Display in library.

10. Space Careers. Make a list of people who work to design and fly rockets. Include scientists, engineers, technicians, as well as astronauts. Ask children which jobs interest them most.

11. Star Search. Show children pictures of the Milky Way galaxy, and star charts. Point out the constellations. Have children complete a word search puzzle with these terms.

12. Starscopes. Give each child an empty toilet paper tube. Tape black construction paper over one end. Use toothpicks to carefully prick a few holes into the black paper. Hold up the starscope to the light and look through the uncovered end. It will look like a sky full of stars.

13. My Planet. Ask children to imagine themselves as creatures from another planet. Have each child draw a picture and write a story about the planet. Bind these in a book called "All About My Planet" to keep in the library.

14. Blast Off. Have half of the children squat down on the floor to be rockets. The others at Mission Control can count down from "T-minus 10" to "zero." The rockets can jump up at "blast off." Then let children switch places. You can elaborate this game by letting the rockets blast off in stages (child jumps to his feet, then puts arms up, then runs around the room). The Mission Control children can press make-believe dials and call out directions. Ask children to walk as if they were on the moon, with less gravity. How would they move through space?

15. Closing Ceremony: The United States Space Program. Display models or pictures of NASA rockets and an astronaut suit. Invite a speaker to talk about the United States space program. Show films of rockets blasting off and a moon landing. Display pictures of the planets and how Earth looks from outer space. If outdoors, have a trained person shoot off model rockets.

Theme-Related Books

For Younger Readers

Burton, Byron. *I Want to Be an Astronaut*. Crowell, 1988.
Johnson, Crockett. *Harold's Trip to the Sky*. Harper, 1957.
Kroll, Steven. *Space Cats*. Holiday, 1979.
MacDonald, Suse. *Space Spinners*. Dial, 1991.
Marshall, Edward. *Space Case*. Dial, 1980.
Sadler, Marilyn. *Alistair in Outer Space*. Prentice, 1984.
Schoberle, Cecile. *Beyond the Milky Way*. Crown, 1986.

Wildsmith, Brian. *Professor Noah's Spaceship.* Oxford, 1980.
Yolen, Jane. *Commander Toad in Space.* Coward, 1980.

For Older Readers

Cameron, Eleanor. *The Wonderful Flight to the Mushroom Planet.* Little, 1954.
Clark, Margaret Goff. *Barney and the UFOs.* Parents, 1975.
Fisk, Nicholas. *Grinny: A Novel of Science Fiction.* Nelson, 1974.
Harding, Lee. *The Fallen Spaceman.* Harper, 1980.
MacGregor, Ellen. *Miss Pickerell Goes to Mars.* McGraw, 1951.
Mooser, Stephen. *Space Raiders and the Planet of Doom.* Archway, 1983.
Pinkwater, Daniel M. *Fat Men from Space.* Dodd, 1977.
Williams, Jay, and Abrashkin, Raymond. *Danny Dunn and the Voice from Space.*
   Archway, 1979.

Nonfiction

Blocksma, Mary, and Blocksma, Dewey. *Space-Crafting.* Prentice, 1986.
Branley, Franklyn. *The Planets in Our Solar System.* Harper, 1981.
Hansen, Rosanna, and Bell, Robert. *My First Book About Space: Developed in Conjunction with* NASA. Simon and Schuster, 1985.
Keller, Charles. *Astronuts: Space Jokes and Riddles.* Prentice, 1985.
Lord, Suzanne. *A Day in Space.* Scholastic, 1986.
Myring. *Rockets and Space Flight.* Usborne, 1982.
Ride, Sally, and Okie, Susan. *To Space and Back.* Lothrop, 1986.
Ross, Frank, Jr. *The Space Shuttle: Its Story and How to Make Flying Paper Models.*
   Lothrop, 1979.
Sabin, Louis. *Space Exploration and Travel.* Troll, 1985.
Simon, Seymour. *How to Be a Space Scientist in Your Own Home.* Lippincott, 1982.

Films and Videos

Beyond the Stars: A Space Story. LCA/COR, 12 mins.
Jetsons: The Movie. MCA, 82 mins.
Minnie's Science Field Trip: Johnson's Space Center. DIS/COR, 18 mins.
Satellites of the Sun. NFBC, 12 mins.
Spaceborne. PYR, 14 mins.

——————— PET PARADE ———————

(Pets)

If being bored is your pet peeve, don't let it happen to you this
summer—come to _____ Library instead! Whether you own a pet

or not, you're sure to have a great time. Learn about jar pets and watch them grow. Design an aquarium. Play the Pet Matching Game. Create your own pet rock and pet monster. Run our pet store. Participate in our Pet Show and lots of other pet projects. Don't miss the fun! Join the **Pet Parade** *at _____ Library today!*

Promotional Items

1. Sign reading "Pet Registration" for check-out area
2. "Pet Owner's Permits" (membership cards)
3. Dog dish cut-outs (for books read)
4. Reading log entitled "Pet Projects"
5. "Pet Parade" bookmarks
6. Pet Care Professional certificates (certificates of participation)
7. Animal figurines (game prizes)

Activities

1. Bulletin Board. Post pictures of all types of pets in a long line, as in a parade. The line may curve as needed to make the best use of space. Post cut-outs of small band instruments, batons, flags, etc., with some of the pets. Add confetti and streamers. Caption: PET PARADE.

2. Reading Incentive Game: Polly on the Loose. Draw a large picture of a house interior, with various rooms sectioned off. Sketch in furniture to indicate the different rooms. In one room, draw an open bird cage. Pace a trail throughout the house, eventually leading back to the cage. Tell children that someone left Polly the Parakeet's cage open. For every X books read by the group, advance Polly one square. (You may want to add people cut-outs to chase Polly around the house.) Readers will win a prize if Polly is safely back in her cage by the closing ceremony.

3. Jar Pets. Display several wild animal pets (toads, snails, crickets, etc.) for children to observe throughout the summer. Label each jar with the type of animal. Let children feed and care for them. Post a growth chart for each animal and let children monitor the pets' progress.

4. Pet Poll. Ask children who own pets to bring in photos of themselves and their pets to display in the library. Take a poll of children who own (or would like to own) different types of pets. Which animal is the most common where you live?

5. Pet Expert. Invite a veterinarian or other animal expert to speak to children about pet care. Have a discussion on how to choose a pet that is right for you.

6. Rodent Pets. Show pictures of rodent pets (hamsters, gerbils, rabbits, etc.). Or you may want to keep some live pets in the library during the summer. (Ask children who don't have pets at home if they would like to feed and care for them.) Let children make thumbprint gerbils. Dip a thumb in brown poster paint, and press onto construction paper. Draw on other features (whiskers, ears, etc.) and surroundings.

7. Dog Word Search. Show pictures of several types of dogs. Ask children to tell you their favorites. Have children complete a word search puzzle of types of dogs. Word searches can also be done for types of pet birds, fish, and cats.

8. Favorite Cats and Dogs. There are many cats and dogs in fiction. Ask children to tell you as many as they can recall. List all names. Then ask children to decide which ones they would like to have as pets and why. Have each child draw a picture and write a story about him and his chosen pet.

9. Cat Pictures. Show children photos of several types of cats. Give children cat pictures to color. Have each child make up a name for his cat and write it under the picture. Then provide stamps with a cat's paw print or cat stickers with which children can design a frame around their pictures.

10. Aquariums. Let children draw and cut out pictures of many types of fish. Glue them to blue or green construction paper to make aquariums. Children may add pictures of starfish, coral, or other aquarium decorations to accompany their pet fish.

11. Pet Matching Game. Post pictures of various animals on a wall. Show pictures of pet foods and let children match the food to the correct animal. Match pet homes or sleeping places to the correct pets. Play recordings of animal sounds and have children identify the pet. Match paw or footprints.

12. Pet Monsters. Provide scraps of paper, markers, stickers, and other art supplies. Let children design, draw and build their own pet monsters. Features from various pets (wings, long legs, scales, etc.) may be combined. Have children make up names for their monsters and tell a little about them.

13. Pet Store. Choose children to be the salesperson and the customer. Other children can pretend to be animals for sale. How does the salesperson help the customer choose a pet? What other things, besides the animal itself, does the customer need to buy? Let children take turns play-acting different roles.

14. Pet Rocks. Supply clean, smooth stones in an assortment of sizes. Let children glue stones together to look like animals. Paint on eyes and other features.

15. Closing Ceremony: Pet Show. Invite each child to bring in a favorite stuffed animal. Stage pet contests, such as a race for the fastest animal (children race, holding their pets), highest jumper (children toss pets in the air), etc. Children can perform pet tricks with their toys. Have a pet parade and give ribbons to all stuffed animals.

Theme-Related Books

For Younger Readers

Balian, Lorna. *The Aminal.* Abington, 1972.
Chalmers, Mary. *Six Dogs, Twenty-Three Cats, Forty-Five Mice, and One Hundred Sixteen Spiders.* Harper, 1986.
Ferguson, Alane. *That New Pet!* Lothrop, 1986.
Gackenbush, Dick. *What's Claude Doing?* Clarion, 1984.
Joerns, Consuelo. *Oliver's Escape.* Four Winds, 1984.
Kellogg, Steven. *Can I Keep Him?* Dial, 1971.
Parish, Peggy. *No More Monsters for Me.* Harper, 1981.
Raskin, Ellen. *Franklin Stein.* Atheneum, 1972.
Simon, Norma. *Cats Do, Dogs Don't.* Whitman, 1986.
Viorst, Judith. *The Tenth Good Thing About Barney.* Atheneum, 1971.

For Older Readers

Atwater, Richard, and Atwater, Florence. *Mr. Popper's Penguins.* Little, 1966.
Carris, Joan. *Pets, Vets, and Marty Howard.* Harper, 1984.
Cleary, Beverly. *Henry and Ribsy.* Morrow, 1954.
Farley, Walter. *The Black Stallion.* Random, 1941.
Haywood, Carolyn. *Eddie's Menagerie.* Morrow, 1978.
Howe, Deborah, and Howe, James. *Bunnicula.* Atheneum, 1979.
Pearce, Philippa. *The Battle of Bubble and Squeak.* Dutton, 1969.
Rawls, Wilson. *Where the Red Fern Grows.* Doubleday, 1961.
Singer, Marilyn. *Tarantulas on the Brain.* Harper, 1982.
Wolkoff, Judie. *Wally.* Bradbury, 1977.

Nonfiction

Arnold, Caroline. *Pets Without Homes.* Clarion, 1983.
Barwell, Eve. *Make Your Pet a Present.* Lothrop, 1977.
Broekel, Ray. *Gerbil Pets and Other Small Rodents.* Childrens, 1983.
Joseph, Joan. *Pet Birds.* Watts, 1975.
LaBarge, L. *The Pet House Book.* Butterick, 1977.
Polikoff, Barbara. *My Parrot Eats Baked Beans: Kids Talk About Their Pets.* Whitman, 1988.
Sabin, Louis. *All About Dogs as Pets.* Messner, 1982.
Seltzer, Meyer. *Petcetera: The Pet Riddle Book.* Whitman, 1989.
Simon, Seymour. *Pets in a Jar.* Viking, 1975.
Stevens, Carla. *Your First Pet.* Macmillan, 1974.

Films and Videos

Best Friends. FIV, ten 5 min. films.
The Day Jimmy's Boa Ate the Wash. RR, 30 mins.
Friend for Life. PYR, 15 mins.
Pet Show. LCI/COR, 13 mins.
The Puppy Who Wanted a Boy. COR, 23 mins.

— UNCOVER HIDDEN TREASURE — AT THE LIBRARY

(Pirates)

Avast, maties! It's time to set sail for a summer of fun and adventure. Become a swashbuckling pirate. Learn about the dangers and excitement of life at sea. Follow a pirate map and search for hidden booty. Create your own treasure chest. You may sail the seven seas, but you won't find a greater time than what _____ Library has in story for you. So join Captain Book and **Uncover Hidden Treasure at the Library!**

Promotional Items

1. Sign reading "Captain Book's Locker" for check-out area
2. "Official Member—Captain Book's Crew" cards (membership cards)
3. Pirate ship cut-outs (for books read)
4. Reading logs entitled "Captain Book's Log"
5. "Uncover Hidden Treasure at the Library" bookmarks
6. Swashbuckling Pirate Awards (certificates of participation)
7. Poster of Captain Book's Treasure Hunt Game with directions for home play (game prizes)

Activities

1. Bulletin Board. Draw or paste a picture of a large open treasure chest. On yellow paper coins, write the titles of fiction and nonfiction books about pirates and life at sea. Paste coins to look as if they are overflowing the chest, and spilling out all around it. Caption: UNCOVER HIDDEN TREASURE AT THE LIBRARY.

2. Reading Incentive Game: Captain Book's Treasure Hunt. Draw a treasure map. Start at a pirate ship which has landed, and end at "X Marks the Spot." Along the way, mark places with names such as "Pirates' Cove," "Skull and Crossbones Valley," "Shipwreck Cliff," etc. Pace off distances between places with squares. For every X books read by the group, advance a pirate marker one square. Readers will win a prize if the pirate reaches "X Marks the Spot" by closing ceremony.

3. Skull and Crossbones. Give children white paper on which a skull and crossbones has been drawn. Let them cut out the designs and glue them onto black construction paper. Attach dowels to make pirate flags. Discuss what the skull and crossbones sign means now.

4. Pirate Terms. Give children a fact sheet of famous fictitious characters and pirate terms (Long John Silver, Davy Jones's locker, pieces-of-eight, plank, etc.). Have readers complete a crossword puzzle with these terms.

5. Treasure Chests. Give each child a shoe box. Cover the box and lid with black construction paper. Paste strips of gold paper at the edges. Paste on pieces of crumpled-up tissue paper for jewels. Add a big cardboard lock and handles.

6. Pirate Places. Locate on a world map countries from which pirate ships came. Discuss: What did pirates do for a living? Why do we like to read about them?

7. Sailor Talk. Explain that pirates were sailors. Invite a speaker to talk to children about the life of a sailor at sea. Perhaps the speaker can demonstrate how to tie knots, navigate a ship, etc.

8. Pirate Treasure. Read a pirate story in which there is a buried treasure. Let children write and illustrate their own stories. Or, they can draw their own treasure maps.

9. Pirate Ship. Display a model or show pictures of a pirate ship. Tell children the nautical terms for the parts of a ship (rigging, bow, starboard, port, crow's nest, deck, etc.). How do pirates steer the ship? Where and how would they sleep?

10. Sea Hazards. Discuss some of the hazards of life at sea. Define terms such as scurvy, mutiny, becalmed seas, delirium, tidal wave, shipwreck, seasickness, etc. Have readers complete a word search puzzle with these terms.

11. Costumes. Make pirate costumes with children. Attach thin black elastics (used for masks) to black cardboard eye patches. Make pirate hats out of folded newspapers. Tie a scarf around each child's waist. Discuss other items pirates might wear.

12. Buckle Those Swashes! Pirates are always described as being "swashbuckling," but what does that mean? Ask children to tell you what they think "swashbuckling" means. What's a swash? How or why do you buckle it? This can be an exercise in creative word play.

13. Pirate Sing-Along. Sing pirate songs with children. Play pirate songs from the play and Disney versions of "Peter Pan," as well as sailor folksongs such as "Sailing, Sailing" and "Up She Rises."

14. Real Treasures. Tell children that a treasure need not be gold or jewels. It can be anything that is of value to a person. Give each child a piece of paper with a large sketch of a treasure chest. Tell them to write in the chest the treasure they would like to find there. The contents need not be material things (example: peace).

15. Closing Ceremony: Treasure Hunt. Children may wear pirate costumes. Plan a treasure hunt where children can gather foil-covered chocolate coins.

Theme-Related Books

For Younger Readers

Baum, Louis. *Juju and the Pirate*. Harper, 1984.
Burningham, John. *Come Away from the Water, Shirley*. Crowell, 1977.
Faulkner, Matt. *The Amazing Voyage of Jackie Grace*. Scholastic, 1987.
Greene, Carol. *The Little Old Ladies Who Loved Cats*. Harper, 1991.
Hasely, Dennis. *The Pirate Who Tried to Capture the Moon*. Harper, 1983.
Hutchins, Pat. *One-Eyed Jake*. Greenwillow, 1979.
Kroll, Steven. *Are You Pirates?* Pantheon, 1982.
McNaughton, Colin. *Anton B. Stanton and the Pirats*. Benn, 1979.
Mahy, Margaret. *The Man Whose Mother Was a Pirate*. Viking, 1986.
Wolcott, Patty. *Pirates, Pirates, Over the Salt, Salt Sea*. Addison, 1981.

For Older Readers

Arden, William. *The Mystery of the Purple Pirate*. Random, 1982.
Barrie, James M. *Peter Pan*. Scribner's, 1980.
Beatty, Jerome, Jr. *Matthew Looney and the Space Pirates*. Addison, 1972.
Gardner, Cliff. *Black Caesar, Pirate*. Peachtree, 1980.
Giff, Patricia Reilly. *The Gift of the Pirate Queen*. Dell, 1983.
Haynes, Betsy. *The Ghost of the Gravestone Hearth*. Nelson, 1977.
Kraske, Robert. *The Sea Robbers*. HBJ, 1977.
Mahy, Margaret. *The Great Piratical Rumbustification*. Godine, 1986.
Stevenson, Robert Louis. *Treasure Island*. Putnam, 1947.
Wibberly, Leonard. *The Crime of Martin Coverly*. Farrar, 1980.

Nonfiction

Cole, William, editor. *The Sea, Ships and Sailors: Poems, Songs, and Shanties*. Viking, 1967.
Day, A. *Pirates of the Pacific*. Meredith, 1968.
Glasscock, Paula, and Weber, Sally. *Castles, Pirates, Knights and Other Learning Delights!* Good Apple, 1980.
McCall, Edith. *Pirates and Privateers*. Childrens, 1980.
Marsh, Carole. *Avast Ye Slobs! The Book of Silly Pirate Trivia*. Gallopade, 1986.
Snow, Edward Rowe. *Pirates and Buccaneers of the Atlantic Coast*. Yankee, 1944.
Stein, R. Conrad. *The Story of the Barbary Pirates*. Childrens, 1982.
Wheeler, Richard. *In Pirate Waters*. Crowell, 1969.
Williams, Guy. *The World of Model Ships and Boats*. Putnam, 1971.

Films and Videos

Captain Kidd. MAC, 26 mins.
The Pirates of Penzance. MCA, 112 mins.
Sunken Treasure. RR, 30 mins.

— GET PROGRAMMED TO READ —

(Robots)

Notice to all intelligent life forms: The humanoids at _____
Library have designed this summer's program to include many fun
activities for reading robots. Find out how robots work and what
they are used for. See robots from science fiction and real life.
Design your own robots. You can even be a robot! Don't short-
circuit your brain cells this summer. Recharge them at _____
Library and **Get Programmed to Read!**

Promotional Items

1. Sign reading "Control Center" for check-out area
2. "Brain Cells Recharger" cards (membership cards)
3. Robot cut-outs (for books read)
4. Reading logs entitled "Programmed Instructions"
5. "Get Programmed to Read" bookmarks
6. Reading Robot Awards (certificates of participation)
7. Transformers, or other toys that change into robots (game prizes)

Activities

    1. Bulletin Board. Post pictures of various robots from TV, movies, books, cartoons, etc. Label them with their names and/or where they are from, as applicable. Paste tiny pictures of open books on each one, to look as though the robots are reading. Caption: GET PROGRAMMED TO READ!
    2. Reading Incentive Game: Amazing Robot. Draw a maze. Place a small robot carrying a book at START (the library). At END, draw a picture of a child at home. Pace off dots throughout the entire maze, including the wrong turns. Advance the robot one dot for every X books read by the group. Let the children decide which way the robot should go. Readers will win a prize if the book is delivered to the child by the closing ceremony.
    3. Famous Robots. Refer to bulletin board pictures and discuss roles of famous robots of movies, TV, and books (Robbie the Robot, R2D2, etc.). Have children complete a word search puzzle of fictional robots.
    4. Geometric Robots. Give children sheets of construction paper. Provide geometric shapes in various sizes and colors of paper for children to create robot pictures.
    5. Your Own Creation. Read *Get Ready for Robots* by Patricia Lauber. Ask

children: If they could invent a robot, what would it do? Have them draw and explain their robot creations.

6. Robot Safety. Discuss the care and handling of robots. Ask children to tell you how they would keep their robots in good working order (check wires and connections, oil it, etc.). What are some possible dangers? (Short circuits, getting it wet, etc.) Make a list of some general operating rules.

7. Robotic Terms. Give readers a fact sheet of terms used in robotics (program, sensors, bionic, android, etc.). Have children complete a crossword puzzle with these terms.

8. Robot or Not? Show some *Inspector Gadget* cartoons to the children. Is Gadget a human, robot, cyborg, bionic man, or something else? Let children state their opinions and reasons.

9. Mr. Machine. Robots are programmed machines that move. Supply lots of old magazines. Let children cut out pictures of all types of machines. They can glue these onto oak tag to make Mr. Machine robots. Display in library.

10. Build Your Own. Provide Tinker Toys, Erector Sets, and other building toys and let children construct robots.

11. Be a Robot. Tell children to pretend they are robots. How would they move and talk? Let children perform simple tasks (walking, picking things up, etc.) as if they were robots.

12. Where No Man Has Gone Before. Robots are often used to go places where humans can't go, such as deep underwater or outer space. Show some photographs taken by such robots (the Mars Lander, etc.). Why couldn't humans have taken these pictures? Where else can robots go that humans can't? Ask children to think of a place they would like to send a robot. Draw a picture of the idea.

13. Readable Robots. Robots in fiction are either helpful to humans or monsters. Let children write and illustrate their own robot stories, with robots as good guys or bad guys. Bind these stories into a book to keep in the library.

14. Robot Costumes. Help children cut arm and neck holes in large brown paper bags or cardboard boxes. They can draw on designs or glue on buttons, pipe cleaners, paper cups, and other items to make robot costumes.

15. Closing Ceremony: Meet a Robot. Invite an expert to bring in a simple remote control robot to show children. Explain how it works, using diagrams of its interior and listing the steps taken to build it. Let children take turns working the robot.

Theme-Related Books

For Younger Readers

Bunting, Eve. *The Robot Birthday.* Dutton, 1980.
Christelow, Eileen. *Mr. Murphy's Marvelous Invention.* Clarion, 1983.
Cole, Babette. *The Trouble with Dad.* Putnam, 1986.

Gage, Wilson. *Down in the Boondocks.* Greenwillow, 1977.
Hoban, Lillian, and Hoban, Phoebe. *The Laziest Robot in Zone One.* Harper, 1983.
Krahn, Fernando. *Robot-Bot-Bot.* Dutton, 1979.
Kroll, Steven. *Otto.* Parents, 1983.
Pienkowski, Jan. *Robot.* Delacorte, 1982.

For Older Readers

Asimov, Janet, and Asimov, Isaac. *Norby: The Mixed-Up Robot.* Walker, 1984.
Beatty, Jerome, Jr. *Maria Looney and the Remarkable Robot.* Avon, 1978.
Bellairs, John. *The Eyes of the Killer Robot.* Dial, 1986.
Hughes, Ted. *The Iron Giant: A Story in Five Nights.* Harper, 1987.
Slote, Alfred. *My Robot Buddy.* Lippincott, 1975.
Stamper, Judith B. *Autobot Alert!* Ballantine, 1986.
Waddell, Martin. *Harriet and the Robot.* Joy St., 1987.
Wilkes, Marilyn. *C.L.U.T.Z.* Dial, 1982.
Yolen, Jane. *The Robot and Rebecca and the Missing Owser.* Knopf, 1981.

Nonfiction

Chester, Michael. *Robots: Fact Behind the Fiction.* Macmillan, 1983.
Cummings, Richard. *Make Your Own Robots.* McKay, 1985.
Elting, Mary. *The Answer Book About Robots and Other Inventions.* Putnam, 1984.
Keller, Charles. *Ohm on the Range: Robot and Computer Jokes.* Prentice, 1982.
Knight, David C. *Robotics: Past, Present, and Future.* Morrow, 1983.
Lauber, Patricia. *Get Ready for Robots!* Crowell, 1987.
Lindblom, Steven. *How to Build a Robot.* Crowell, 1985.
Metos, Thomas H. *Robots A to Z.* Messner, 1980.
Ryder, Joanne. *C-3PO's Book About Robots.* Random, 1983.

Films and Videos

Ballet Robotique. PYR, 8 mins.
Inspector Gadget. Vols. 1–4, FHE, 90 mins. each.
Robotics: The Future Is Now. AIMS, 20 mins.
Romie-O and Julie-8. WAR, 25 mins.
Short Circuit. (Rated PG.) CBS, 98 mins.
Star Wars. CBS, 121 mins.

—————— SEA READS ——————

(The Sea, Marine Life)

Splish, splash! _____ Library is just swimming with lots of
fun activities for you this summer. Identify sea shells and make

shell jewelry. Create your own aquarium and sand art designs. Learn about different kinds of water transportation, marine life, and mythical sea creatures. Help our submarine dive 20,000 leagues under the sea. Come to our indoor beach party. So spend this summer by the sea. Catch a wave to _____ Library and gather some **Sea Reads!**

Promotional Items

1. Sign reading "Lifeguard Station" for check-out area
2. "Beachcomber Passes" (membership cards)
3. Starfish cut-outs (for books read)
4. Reading logs entitled "Ship's Log"
5. "Sea Reads" bookmarks
6. Sea Star Awards (certificates of participation with a starfish imprint)
7. Inflatable beach balls (game prizes)

Activities

1. Bulletin Board. Cover the area with paper waves. Post a cut-out of a rowboat atop the water. In the boat, draw a fishing line and post a picture of a child reading. In the water, post cut-outs of various types of fish. Write the name of a fiction or nonfiction book about the sea or marine life on each fish. Caption: SEA READS.

2. Reading Incentive Game: 20,000 Leagues Under the Sea. Cover the lower three-quarters of the area with blue paper to indicate water. On the left, above the water, draw a dock (START) from which a submarine playing piece will leave. At the right, measure from the surface (0) to the bottom (20,000 leagues under the sea). Draw a cave destination (END) in the bottom right corner. Pace off bubbles throughout the sea, making the playing area as elaborate as you wish (secret caves, sunken pirate ships, coral reefs, etc.). Advance the submarine one bubble for every X books read by the group. Readers will win a prize if the game is completed by the closing ceremony.

3. Ocean Life. Give readers fact sheets about ocean life, divided into four categories: birds, mammals, plants, and fish/shellfish. Have readers complete one or more word search puzzles with these terms.

4. Shells, Etc. Bring in sea shells, starfish, coral, sponges, and other examples of sea life to show children. Let children use labeled photographs to identify the shells, etc. Allow children to handle these (carefully). Can they really hear the waves coming in when they hold a conch shell to their ears?

5. Necklaces. Let children string together some small shells in which holes have been drilled to make sea shell necklaces.

6. Sea Terms. Give readers a fact sheet defining different sea-related terms (tide, wave, whirlpool, salt water, marine, etc.). Have children complete a cross-word puzzle of these terms.

7. Beach Fun. Read a book about going to the beach. Ask children what they like to do at the beach. Make a list of beach safety rules.

8. Sand Art. Provide clear plastic cups and several shades of colored sand. Let children pour layers of the various colors to make sand art designs. Cover completed artwork with plastic wrap and caution children not to shake the cups.

9. Water on the Globe. Nearly two-thirds of the earth's surface is covered by water. On a world map, have children locate the seven oceans and examples of a river, lake, strait, sea, tributary, etc.

10. Water Vessels. Display models or show pictures of types of water transportation (rafts, canoes, rowboats, submarines, etc.). Discuss their uses. Invite an expert to talk about shipbuilding, sails, navigation, or another boat-related topic.

11. Sea Myths. There are many mythical creatures, such as mermaids, which supposedly live in the sea. Compile a list of fictional sea creatures with the children. Let them write and illustrate their own stories of one of these, or make up their own type of sea life.

12. Aquariums. Provide paper cut-outs of several types of aquarium life and decorations. Let children paste these on blue oak tag to create their own aquarium scenes. Display in library.

13. Careers Game. Play a matching game to teach children about some sea-related careers. Prepare three sets of cards: (a) Pictures of workers with their appropriate attire and props (marine biologist, fisherman, diver, sailor, etc.); (b) the name of each job; and (c) cards detailing some aspect of each job. Post the workers' pictures (a). Let children match the cards from (b) and (c) to the correct pictures. Can the children think of any other sea-related jobs?

14. Sea Foods. Provide lots of old magazines. Let children cut pictures of seafood dishes and paste them onto oak tag to make collages. Display in library.

15. Closing Ceremony: Beach Party. Set up games and activities which signify some popular beach and water pastimes. Examples: (a) Give children a toy fishing pole and three chances to catch plastic fish in a tub of water; (b) Provide wind-up boats and let children race them across a tub of water; (c) Let children paint designs on "surfboards" (wooden tongue depressors); (d) Provide a sandbox and toys for children to play with; (e) Play surfer music and teach children how to do the 1960s dance "The Swim."

Theme-Related Books

For Younger Readers

Ardizzone, Edward. *Little Tim and the Brave Sea Captain*. Oxford, 1955.

Berenstain, Stan, and Berenstain, Jan. *The Bears' Vacation.* Random, 1968.
Carrick, Carol. *Dark and Full of Secrets.* Clarion, 1984.
Cole, Sheila. *When the Tide Is Low.* Lothrop, 1985.
Himmelman, John. *Montigue on the High Seas.* Viking, 1988.
Lionni, Leo. *Swimmy.* Pantheon, 1963.
Marshall, Edward. *Three by the Sea.* Dial, 1981.
Peet, Bill. *Cyrus the Unsinkable Sea Serpent.* Houghton, 1975.
Ricciuti, Edward R. *Donald and the Fish That Walked.* Harper, 1974.
Waber, Bernard. *I Was All Thumbs.* Houghton, 1990.

For Older Readers

Aiken, Joan. *The Kingdom Under the Sea.* Penguin, 1986.
Boston, L.M. *The Sea Egg.* HBJ, 1967.
Holling, Holling C. *Paddle-to-the Sea.* Houghton, 1941.
Lisle, Janet Taylor. *The Lampfish of Twill.* Orchard, 1991.
Loeper, John. *The Golden Dragon.* Atheneum, 1978.
Manus, Willard. *Sea Treasure.* Doubleday, 1961.
Sperry, Armstrong. *Call It Courage.* Macmillan, 1940.
Turner, Susan. *Lost at Sea.* Raintree, 1982.
Warner, Gertrude Chandler. *Mystery in the Sand.* Whitman, 1971.

Nonfiction

Arthur, Alex. *Eyewitness Books: Shells.* Knopf, 1989.
Beauregard, Sue, and Fairchild, Jill. *Ocean Plants.* Cypress, 1982.
Bendick, Jeanne. *Exploring an Ocean Tide Pool.* Garrard, 1976.
Goudey, Alice E. *Houses from the Sea.* Scribner's, 1959.
Hogner, Dorothy C. *Sea Mammals.* Harper, 1979.
Hosking, Eric J. *Sea Birds of the World.* Facts on File, 1984.
Myers, Arthur. *Sea Creatures Do Amazing Things.* Random, 1981.
Paige, David. *A Day in the Life of a Marine Biologist.* Troll, 1981.
Podendorf, Illa. *Animals of Sea and Shore.* Childrens, 1982.
Ronai, Lili. *Corals.* Crowell, 1976.
Seymour, Peter. *What Lives in the Sea.* Macmillan, 1985.
Simon, Seymour. *How to Be an Ocean Scientist in Your Own Home.* Lippincott,
    1988.

Films and Videos

Broderick. PHX, 9 mins.
Dive to the Coral Reefs. RR, 30 mins.
The Restless Sea. DIS/COR, 36 mins.
The Treasures of the Grotoceans. NFBC, 16 mins.
A Trip to the Aquarium. CHUR, 14 mins.
20,000 Leagues Under the Sea. DIS, 126 mins.
The Undersea World of Jacques Cousteau. CHUR, 24 films, 20–25 mins. each.

— SUMMER ON THE HIGH SEAS —

(Ships, Boating)

Ships ahoy! That's what this summer is all about at _____ Library. Examine all types of seagoing vessels, from ancient times up to the present. Build a raft and power a galley. Chart the sea voyages of famous explorers. Learn about pleasure boats and seafaring careers. Design a cruise ship and make a marine collage. Help our clipper ship deliver tea from China. Create your own ship's flag and navy badges. Explore our Ship Museum. You will be in ship-shape this **Summer on the High Seas!**

Promotional Items

1. Sign reading "Ship's Bridge" for check-out area
2. "Crew Member" cards (membership cards)
3. Submarine cut-outs (for books read)
4. Reading logs entitled "Captain's Log"
5. "Summer on the High Seas" bookmarks
6. Seafarer certificates (certificates of participation)
7. Wind-up toy boats; sailor hats (game prizes)

Activities

1. Bulletin Board. Cover two-thirds of the area with paper waves. In the center, atop the waves, place a large cut-out of a cruise ship with the names or headshots of club members on it. Place smaller cut-outs of modern United States ships and boats throughout the waves. Label each one with the title and author of a fiction or nonfiction book about sea voyages, ships and boats, or people who work on them. Caption: SUMMER ON THE HIGH SEAS.

2. Reading Incentive Game: Clipper Cargo. Post a world map. Pace off a route from New York, around the tip of Africa, to China. Place two square cut-outs marked "tea" or two tea bags at China. Continue the route from China to San Francisco, around the tip of South America, and back to New York. Use a cut-out of a clipper ship as the marker. Advance the clipper one space for every X books read by the group. When it reaches China, put the tea cargo on the ship. Drop off one load of tea in San Francisco, and bring the other to New York. Readers will win a prize if the clipper ship completes its voyage by the closing ceremony.

3. Ancient Ships. Post pictures, in chronological order, of various ships throughout history. Label each one with the type of ship, nation that built it, when and how it was used, and other interesting features. Ask children to draw a picture or write a story about an adventure on a ship of their choice.

4. Houseboats. Let children glue popsicle sticks together to make rafts. Cut a door opening on one side of a half-pint milk carton. Glue the carton onto the center of the raft to make a houseboat. Show children pictures of houseboats, sampans, and other seagoing vessels in which people live.

5. Row Your Boat. Ancient ships called galleys were powered by slaves. Each held an oar with both hands, and they rowed all at the same time. Have children pretend to row galleys. Sit ten children on mats on the floor arranging them in five pairs, one pair behind another, to form two long lines. Tell them to row pretend oars, five to the right and five to the left. Have someone call out a rhythm so everyone rows together. Then tell children to slide backwards each time they row. Line up several galleys and have them race across the room. Sing a few rounds of "Row, Row, Row Your Boat" to relax after the races.

6. Famous Voyages. Give readers a fact sheet of famous historical seafaring explorers and ships (Christopher Columbus, Sir Francis Drake, *Mayflower*, etc.). Trace their famous voyages on a world map. (If possible, use maps from the appropriate time period.)

7. Flags. Show pictures of ships' flags, past and present, from around the world. Include flags of the navy, merchant, and passenger lines, plus semaphore flags, storm warning flags, and international alphabet flags. Tell children to imagine they have their own fleets. Have each child design a flag or combination of flags to fly on his ships. Display in library.

8. Nautical Terms. Give children a fact sheet of nautical terms and ship parts (knot, starboard, helm, anchor, etc.). Have children complete a crossword puzzle with these terms.

9. Toy Boats. Show children several plastic and wind-up toy boats. Explain what type each one represents. Then provide a water table and let children play with the boats.

10. Marine Collages. Let children glue small seashells, bits of netting, rope knots, and cut-outs shaped like anchors, helms, and fish to pieces of oak tag. Glue rope frames along the edges of the collages.

11. Ship Mates. Post pictures of modern boats and ships. Ask children to name some jobs of people who work on navy ships, submarines, fishing boats, merchant vessels, cruise ships, barges, etc. List all jobs on a chalkboard. What are some other ship-related jobs? (Boat-building, dock workers, etc.)

12. Navy Uniforms. Show pictures of United States Navy uniforms and insignia. Provide cut-outs of stars, eagles, and stripes. Let children glue these onto stick-on patches to make navy badges.

13. Pleasure Boats. Have children complete a word search puzzle of types of modern sailboats and sporting boats.

14. Cruise Ships. Some people vacation on modern luxury passenger ships. Ask children to design a cruise ship by listing all the features they would want for a great vacation. Then show pictures and diagrams of the *Queen Elizabeth II.* How does it measure up to their expectations? Let children write and illustrate stories about their ideal seafaring vacations.

15. Closing Ceremony: Ship Museum. Invite hobbyists who build and collect model ships to bring some in to show the children. Display all types of ships and boats, plus other marine artifacts (navigational charts, figureheads, fishing nets, buoys, etc.). Have people speak about boating safety and show how to tie knots, cast a fishing reel, and other simple seafaring skills.

Theme-Related Books

For Younger Readers

Allen, Pamela. *Who Sank the Boat?* Coward, 1983.
Crews, Donald. *Harbor.* Greenwillow, 1982.
Domanska, Janina. *I Saw a Ship A-Sailing.* Macmillan, 1972.
Gramatky, Hardie. *Little Toot.* Putnam, 1939.
Haas, Irene. *The Maggie B.* McElderry, 1975.
Joerns, Consuelo. *The Foggy Rescue.* Four Winds, 1980.
Lattimore, Deborah Nourse. *The Lady with a Ship on Her Head.* HBJ, 1990.
Lorenz, Graham. *Song of the Boat.* Crowell, 1975.
Maestro, Betsy. *Ferryboat.* Crowell, 1986.
Van Allsburg, Chris. *The Wreck of the Zephyr.* Houghton, 1973.
Williams, Vera B. *Three Days on the River in a Red Canoe.* Greenwillow, 1981.

For Older Readers

Cabral, Olga. *So Proudly She Sailed.* Houghton, 1981.
Cole, Lois Dwight. *Linda Goes on a Cruise.* Coward, 1958.
Flory, Jane. *The Great Bamboozlement.* Houghton, 1982.
Norling, Josephine. *Pogo's Sea Trip.* Holt, 1949.
Rounds, Glen. *Mr. Yowder and the Steamboat.* Dell, 1980.
Weller, Frances Ward. *Boat Song.* Macmillan, 1987.
Zhitkou, Boris. *How I Hunted the Little Fellows.* Dodd, 1979.

Nonfiction

Ancona, George. *Freighters: Cargo Ships and the People Who Work Them.* Crowell, 1985.
Berenstain, Michael. *The Ship Book.* McKay, 1978.
Brown, Walter, and Anderson, Norman. *Sea Disasters.* Lippincott, 1981.
David, Andrew, and Moran, Tom. *River Thrill Sports.* Lerner, 1983.
Franklin, Walker. *Famous American Ships.* Simon and Schuster, 1958.
Gibbons, Gail. *Boat Book.* Holiday, 1983.

Huff, Barbara. *Welcome Aboard! Traveling on an Ocean Liner.* Clarion, 1987.
Scott, Geoffrey. *Egyptian Boats.* Carolrhoda, 1981.
Vandervoort, Thomas J. *Sailing Is for Me.* Lerner, 1981.
Weiss, Harvey. *Submarines and Other Underwater Craft.* Harper, 1990.
Williams, Guy R. *The World of Model Ships and Boats.* Putnam, 1971.

Films and Videos

Boats and Ships. BRIT, 14 mins.
Great Explorers. (4 films), NGEO, 13–15 mins. each.
Ships. DIS/COR, 15 mins.
Steamboat Willie. DIS/COR, 8 mins.
Yellow Submarine. MGM/UA, 85 mins.

—— SEE WHAT'S IN STORE ——
AT THE LIBRARY

(Shopping, Stores)

*If you like to shop, _____ Library is the place to hang out
this summer. Get your charge card and checkbook and hit the
mall. Make a cash register and shop at the supermarket. Participate in a consumer poll. Let your fingers do the walking
through the Yellow Pages. Place a catalog order. Take advantage
of mark-downs and sales. Load your shopping cart with goodies.
Join our shopping Mall Scavenger Hunt. Come **See What's in
Store at the Library!***

Promotional Items

1. Sign reading "Check-Out Counter" for check-out area
2. "Charge Cards" (membership cards; see activity #3)
3. Shopping cart cut-outs (for books read)
4. Reading logs entitled "Shopping List"
5. "See What's in Store at the Library" bookmarks

6. Smart Shopper Awards (certificates of participation)
7. Plastic squeeze change purses or velcro wallets (game prizes)

Activities

1. Bulletin Board. Post various-sized cut-outs in the shapes of stores, and label each with the type of shop it represents. In the display window of each store, list the titles and authors of two or three related books. Caption: SEE WHAT'S IN STORE AT THE LIBRARY!

2. Reading Incentive Game: Department Store. Draw a diagram of a large department store. Clearly label each department and the main entrance. Pace off a trail from the entrance, hitting all the departments, and returning to the entrance. Use a shopping bag cut-out as a marker. Advance the bag one space for every X books read by the group. Readers will win a prize if the trail has been completed by the closing ceremony.

3. Charge Cards. Give each child a piece of oak tag, 3⅜″ × 1⅛″ — the size of a charge card. At the top of the card, stamp the library's name and/or logo. Underneath that, print, "Personal Charge Card." Then print the child's code number and name. Have the child sign the back. This will serve as the membership card.

4. Shops Around. Have children complete word search puzzles of stores that sell things (hardware, bakery, pet store, etc.) and shops that offer services (post office, bank, dry cleaner, barber, etc.).

5. Checkbooks. Give each child ten slips of paper, 6″ × 3¼″, on which the lines for date, signature, etc., plus the name and address of the library (where the bank's name would go on a check) have already been printed. Have children print their names in the upper left corner, and number their checks 1 to 10 in the upper right corner. Then let them staple their checks into a pack. Teach children how to write out a check. Show them a transaction register, and a bank printout of a checking account.

6. Let Your Fingers Do the Walking. Post a large local area map on one wall. Tell children to look through the Yellow Pages of the local phone book to find stores in which to purchase several named items. After they find a store in the book, have them locate the store on the map.

7. Cash Registers. Cut the bottom half of an egg carton to fit inside a shoe box. This will hold change. Cut a slit near one end of the box lid as wide as adding machine tape. Place a roll of tape in the box and pull through the slit in the lid. Turn the box so that the tape end of the lid is away from you. Label stick-on dots with numbers 0 through 9, +, −, "tax" and "total." Arrange on box lid. Jingle bells may be glued inside the lid so the register will ring up sales. Children can take turns playing cashier of different types of shops. Have them write each sale total on the tape, tear it off, and give the customer his receipt.

8. Supermarket. Supply lots of pre-cut grocery coupons separated into several open boxes which represent the various aisles or departments in a supermarket (dairy, baked goods, health and beauty aids, etc.). Have children pretend these coupons are the actual items. Let each child pick ten items to buy. They can bring these to a child acting as a cashier who will ring up the sale using the "cents off" of each coupon as the price of that item. Shoppers can practice writing a check to pay for the purchase.

9. Sales. Show children different newspaper, magazines, and direct mail advertisements for sales promotions. Note some of the gimmicks Tused (percent off the price, "limited time only," rebates, etc.). Supply art materials and let children make sales posters for any items or type of store they choose. Display in library.

10. Catalog Shopping. Provide several mail-order catalogs for children to browse through. Divide a chalkboard into two columns labeled "Advantages" and "Disadvantages." Ask children to list some advantages and disadvantages of catalog shopping. Let children practice filling in a catalog order form or pretend to phone in an order.

11. Cart It Away. Give children large pieces of oak tag on which the outline of a shopping cart has been drawn. Supply lots of newspaper ad inserts and old magazines. Have each child decide on a certain type of store in which to go shopping (candy, clothing, furniture, car dealership, etc.). Let them cut out appropriate pictures and glue them into their shopping carts.

12. May I Help You? Have children complete a crossword puzzle of people who work in stores (butcher, jeweler, florist, etc.).

13. UPC Code-Art. Provide several UPC codes cut from product labels or coupons. Briefly explain their use. Then have children use these to make funny pictures. (Bar codes used as teeth, moustaches, TV static, footprints, etc.) Children can glue UPC codes onto paper and draw additional features around them. Add humorous captions and display in library.

14. Let the Buyer Beware. Show children *Zillions* (Consumer Reports for kids) and similar magazines that rate or recommend products. Then have children compare some items with which they are familiar. List several brands (and prices, if known) of one type of item (like sneakers) on a chalkboard. Ask children to rate various aspects of the product (style, comfort, support, durability, value, etc.). Which products would children recommend?

15. Closing Ceremony: Shopping Mall Scavenger Hunt. Set up areas in the library to represent various specialty shops in a mall. Give each child a shopping bag and the same list of things to "buy." Each child must go to every shop (not necessarily in order), purchase the required item with his charge card, place it in his shopping bag, and cross it off his list. Items can include a toy ring from the jeweler, pretend stamps from the post office, a jellybean from the candy store, etc. When the child has finished, a "security guard" will inspect the shopping bag to make sure all the required items are in it. Ask parents to be clerks in the shops, and help the children with their pretend purchases. This is not a race, so children do not have to rush.

Theme-Related Books

For Younger Readers

Anno, Mitsumaso, *Anno's Flea Market..* Philomel, 1984.
Burningham, John. *The Shopping Basket.* Crowell, 1980.
deReginiers, Beatrice Schenk. *Waiting for Mama.* Clarion, 1984.
Grossman, Bill. *Tommy at the Grocery Store.* Harper, 1989.
Lobel, Anita. *On Market Street.* Greenwillow, 1981.
Meddaugh, Susan. *Witch's Supermarket.* Houghton, 1991.
Pearson, Tracey Campbell. *The Storekeeper.* Dial, 1988.
Rosen, Winifred. *Henrietta and the Day of the Iguana.* Four Winds, 1978.
Schick, Eleanor. *Jody on His Own.* Dial, 1982.
Smith, Barry. *Tom and Annie Go Shopping.* Houghton, 1990.

For Older Readers

Clymer, Eleanor. *How I Went Shopping and What I Got.* Holt, 1972.
Hicks, Clifford B. *Alvin's Swap Shop.* Holt, 1976.
Merrill, Jean. *The Pushcart War.* Childrens, 1964.
Peck, Richard. *Secrets of the Shopping Mall.* Delacorte, 1979.
Taylor, Sydney. *All-of-a-Kind Family Downtown.* Follett, 1972.
Van Leeuwen, Jean. *The Great Cheese Conspiracy.* Random, 1969.
Wain, John. *Lizzie's Floating Shop.* Merrimack, 1984.

Nonfiction

Dean, Jennifer B. *Careers in a Department Store.* Lerner, 1973.
Field, Rachel. *General Store.* Little, 1988.
Fisher, Leonard Everett. *The Peddlers.* Moffa, 1968.
Gibbons, Gail. *Department Store.* Harper, 1984.
Kalman, Bobbie. *Early Stores and Markets.* Crabtree, 1981.
Sawyer, Jean. *Our Village Shop.* Putnam, 1984.
Schwartz, Alvin. *Stores.* Macmillan, 1977.
Seidelman, James E. *Shopping Cart Art.* Crowell, 1970.

Films and Videos

Adventure Enough. PHX, 12 mins.
Martha Ann and the Mother Store. CHUR, 16 mins.
Not So Fast, Songololo. WW, 8 mins.
Scrooge McDuck and Money. DIS/COR, 16 mins.

———— GO UNDERCOVER ————
WITH A BOOK

(Spies, Detectives)

*Enemy agents have stolen top secret plans from _____ Library. We need our best undercover agents to solve the crime. Report to Library Headquarters and receive your ID and case file. Put together a spy kit and disguises. Track down a suspect. Analyze various substances in our special crime lab. Follow clues and decipher the secret message. A world of intrigue awaits you this summer when you **Go Undercover with a Book.***

Promotional Items

1. Sign reading "Library Headquarters" for check-out area
2. "Undercover Agent IDs" (membership cards; see activity #3)
3. Magnifying glass cut-outs (for books read)
4. Reading logs entitled "Case File"
5. "Go Undercover with a Book" bookmarks
6. Master Spy certificates (certificates of participation)
7. Magnifying glass, glasses-and-nose disguises (game prizes)

Activities

1. Bulletin Board. On the left, draw a tall street lamp with a suspicious-looking figure in a trench coat standing beneath it. On the right, draw a brick wall with a smaller figure in a trench coat leaning against it. Both figures are reading books. Above center, draw a large magnifying glass. In it, write the caption: GO UNDERCOVER WITH A BOOK.

2. Reading Incentive Game: Track Down the Clues. Post a large street map of the area around the library. Draw a trail of a man's shoeprints leading from the library (START) to various places on the map. Indicate with a "?" these places and the hideout (END). Next to the map, post a sign that says, "Top Secret Plans." Under it, place several blank pieces of paper—one for each letter to the secret message—leaving a space between words. For every X books read by the group, advance the marker (a trenchcoat) one shoeprint. Each time the marker reaches a "?," draw a symbol on one of the blank papers. Readers will win a prize if all the symbols are filled in by the closing ceremony. Make up a code for the symbols (example: @ = A, # = B, $ = C, etc.). See activity #15 for details about decoding the message. The secret plans may be an announcement of next year's summer reading theme, or another message of your choice.

3. Undercover Agent ID. Take headshot photos of club members. Let them glue these in the upper right corner of blank 3″ × 5″ index cards. With black ink, put the child's right thumbprint next to the picture and have him sign his name. The card will state that the bearer is an Undercover Agent for _____ Library. Give each child his ID along with an Undercover Agent badge.

4. Spy Terms. Give children a fact sheet defining various spy or detective terms (suspect, briefing, lead, intercept, etc.). Have readers complete a crossword puzzle with these terms.

5. Guessing Games. Play some guessing games with children: (a) "I Spy" (children try to guess an object in the room); (b) "Twenty Questions" (children can ask twenty yes or no questions to guess the identity of an object or person); (c) "Hot-Cold" (children try to find a certain object in the room; they are "hot" if they are close to it, and "cold" if they are far from it); etc.

6. Secret Message. Ahead of time, write a message in lemon juice on white paper. It will be invisible when dry. Later, show children the paper and tell them a fellow agent sent a secret message. To reveal it, hold the paper over a hot light bulb (be careful!). Provide paper, brushes, and lemon juice so children can write their own invisible messages. Send them home with instructions for parents.

7. Fictitious Sleuths. Give readers a fact sheet of popular juvenile sleuths who are featured in their own series (Nancy Drew, Nate the Great, etc.). Have children complete a word search puzzle with these names.

8. Solve It Yourself. Read several short mystery stories and let children solve them. Have the person(s) who solved the mysteries list the clues and explain how they were interpreted.

9. Codes and Puzzles. Give children code sheets, with A = 1, B = 2, C = 3, etc. (or another code of your choice), along with several coded messages for them to decipher. Pass out some mazes for readers to solve. Have children create their own messages, mazes, or puzzles. Print some of them in a booklet to hand out at the closing ceremony.

10. Disguises. Provide various clothing items and accessories, wigs, fake noses, etc. Let children try on items to make disguises. Who or what are they supposed to be? How would that person walk, talk, etc.?

11. Observation Skills. Hand out several activity sheets to train the children's powers of observation: (a) Identify suspicious subjects in a "What's wrong with this picture?" page. (b) Stare at a picture for two minutes. Then hide it and answer questions about the picture to see what is remembered. (c) Circle the discrepancies between two almost-identical pictures. (d) Look at a map with trails of different footprints going in various directions. Track a suspect's prints from the crime scene to his hideout.

12. Spy Kits. Provide lots of magazines. Tell children to think about what equipment they could use as secret agents. Let them cut out items and paste them on paper, with an explanation for each one's use. Encourage creativity, such as: sunglassees — to hide your identity; pen — which shoots a laser beam; watch — which is also a two-way radio; camera — to take photos of suspects; umbrella — which doubles as a mini-copter; etc.

13. Crime Prevention. Invite a detective or police officer to fingerprint children. Discuss personal safety and list some crime-prevention tips (don't talk to strangers, etc.). Let children take home their ID prints and safety tips.

14. Crime Lab. Ask children to list some methods detectives use to analyze clues. Set up a crime lab and let children conduct some simple tests themselves: (a) Dust a glass for fingerprints; (b) Compare the smell on a handkerchief with five scented index cards; (c) Use a magnifying glass to match torn fibers with scraps of material; (d) Match a drawing of a suspect to its photo mugshot; etc.

15. Closing Ceremony: Decode the Secret Message. Ahead of time, write each symbol that was used in Activity #2 on one side of a blank index card. On the other side, write the letter which that symbol represents. Hide these cards in various places in the library. Then tell children they must find these cards in order to decipher the game message and reveal the top secret plans. Write each symbol and the letter it represents on a chalkboard as the cards are found and given to you. When all the cards have been found, children can use the code to decipher the top secret message. Declare the children Master Spies when the code is cracked, and award prizes.

Theme-Related Books

For Younger Readers

Alexander, Sue. *World Famous Muriel.* Little, 1983.
Kellogg, Steven. *The Mystery of the Missing Red Mitten.* Dial, 1974.
Lewis, Thomas P. *Mr. Sniff and the Motel Mystery.* Harper, 1984.
Lexau, Joan M. *The Homework Caper.* Harper, 1960.
Massie, Diane Redfield. *Chameleon Was a Spy.* Harper, 1979.
Sharmat, Marjorie. *Nate the Great.* Putnam, 1972.
Smith, Jim. *Alphonse and the Stonehenge Mystery.* Little, 1980.
Stefanec-Ogren, Cathy. *Sly, P.I.: The Case of the Missing Shoes.* Harper, 1989.
Yolen, Jane. *Piggins.* HBJ, 1987.

For Older Readers

Dixon, Franklin W. *The Hardy Boys* (series). Grosset.
Fitzhugh, Louise. *Harriet the Spy.* Harper, 1964.
Hass, E.A. *Incognito Mosquito, Private Insective.* Random, 1985.
Hildick, E.W. *The Case of the Condemned Cat.* Macmillan, 1975.
Keene, Caroline. *Nancy Drew* (series). Grosset.

O'Connell, Jean S. *The Dollhouse Caper.* Crowell, 1976.
Raskin, Ellen. *The Westing Game.* Dutton, 1978.
Simon, Seymour. *Einstein Anderson, Science Sleuth.* Viking, 1980.
Sobol, Donald. *Encyclopedia Brown, Boy Detective.* Lodestar, 1963.
Titus, Eve. *Basil of Baker Street.* McGraw, 1958.

Nonfiction

Albert, Burton, Jr. *Code Busters!* Whitman, 1985.
Butler, William. *The Young Detective's Handbook.* Little, 1981.
Hindley, Judy, and King, Colin. *Fakes and Forgeries.* Usborne, 1979.
Martini, Teri. *The Secret Is Out: True Spy Stories.* Little, 1990.
Paige, David. *A Day in the Life of a Police Detective.* Troll, 1981.
Rawson, Christopher, et al. *Disguise and Make-Up.* Usborne, 1978.
Selsam, Millicent. *How to Be a Nature Detective.* Harper, 1963.
Sobol, Donald. *Encyclopedia Brown's Book of Wacky Spies.* Morrow, 1984.
Thomson, Ruth, and Hindley, Judy. *Tracking and Trailing.* Usborne, 1978.
Travis, Falcon, and Hindley, Judy. *Secret Messages.* Usborne, 1978.

Films and Videos

Cloak and Dagger. (Rated PG.) MCA, 101 mins.
Encyclopeda Brown: One Minute Mysteries. HI, 30 mins.
The Great Muppet Caper. CBS, 98 mins.
Mystery on the Docks. RR, 30 mins.
Nate the Great Goes Undercover. CHUR, 10 mins.

—— HAVE A PRIME TIME ——
AT THE LIBRARY

(Television)

*If you like TV, then you'll love _____ Library this summer.
Switch us on and learn about television production and special
effects. Make a microphone and a TV set. Invent future uses for
television. Be in a commercial. Create your own television series.
Vote for your favorite shows in the Emmy Awards and play "The
Ratings Game." You're sure to* **Have a Prime Time at the
Library!**

Promotional Items

1. Sign reading "Station (library's initials)-TV Control Room" for check-out area
2. "Station (library's initials)-TV Crew Member" (membership cards)
3. TV set cut-outs (for books read)
4. Reading logs entitled "Program Guide"
5. "Have a Prime Time at the Library!" bookmarks
6. Video Whiz-Kid Awards (certificates of participation)
7. T-Shirt transfers with the "Station (library's initials)-TV" logo (game prizes)

Activities

1. Bulletin Board. Draw a large TV set. On the screen, write "Station (library's initials)-TV." Post pictures of television equipment, scenes from TV shows, and TV-related books around the TV set. Caption: HAVE A PRIME TIME AT THE LIBRARY.

2. Reading Incentive Game: TV Transmission. Draw a picture of a TV station and transmitter. Above and to the right, draw a communications satellite. Further to the right, draw another TV station and transmitter. To the right of that, draw a home with a satellite dish. Connect the transmitters, satellite, and dish with lines drawn as wavelengths. Use a circle with red, green, and blue dots as the marker. Start the marker at the first transmitter. Advance it one peak on the wavelengths for every X books read by the group. Readers will win a prize if the marker reaches the satellite dish by the closing ceremony.

3. TV Equipment. Show children pictures of or actual TV production equipment (microphone, tripod, cables, camera, etc.). Have children complete a crossword puzzle with these terms.

4. Microphones. Glue one end of a paper towel tube into a small white paper cup. Glue silver glitter onto the cup. Children can practice interviewing each other while speaking into their microphones.

5. Commercials. Ask each child to pick a favorite book, then make up a commercial advertising the book. If video equipment is available, tape these commercials to show at the closing ceremony.

6. Emmy Awards. List several categories for which Emmy Awards are given, or let children make up categories (Best Cartoon, Best Child Actor, Best Theme Song, etc.). Children can vote for the winners. Print the list of winners and distribute at the closing ceremony.

7. TV Sets. Give each child two sheets of oak tag, 12" high and 13" wide, to make TV sets. On one sheet, cut a rectangular hole, leaving 1" on the right, left, and top edges, and 2½" on the bottom. This is the TV screen. Glue paper circles underneath the screen for dials, and label them, "volume," "contrast," "on/off," etc. Staple the top and bottom edges of the TV set to the back-up sheet, leaving the right and left sides open. Let children draw pictures on paper 8½″ high and 11″ wide. Slide the pictures through an open side of the TV, so the pictures appear on the screen.

8. TV Series. Read a book belonging to a series or let children pick a book. Discuss how they would turn this concept into a TV series. What sets would be needed? Who would the main and recurring characters be? Who would be cast in the roles? What would the name of the series be?

9. TV Stations. Give children a list of TV stations in your state. Have them locate these places on the state map.

10. TV Terms. Give children a fact sheet on television production terminology (on location, action, transmit, etc.). Have them complete a word search puzzle with these terms.

11. Special Effects. Video images can be edited to create many special effects. One type is called chromakey, in which one image is combined with a different background, such as a weather forecaster over a map. Let children create their own special effects pictures. Provide some old magazines. Pick a background picture, such as a lake. Carefully cut out another picture, such as a man, and paste it on the background to give a special effect (a man walking on water). Encourage children to invent magical or crazy effects, such as a large bird chasing a small cat. Children can slide these pictures into their TV sets (activity #7).

12. TV Careers. There are many types of careers in television. Divide a chalkboard into three areas and label them: (a) "Making equipment"; (b) "On the set"; and (c) "In the control room." Describe several jobs and let children decide in which group they belong. Examples: (a) factory worker, electronics engineer; (b) cameraman, actor, set designer; (c) vision mixer, technical director; etc.

13. Future TV. TV is not just for entertainment anymore. Technology has made other uses for TVs possible. Have children name some other uses (as computer monitors, for video games, home shopping, etc.). Ask children to brainstorm other possible uses for TVs in the future. Have children illustrate their ideas.

14. New Shows. Divide children into groups. Tell each group to create their own idea for a TV show. It can be any type—soap opera, cartoon, sitcom, science fiction, etc. Each show must have a title, a brief description of its concept, and a list of characters. Decide whether the show is one hour or a half-hour long, what night and time slot it will be on, and who the audience would be. Then give a brief description of one episode of the show. Bind these TV show ideas into a book called "New This Fall on (library's initials)-TV" to keep in the library.

15. Closing Ceremony: The Ratings Game. A librarian game show host will name several TV shows that children watch. The host will interview three children (representing different age groups) for their opinions of each show. Then have the entire group vote by raising hands to rate the show as: (a) Must watch; (b) Will watch sometimes; (c) Will watch if nothing better is on; or (d) No way would I watch that. Determine the all-around favorite and least-liked shows. In between rounds, play videos of book commercials done earlier by the children (activity #5).

Theme-Related Books

For Younger Readers

Adams, Barbara. *Can This Telethon Be Saved.* Dell, 1987.
Adler, David A. *Cam Jansen and the Mystery of the Television Dog.* Viking, 1981.
Barden, Rosalind. *TV Monster.* Crown, 1989.
Freeman, Don. *The Paper Party.* Viking, 1974.
Kunnas, Mauri. *Ricky, Rocky, and Ringo on TV.* Crown, 1987.
McPhail, David. *Fix-It.* Dutton, 1984.
Rosen, Winifred. *Ralph Proves the Pudding.* Doubleday, 1972.
Wright, Betty R. *The Day Our TV Broke.* Raintree, 1980.

For Older Readers

Adams, Barbara. *On the Air and Off the Wall.* Dell, 1986.
Angell, Judie. *First the Good News.* Bradbury, 1982.
Byars, Betsy. *The TV Kid.* Viking, 1976.
Conford, Ellen. *You Never Can Tell.* Little, 1984.
Girion, Barbara. *Prime Time Attraction.* Dell, 1987.
Harris, Mark J. *Confessions of a Prime Time Kid.* Lothrop, 1985.
Heide, Florence Parry. *The Problem with Pulcifer.* Lippincott, 1982.
Manes, Stephen. *The Boy Who Turned into a TV Set.* Avon, 1983.
Paterson, Katherine. *Come Sing, Jimmy Jo.* Lodestar, 1985.
West, Dan. *The Day the TV Blew Up.* Whitman, 1988.

Nonfiction

Beal, George. *See Inside a Television Studio.* Watts, 1978.
Charren, Peggy, and Hulsizer, Carol. *The TV-Smart Book for Kids: Puzzles, Games, and Other Good Stuff.* Dutton, 1986.
Cheney, Glenn Alan. *Television in American Society.* Watts, 1983.
Drucker, Malka, and James, Elizabeth. *Series TV: How a Television Show Is Made.* Clarion, 1983.
Fields, Alice. *Television.* Watts, 1980.
Fenten, D.X., and Fenten, Barbara. *Behind the Television Scene.* Crestwood, 1980.
Griffin-Beale, Christopher, and Gee, Robin. *TV and Video.* Usborne, 1982.
Hallenstein, Kathryn. *I Can Be a TV Camera Operator.* Childrens, 1984.
Jasperson, William. *A Day in the Life of a Television News Reporter.* Little, 1981.
Scott, Elaine. *Ramona: Behind the Scenes of a Television Show.* Morrow, 1988.

Films and Videos

The Bionic Bunny Show. RR, 30 mins.
The Electronic Rainbow. PYR, 23 mins.
Of Muppets and Men. FIV, 52 mins.
Sooper Goop. CHUR, 10 mins.
TV or Not TV? BARR, 15 mins.

—— READERS' THEATER ——

(Theater)

Attention! Casting Call! Broadway has come to _____
Library this summer. Explore the theater: Learn about different
types of plays. Find out what goes on backstage as well as onstage.
Make set pieces and props. Create a costume and try on stage
make-up. Be a mime and read a script. Design a theater program.
See a professional drama production. If you're looking for fun this
*summer, try out **Readers' Theater!***

Promotional Items

1. Sign Reading "Box Office" for check-out area
2. "Member of _____ Library Theater Guild" cards (membership cards)
3. Star cut-outs (for books read)
4. Reading logs entitled "Script"
5. "Readers' Theater" bookmarks
6. Tony Award certificates (certificates of participation)
7. "Readers' Theater" T-shirt transfers (game prizes)

Activities

1. Bulletin Board. Draw curtains along the top and sides of the area to represent a proscenium stage. Above the stage, write "_____ Library Presents . . . ." On the stage, post cut-outs of books, one for each letter of the caption: READERS' THEATER.

2. Reading Incentive Game: Production Schedule. Post a giant calendar of the exact number of days of the summer reading promotion. Label it, "Production Schedule." Next to it, list in order all the things that need to be done when producing a play (choose play, hire director, make budget, cast parts, etc.). For every X books read by the group, write in the appropriate date on the calendar another production item that was accomplished. (More than one item can be on a date.) Readers will receive a prize if all the items have been written onto the calendar by "Opening Night" (the closing ceremony).

3. Mime. Have children do simple exercises to introduce them to acting and pantomime. (a) Mime various emotions, first by using facial expressions only, then by their walk, then with their entire bodies. (b) Act like different animals. (c) Pretend to play sports or games. (d) Mime some everyday activities (read a newspaper, clean a window, open and close a door, etc.). (e) Pair up children and have them face each other to do a mirror exercise.

4. Theater Terms. Give children a fact sheet of theater terms (scene, cue, audience, etc.). Show pictures of theaters and stages. Have children complete a crossword puzzle of these terms.

5. Comedy/Tragedy. Make cardboard templates of a comedy mask and a tragedy mask, each about 7 inches long and 5 inches wide, with holes cut out for eyes and mouths. Let children trace one of each, using two different colors of construction paper. Cut out the masks, including the eyes and mouths. Glue the masks, overlapping slightly, onto a third color paper (in the classic comedy/tragedy pose). The masks may be embellished with glitter.

6. Play Types. Have readers complete a word search puzzle of types of plays (comedy, tragedy, farce, musical, etc.).

7. Costumes. Provide lots of "grown-up" clothes and fancy accessories— gowns, ties, hats, costume jewelry, shoes, etc. Let children dress up in a costume of their own design. Then, one at a time, let them act (with words and movement) the way their character would act. The others should try to guess who or what that person is. Or, assign each child a character and have them find an appropriate costume.

8. Make-up. Show children a theater make-up kit. Explain the purpose of each type (pancake, greasepaint, etc.). How does theater make-up differ from regular street make-up? How is it similar? Ask for volunteers, and use make-up to make them look old, handsome, etc.

9. Mini-Flats. Explain that the walls of a set are usually not real walls, but flats. To make a miniature flat, glue four wooden popsicle sticks into a square frame and let dry. Cut a square of plain paper, slightly larger than the frame. Lay the frame onto the center of the paper. Fold the paper over the edges of the frame and tape securely, so there are no bulges or wrinkles. Turn over the flat, and paint a scene of your choice, being careful not to punch a hole in the paper. Show a real flat to the children.

10. Lighting. Display different types of stage lighting (fresnels, footlights, spots, etc.). Show children how gels are added to change the color of a light. Show a diagram of how lights are hung. How does lighting affect a scene? Shine a stage light on some children and ask them how it feels.

11. Stage Props. Tell children that fake props are often substituted for the real thing in a play. Help children create some stage props (like papier-maché rocks) or phony food (like cardboard pizza) that could be used in a play.

12. Off-Broadway. Give readers a list of noted off-Broadway theater companies and their locations (The Guthrie Theater of Minneapolis, Minnesota; Long Wharf Theater of New Haven, Connecticut, etc.). Have children find these cities on a map of the United States.

13. Scripts. Show children what a script looks like. Then choose selections from a children's play. Assign children roles and have them read for the

group. If possible, have them perform a readers' theater piece at the closing
ceremony.

14. Programs. Let children examine some theater programs. Explain the
different on- and off-stage jobs, emphasizing that they are all important. Post a large
program for a popular play with all the jobs listed, but no names given. Ask for
volunteers and fill in children's names for the various acting and non-acting jobs.
Include lots of chorus and backstage jobs so everyone can be listed in the program.
Ask each child to draw a design for the program cover.

15. Closing Ceremony Performance. Invite a children's theater group to
perform. After the show, let the readers speak to the theater people about what it's
like to do a play. Let the reader's theater children perform their play.

Theme-Related Books

For Younger Readers

Blake, Quentin. *The Story of the Dancing Frog.* Knopf, 1985.
Brandenberg, Franz. *Nice New Neighbors.* Greenwillow, 1977.
Freeman, Don. *Will's Quill.* Viking, 1975.
Giff, Patricia Reilly. *The Almost Awful Play.* Penguin, 1985.
Haas, Irene. *The Little Moon Theater.* Macmillan, 1981.
Hoffman, Mary. *Amazing Grace.* Dial, 1991.
Holabird, Katharine. *Angelina on Stage.* Potter, 1986.
Isadora, Rachel. *Jesse and Abe.* Greenwillow, 1981.
Nixon, Joan Lowery. *Gloria Chipmunk, Star!* Houghton, 1990.
Wharton, Thomas. *Hildegard Sings.* Farrar, 1991.

For Older Readers

Auch, Mary J. *Glass Slippers Give You Blisters.* Holiday, 1989.
Blume, Judy. *The One in the Middle Is a Green Kangaroo.* Bradbury, 1981.
Cross, Gillian. *The Dark Behind the Curtain.* Oxford, 1987.
Gormley, Beatrice. *Fifth Grade Magic.* Dutton, 1982.
Holmes, Barbara Ware. *Charlotte Shakespeare and Annie the Great.* Harper, 1989.
Howe, James. *Stage Fright: A Sebastian Barth Mystery.* Macmillan, 1986.
Martin, Ann M. *Stage Fright.* Holiday, 1984.
Phelan, Terry Wolfe. *The S.S. Valentine.* Four Winds, 1979.
Robinson, Barbara. *The Best Christmas Pageant Ever.* Harper, 1972.
Singer, Marilyn. *Twenty Ways to Lose Your Best Friend.* Harper, 1990.

Nonfiction

Babcock, Dennis, and Boyd, Preston. *Careers in the Theater.* Lerner, 1985.
Bauer, Caroline Feller. *Presenting Reader's Theater.* Wilson, 1987.
Belville, Cheryl. *Theater Magic: Behind the Scenes at a Children's Theater.* Carolrhoda,
    1985.
Brokering, Lois. *Resources for Dramatic Play.* Fearon, 1989.

Bruun-Rasmussen, Ole, and Petersen, Grete. *Make-up, Costumes and Masks for the Stage.* Sterling, 1976.

Campbell, Patricia J. *Passing the Hat: The Life of Street Performers in America.* Delacorte, 1981.

Goffstein, Brooke. *An Actor.* Harper, 1987.

Judy, Susan, and Judy, Stephen. *Putting on a Play: A Guide to Writing and Producing Neighborhood Drama.* Scribner's, 1982.

Powers, Bill. *Behind the Scenes of a Broadway Musical.* Crown, 1982.

Smith, Betsy Covington. *A Day in the Life of an Actress.* Troll, 1985.

Films and Videos

The Art of Silence: Pantomimes with Marcel Marceau. BRIT, 4 films 29–35 mins. each.
Beware, Beware, My Beauty Fair. PHX, 29 mins.
A Chair for My Mother. RR, 30 mins.
The Muppets Take Manhattan. CBS, 94 mins.
Puppets: How They Happen. FILM, 18 mins.

— PLAYTIME AT THE LIBRARY —

(*Toys and Games*)

You will have a toy-riffic time this summer at _____ Library. Fill up your toy chest and make beanbags. Vote for your favorite toys and games. Make clothespin dolls and button spinners. Play card games and pick-up straws. Try to solve the puzzler and other guessing games. Come to the Playground Party and join the fun. So if you're game for a good time, sign up now for **Playtime at the Library.**

Promotional Items

1. Sign reading "Playground" for check-out area
2. "Gaming Permits" (membership cards)
3. Building block cut-outs (for books read)
4. Reading logs entitled "Game Pieces"
5. "Playtime at the Library" bookmarks
6. Toy-riffic Kid Awards (certificates of participation)
7. Word games and puzzle books (game prizes)

Activities

1. Bulletin Board. Post pictures from children's books and other media about toys, games, and play. Also post pictures of the toys that will be made during the summer. Caption: PLAYTIME AT THE LIBRARY.

2. Reading Incentive Game: Puzzler. Draw a picture or choose a poster to use, then cut it up to make a jigsaw puzzle. (Pieces can be square or odd-shaped.) On one wall, draw the outline of the puzzle, with each piece traced in its place. Save the pieces where they cannot be seen. For every X books read by the group, post one puzzle piece in its place on the wall. Skip around; don't place pieces in order. Readers will win a prize if the puzzle is completed by the closing ceremony. You can also let children submit written guesses as to what the completed picture will be. Award a separate prize to the first person to guess correctly.

3. Pick-Up Straws. Divide children into small groups and have them sit in a circle. Give each group a box of plastic straws. Dump the straws into the center of each circle. The object of the game is to pick up one straw at a time, without disturbing the others. Each child takes a turn. If he picks up a straw successfully, he can keep picking up straws until he misses. Then the next child takes a turn. The person who ends up with the most straws at the end of the game is the winner.

4. Spinners. Give each child a large two- or four-hole button and a 24″ length of string. Help children thread the string through one hole of the button, then back through the opposite hole. Tie the ends of the string together. Slide the button to the middle of the loop of string. Help children loop one end of the string around the middle finger of the left hand, and the other end around the middle right finger. Twirl the button around several times so the string becomes tightly twisted. Then pull both hands apart and together, back and forth. The button in the middle will spin around until the string is unwound.

5. "Real" Toys. Read *Corduroy*, by Don Freeman. Ask children if they have a special stuffed animal or doll that seems real. Have them write a story or draw a picture of an imaginary adventure with a favorite doll or stuffed animal.

6. Toy Store. Sit children in a circle and play a memory game with them. One person starts with, "I went to the toy store and I bought (names a toy)." The next person repeats the phrase, names the toy, and adds a new one. Keep going in this fashion around the circle. See who can remember the most toys in the list.

7. Toy Chest. Provide lots of old magazines. Give each child a piece of oak tag on which the outline of an open toy chest has been drawn. Let children cut out pictures of toys they would like to have and glue them into their toy chests.

8. Favorite Toys. Ask each child to name one favorite toy. List these on the board. Then take a poll and note how many children own each toy. Which toy is the most popular? Why? You can also take a poll of favorite games.

9. Video Games. Have children complete a word search puzzle with the names of popular video games.

10. Beanbags. Give each child an old plain-colored sock (tube socks are best) that does not have holes. Children can draw designs on them with felt-tip markers. Let children fill each sock about half full with seeds and beans. Tie the sock tightly closed with a piece of string. Children can play catch or basketbag (like basketball), or make up another beanbag game.

11. Toys from the Past. Display toys or pictures of toys that were popular in the past (hula-hoops, Rubik's Cubes, Mr. T dolls, etc.). Note some other toys and games that have been around a long time (yo-yos, Monopoly, Barbie dolls, etc.). Ask children why they think some toys and games stay popular and others don't.

12. Clothespin Dolls. Give each child a wooden slot-type clothespin. With colored felt-tip markers, draw a mouth, eyes, nose, and hair on the round knob. Twist a pipe cleaner around the neck of the clothespin to make arms. Color boots or shoes on the two lower tips. Children can color different shirt and pants designs to make their dolls unique.

13. Card Games. Divide children into small groups and give each group a deck of playing cards. Teach them how to play a simple card game, such as Crazy Eights or Go Fish.

14. Riding Toys. Ask children to name some riding toys (bicycles, go-karts, rocking horses, battery-operated cars, etc.). Let them draw a picture of their favorite riding toy, or design a new one. Display in library.

15. Closing Ceremony: Playground Party. Play several movement games with children, such as musical chairs, ring-around-the-rosie, duck-duck-goose, giant steps, wonder ball, etc. Older children may prefer to play guessing games such as I spy or hangman, or board games.

Theme-Related Books

For Younger Readers

Andersen, Hans Christian. *The Steadfast Tin Soldier.* Clarion, 1979.
Browne, Anthony. *Gorilla.* Knopf, 1985.
Freeman, Don. *Corduroy.* Viking, 1968.
Goffstein, M.B. *Me and My Captain.* Farrar, 1974.
Lionni, Leo. *Alexander and the Wind-Up Mouse.* Pantheon, 1969.
Rayner, Mary. *Crocodarling.* Bradbury, 1985.
Van Allsburg, Chris. *Jumanji.* Houghton, 1981.
Wells, Rosemary. *Max's Toys: A Counting Book.* Dial, 1979.
Ziefert, Harriet. *Goodnight, Everyone.* Little, 1988.
Zolotow, Charlotte. *William's Doll.* Harper, 1972.

For Older Readers

Banks, Lynne Reid. *The Indian in the Cupboard.* Doubleday, 1981.
Duffy, James. *The Revolt of the Teddy Bears.* Crown, 1984.

Field, Rachel. *Hitty: Her First Hundred Years.* Macmillan, 1937.
Hoban, Russell. *The Mouse and His Child.* Harper, 1967.
Peck, Robert Newton. *Trig.* Little, 1977.
Rubinstein, Gillian. *Space Demons.* Dial, 1988.
Sleator, William. *Among the Dolls.* Dutton, 1975.
Snyder, Zilpha Keatley. *The Egypt Game.* Dell, 1986.

Nonfiction

Bourne, Miriam Anne. *Let's Visit a Toy Factory.* Troll, 1987.
Flick, Pauline. *Discovering Toys and Toy Museums.* Legacy, 1977.
Gibbons, Gail. *Playgrounds.* Holiday, 1985.
Joseph, Joan. *Folk Toys Around the World.* Parents, 1972.
Lerner, Mark. *Careers in Toymaking.* Lerner, 1980.
Opie, Iona, et al. *The Treasures of Childhood.* Arcade, 1990.
Radlauer, Ruth, and Radlauer, Edward. *Dolls.* Childrens, 1980.
Todd, Leonard. *Trash Can Toys and Games.* Viking, 1974.
White, Laurence B., Jr. *Science Toys and Tricks.* Harper, 1980.
Williams, J. Alan. *The Kids' and Grown-Ups' Toy-Making Book.* Morrow, 1979.

Films and Videos

Babes in Toyland. DIS, 105 mins.
Corduroy. WW, 16 mins.
Matrioska. NFBC, 5 mins.
Tasha and the Magic Bubble. CENT, 20 mins.
Tchiou Tchiou. BRIT, 15 mins.
The Velveteen Rabbit. RH, 30 mins.

- RIDE THE READING RAILROAD -

(Trains)

All aboard the Reading Railroad! Chug along to the Library Station and pick up your ticket for a summer of fun and adventure. Travel full steam ahead and find out about all types of trains and the people who work with them. Help build our model train display. Design a train of the future. Learn to read train schedules. You can even be a train! _____ Library will keep you on the right track this summer. Climb aboard and **Ride the Reading Railroad!**

Promotional Items

1. Sign reading "Library Station" for check-out area
2. "Train Tickets" (membership cards)
3. Reading logs entitled "Travel Log"
4. Engine cut-outs (for books read)
5. "Ride the Reading Railroad" bookmarks
6. Certificates of Arrival (certificates of participation)
7. Model trains (game prizes)

Activities

1. Bulletin Board. Post on the wall a picture of a long passenger train. Glue headshots of the reading club members onto the train to indicate children who are looking out the windows. Caption: RIDE THE READING RAILROAD.

2. Reading Incentive Game: Train Trip. Draw a railroad track that begins at the "Roundhouse" and extends along a wall of the library to the "Final Destination." For every X books read by the group, advance a train marker one tie along the track. Readers win a prize if the train reaches its destination by the closing ceremony.

3. Model Train Display. Display a model train set. Have children glue popsicle sticks together to make a long tunnel for the train to go under. Let them bring in scenic pieces to add to the railroad community throughout the summer.

4. Cars. Give readers a fact sheet of the different cars in a train (engine, boxcar, caboose, etc.). Have them complete a crossword puzzle with these terms.

5. Group Train. Have each child draw one car of a train on a piece of construction paper. Post the pictures end-to-end to form one long train along the wall.

6. Train Songs. Have children sing and act out "I've Been Working on the Railroad." Play recordings of other train songs and let children sing along.

7. State Tracks. Study a map of your state. Identify railroad tracks with the children. Where do the tracks go? Give children paper and colored markers to draw a map of a train route, either real or imaginary.

8. Trains of the Future. Show children pictures of old trains and modern trains. Have children draw their own "trains of the future." Consider how the train would look, how it would run, where would it go, and what it would carry.

9. Railroad Jobs. Discuss with children the various jobs of people who work on trains. Where does each person work? What are the duties of each job? Have children role-play some jobs.

10. Library Journey. Line up all the children in a row, front-to-back. Have them pretend they are a train, and let them chug around the library. With a librarian as the conductor, stop at various "stations" along the way to point out things of interest, such as the card catalog, the reference desk, the magazine area, the poetry section, etc. Take advantage of the opportunity to acquaint readers with many areas and features of the library.

11. Types of Trains. Give an illustrated talk about different types of trains (freight, passenger, trolley, steam, subway, etc.). Have children complete a word search puzzle of types of trains.

12. Train Construction. Use pint and quart size milk cartons to make train cars. Cut some in half vertically and lay on their sides to be flat cars. Cover all cartons with construction paper. Let children color them to look like various train cars. Glue on cardboard wheels and link cars together with pipe cleaners. Then have children glue popsicle sticks together to make a train track. Display the train on the track.

13. I Think I Can. Assign children roles as toys and trains and have them act out Watty Piper's *The Little Engine That Could.*

14. Railroad Station. Have children set up an area to look like a railroad station. Display train schedules and show children how to read them. Assign children roles as the ticket-seller, passengers, and the conductor, and have them play-act boarding a train.

15. Closing Ceremony: Railroad Hobby. Invite a hobbyist to display several types of model electric trains and give a talk on how children can get into the hobby. Show how trains are set up. Display hobby magazines. Let children run some trains themselves.

Theme-Related Books

For Younger Readers

Barton, Byron. *Trains.* Crowell, 1986.
Benson, Kathleen. *Joseph on the Subway Trains.* Crowell, 1981.
Brown, Margaret Wise. *Two Little Trains.* Harper, 1949.
Ehrlich, Amy. *The Everyday Train.* Dial, 1977.
Howard, Elizabeth Fitzgerald. *The Train to Lulu's.* Holiday, 1981.
Rosenberg, Liz. *Adelaide and the Night Train.* Harper, 1989.
Steptoe, John. *Train Ride.* Harper, 1971.
Van Allsburg, Chris. *The Polar Express.* Houghton, 1985.

For Older Readers

Bemelmans, Ludwig. *Quito Express.* Viking, 1965.
Coren, Alan. *Railroad Arthur.* Little, 1978.
Cross, Gilbert B. *Terror Train!* Macmillan, 1987.
Fleischman, Sid. *Me and the Man on the Moon-Eyed Horse.* Little, 1977.
Fleming, Susan. *Trapped on the Golden Flyer.* Westminster, 1978.
Hamilton, Dorothy. *The Blue Caboose.* Herald, 1973.
Hyde, Dayton O. *Thunder Down the Track.* Macmillan, 1986.

Rounds, Glen. *Mr. Yowder and the Train Robbers.* Holiday, 1981.
Warner, Gertrude Chandler. *The Boxcar Children.* Whitman, 1950.
Welber, Robert. *The Train.* Pantheon, 1972.

Nonfiction

Ault, Phil. *All Aboard! The Story of Passenger Trains in America.* Dodd, 1976.
Ditzel, Paul C. *Railroad Yard.* Messner, 1977.
Dunbar, Charles S. *Buses, Trolleys and Trams.* Hamlyn, 1967.
Fisher, Leonard Everett. *The Railroads.* Holiday, 1979.
Flatley, Dennis R. *The Railroads: Opening the West.* Watts, 1989.
Meade, Chris. *Careers with a Railroad.* Lerner, 1975.
Pierce, Jack. *The Freight Train Book.* Carolrhoda, 1980.
Radlauer, Edward. *Model Trains.* Childrens, 1979.
Stein, R. Conrad. *The Story of the Golden Spike.* Childrens, 1978.
Yepsen, Roger. *Train Talk: An Illustrated Guide to Lights, Hand Signals, Whistles and Other Languages of Railroading.* Pantheon, 1983.

Films and Videos

Casey Jones. PHX, 11 mins.
Frieght Train. BRIT, 12 mins.
The Little Engine That Could. COR, 10 mins.
The Odyssey of the Pacific. MCA, 82 mins.
Toccata for Toy Trains. PYR, 15 mins.
Trains. DIS/COR, 14 mins.

——— *TREE*T YOURSELF ———
TO A BOOK
(Trees, Forests)

*Branch out for a tree-mendous summer at _____ Library.
Learn about all types of common and exotic trees. Design a tree
house. Create a leaf picture. Draw your own family tree. Put
together a collage of tree products. Find out about life in a tropical
rainforest. Make a block of thinking wood. Come to our Arbor Day
tree-planting ceremony. Log in some time at the library this summer, and* **TREEt Yourself to a Book!**

Promotional Items

1. Sign reading "Branch Office" for check-out area
2. "Tree-Topper ID" (membership cards)
3. Leaf cut-outs (for books read)
4. Reading logs entitled "Reading Log"
5. "TREEt Yourself to a Book" bookmarks
6. Arborist Awards (certificates of participation)
7. Small live trees (game prizes)

Activities

1. Bulletin Board. Post a cut-out of a large tree tunk. Post cut-outs of leaves on the tree. On each leaf, write the name of a reading club member. Draw a picture of a child sitting under the tree, reading a book. Caption: **TREET YOURSELF TO A BOOK.**

2. Reading Incentive Game: Tree Rings. Sketch a large cut-away view of a tree trunk, revealing its annual rings. For every X books read by the group, color in one ring, starting from the center and moving outward. Readers will win a prize if all the rings have been colored in by the closing ceremony.

3. Tree Parts. Give children a sketch of a tree. Help them label the various parts (stem, bark, leaf, roots, bud, etc.). Let children color their pictures, and draw a tree of their own.

4. Tree Groups. Show children pictures of different trees. Have them categorize these into three main groups of trees: broadleaf, needleleaf, and palms. Which trees grow where you live? What are some places that the other trees may be found?

5. Leaf Pictures. Each state in the United States has a state tree. Display pictures of your particular state tree. Bring in several leaves (or needles) from this tree to make pictures. Give each child a 6″ by 7″ piece of wood-grain patterned, adhesive-backed decorating paper. Place it pattern side down and remove the covering paper to reveal the adhesive. Arrange leaves or needles on the adhesive. Over this, press a 6″ by 7″ piece of clear plastic wrap as smoothly as possible. Glue a frame of oak tag or popsicle sticks onto the leaf picture.

6. Unusual Trees. Some trees grow only in certain parts of the world. Locate on a world map the places where these trees grow: banyan, ginko, eucalyptus, redwood, upas, cacao, and any others you may choose. Display pictures of these trees and tell children about their special features.

7. Tropical Rain Forest. Read *The Great Kapok Tree*, by Lynn Cherry. Have children list the animals that live in the tree. How does the tree benefit life on earth? Hand out a labeled sketch of the layers of trees that grow in a tropical rain forest (underbrush, canopy, emergent trees, etc.). Have children color in this page and add some animals.

8. Tree Searches. Have children complete word search puzzles of common broadleaf trees and fruit or edible nut trees.

9. Family Trees. Have children draw pictures of their family trees. Use branches and leaves to include the various relatives.

10. Tree Terms. Give children a fact sheet of tree-related terms (forest, lumber, pruning, evergreen, etc.). Have children complete a crossword puzzle with these terms.

11. Tree Products. Ask children to name some fruits that grow on trees. What else do we get from trees? (Paper, wood, rubber, maple sugar, coffee, etc.) Provide lots of old magazines. Let children cut out pictures of things that we get from trees. Glue these pictures onto oak tag to make collages.

12. Tree Houses. Show children pictures of some real and fictitious tree houses. Divide children into groups and have them design and draw their own tree houses. Display in library.

13. Tree Tales. There are many folk tales and true stories involving trees, such as stories about Johnny Appleseed and Paul Bunyan, or Connecticut's historic Charter Oak Tree. Tell children a tree story that is popular where you live. Let children write their own stories about trees.

14. Thinking Wood. Some people like to rub a smooth piece of wood with their fingers to help them think. Give each child a hand-size block of wood and a sheet of fine sandpaper. Have them sand down their blocks on all sides, until they are perfectly smooth. Provide a few shades of shoe polish and let children stain their wood. Children can rub their thinking woods to help them relax or use their imaginations.

15. Closing Ceremony: Arbor Day Celebration. If possible, arrange to have a tree planted on the library property, or another place where the closing ceremony can be held. Have a guest speaker explain to the children the steps taken to plant and care for a tree. If an outdoor ceremony is not possible, the speaker can demonstrate by planting an indoor tree in a pot. Children should be given instructions on how to plant and care for their own trees. Serve foods that come from tree products (fruit, chocolate, cinnamon buns, etc.).

Theme-Related Books

For Younger Readers

Buscaglia, Leo. *The Fall of Freddy the Leaf.* Holt, 1982.
Cherry, Lynne. *The Great Kapok Tree.* HBJ, 1990.
Fleischman, Paul. *The Birthday Tree.* Harper, 1979.
Gibbons, Gail. *The Seasons of Arnold's Apple Tree.* HBJ, 1984.
Killion, Bette. *The Apartment House Tree.* Harper, 1989.
Romonova, Natalie. *Once There Was a Tree.* Dial, 1985.
Schertle, Alice. *In My Treehouse.* Lothrop, 1983.

Silverstein, Shel. *The Giving Tree.* Harper, 1964.
Tressault, Alvin. *The Dead Tree.* Parents, 1972.
Udry, Janice May. *A Tree Is Nice.* Harper, 1956.

For Older Readers

Brittain, Bill. *Devil's Donkey.* Harper, 1981.
Calhoun, Mary. *Julie's Tree.* Harper, 1990.
Corcoran, Barbara. *Sasha, My Friend.* Atheneum, 1973.
Holling, Holling C. *Tree in the Trail.* Houghton, 1990.
Holman, Felice. *The Blackmail Machine.* Macmillan, 1968.
Levitin, Sonia. *Jason and the Money Tree.* HBJ, 1974.
Richmont, Enid. *The Time Tree.* Little, 1990.
Snyder, Zilpha Keatley. *Below the Root.* Atheneum, 1975.
Taylor, Mildred. *Song of the Trees.* Dial, 1975.

Nonfiction

Bash, Barbara. *Tree of Life.* Little, 1989.
Brandt, Keith. *Discovering Trees.* Troll, 1982.
Brockman, Frank. *Trees of North America.* Western, 1968.
Dowden, Anne Ophelia. *The Blossom on the Bough: A Book of Trees.* Crowell, 1975.
Kirkpatrick, Rena K. *Look at Leaves.* Raintree, 1978.
Kurelek, William. *Lumberjack.* Houghton, 1974.
Mitgutsch, Ali, et. al. *From Tree to Table.* Carolrhoda, 1981.
Newton, James R. *A Forest Is Reborn.* Crowell, 1982.
Price, Christine. *The Arts of Wood.* Scribner's, 1976.

Films and Videos

All About Trees. NGEO, 2 films, 12 mins. each.
Leaves. AIMS, 13 mins.
The Lorax. PHX, 25 mins.
Paul Bunyan. RR, 30 mins.
Trees: How We Identify Them. COR, 11 mins.
Winnie the Pooh and the Honey Tree. DIS/COR, 26 mins.

—— PLAN YOUR VACATION ——
AT THE LIBRARY
(United States Geography, Travel)

Where can you go this summer for a good time? To the library, of course! Our Tourist Information Bureau will introduce you to great vacation spots locally and across the United States. You can add to our calendar of events, choose a resort, and make travel arrangements for your dream vacation. You will set up a suitcase, put together a photo album, and collect souvenirs. Make the most of your summer. **Plan Your Vacation at the Library.**

Promotional Items

1. Sign reading "Tourist Information Bureau" for check-out area
2. "Vacation Club Member IDs" (membership cards)
3. Suitcase cut-outs (for books read)
4. Reading log entitled "Vacation Spots"
5. "Plan Your Vacation at the Library" bookmarks
6. First Class Tourist Awards (certificates of participation)
7. Library souvenir pennants (game prizes)

Activities

1. Bulletin Board. Make a collage of brochures from several tourist attractions across the United States, all clearly labeled. Add a few bus, plane and train schedules and tickets. Caption: PLAN YOUR VACATION AT THE LIBRARY.

2. Reading Incentive Game: Pennant Race. Post a map of the United States. Label small pennant cut-outs with the names of several popular tourist attractions. Use push-pins to post the pennants on their proper locations on the map. Next to the map, post a cut-out of a large suitcase. For every X books read by the group, place one pennant in the suitcase. Readers will win a prize if all the pennants are in the suitcase by the closing ceremony.

3. Send Us a Card. Make sure all children have the library's address. Tell them to mail a picture postcard to the library when they go on vacation during the summer. Display all cards received.

4. Local Fun Spots. Show pictures of some local, inexpensive places where families can take day trips (museums, parks, beaches, etc.). Let children who have visited these spots tell the group about them. Give readers an information sheet with admission prices, hours of operation, and addresses of day trip places.

5. Vacation Photos. Ask children to bring in photographs of themselves from their most recent vacations. Have them mount their photographs on oak tag. Label with children's names and when and where the pictures were taken. Display in library.

6. Big Events. Post a large calendar. Tell children to look in travel guides, newspapers, and other sources to find out where and when major festivals, celebrations, contests, sporting events, and other events of interest in the United States will be held. Mark these events and their locations on the calendar. Include such things as Mardi Gras, Macy's Thanksgiving Day Parade, chili cook-offs, and the Superbowl. This can be an ongoing summer project. The child who notes the event should give a brief explanation about it. At the end of the program, ask children to tell you some of the events they may like to see someday.

7. Activities Puzzle. Have children complete a word search puzzle of things they might do while on vacation (swim, ski, camp out, fish, etc.).

8. Transportation Mobile. People can get to their vacations by car, bus, plane, train, or boat. Give each child two construction paper cut-outs of each of these items, and markers to decorate them with. Staple the matching pieces together halfway around, stuff with newspaper, then staple closed. Hang the shapes on a coat hanger that has been bent into a circle.

9. Pick a Resort. Show children several resort and time-share brochures. Explain how to tell which features are offered at these places. Let each child list some features he would want (indoor swimming pool, two-bedroom unit, a place in the mountains, etc.). Using this list as a guide, have each child choose a resort in which he would like to stay.

10. Photo Album. Provide lots of old magazines. Let children cut out pictures of places they would like to visit and glue them onto sheets of construction paper. On a cover sheet, write, "My Vacation Photo Album." Staple pages to bind like a book.

11. Travel Terms. Give children a fact sheet of travel terms (luggage, reservation, itinerary, etc.). Have them complete a crossword puzzle with these terms.

12. Suitcasees. Provide shirt-size boxes for children to make into suitcases. Carefully tear two corners on the top half so that one of the long side panels is loose. Tape or glue this loose panel to a corresponding panel on the bottom half, so that the box opens and closes like a suitcase. Turn to the opposite panels to attach the handle. Cut a slit in the center of the outer panel, 2½" long by ¾" wide. Cut a strip of pliable cardboard 6" long and ⅝" wide. Punch two holes in the inner panel, matching either end of the length of the slit in the outer panel. Place the handle strip through these holes, and tape ends together inside the inner panel. Close the box and push the handle through the outer panel slit to "lock" the suitcase and to carry it.

13. Tourist Attraction Game Show. Post pictures of the United States tourist attractions that are used in the reading incentive game. Divide children into teams. Use a TV game show format and ask children to identify the sites. Have the child who correctly identifies the attraction locate its place on the map. The team with the most correct answers may be awarded a prize.

14. Souvenir Placemat. Most people collect souvenirs while on vacation. Give children 12" by 16" sheets of construction paper. Let them draw a vacation scene or design of their choice. Then write on it "Official Souvenir Placemat—(name of library), Summer (year)." Laminate or cover front and back with clear adhesive-backed paper to make placemats waterproof.

15. Closing Ceremony: U.S.A. Buffet. Set up a buffet of foods that are typical of different parts of the United States for children to sample (Cincinnati chili, cajun rice, french fries and gravy, etc.). Invite a travel agent to speak to children and pass out travel brochures. Supply addresses of chambers of commerce and tourist information bureaus throughout the country so children can send away for more materials.

Theme-Related Books

For Younger Readers

Anno, Mitsumasa. *Anno's U.S.A.* Philomel, 1983.
Bate, Lucy. *How Georgina Drove the Car Very Carefully from Boston to New York.* Crown, 1989.
Harwood, Pearl. *A Long Vacation for Mr. and Mrs. Bumba.* Lerner, 1971.
Jonas, Ann. *Round Trip.* Greenwillow, 1983.
Kessler, Leonard P. *Are We Lost, Daddy?* Grosset, 1967.
Khalsa, Dayal Kaur. *My Family Vacation.* Clarkson N. Potter, 1988.
McPhail, David. *Emma's Vacation.* Dutton, 1987.
Rockwell, Anne. *On Our Vacation.* Dutton, 1989.
Roffey, Maureen. *I Spy on Vacation.* Four Winds, 1988.
Stevenson, James. *The Sea View Hotel.* Greenwillow, 1978.
Williams, Vera B., and Williams, Jennifer. *Stringbean's Trip to the Shining Sea.* Scholastic, 1988.

For Older Readers

Clements, Bruce. *I Tell a Lie Every So Often.* Farrar, 1984.
Hest, Amy. *Travel Tips from Harry: A Guide to Family Vacations in the Sun.* Morrow, 1989.
Martin, Ann M. *Eleven Kids, One Summer.* Holiday, 1991.
Pellowski, Michael J. *Double Trouble on Vacation.* Willowisp, 1989.
Ressner, Phillip. *Dudley Pippin's Summer.* Harper, 1979.
Robertson, Keith. *Henry Reed's Journey.* Viking, 1963.

Nonfiction

Bauer, Caroline Feller. *Celebrations: Read-Aloud Holiday and Theme Book Program.* Wilson, 1985.
Bernstein, Joanne, and Cohen, Paul. *Riddles to Take on Vacation.* Whitman, 1987.
Brown, Laurene K., and Brown, Marc. *Dinosaurs Travel: A Guide for Families on the Go.* Little, 1988.
Burda, Margaret. *Amazing States.* Good Apple, 1984.
Caney, Steven. *Kids' America.* Workman, 1978.
Clouse, Nancy L. *Puzzle Maps U.S.A.* Holt, 1990.
McKissack, Patricia, and McKissack, Frederick. *Big Bug Book of Places to Go.* Milliken, 1987.

Films and Videos

Babar the Elephant Comes to America. VES, 23 mins.
National Geographic's Guide to the National Parks of the United States. NGEO, 30 mins.
North America: Land of Many Peoples. NGEO, 16 mins.
Sport Goofy's Vacation. DIS, 43 mins.
United States Regions Series. BRIT, 6 films, 17–23 mins. each.

—— READ UP A STORM ——

(Weather)

Did you ever wonder why it rains? What causes hurricanes and tornadoes? Why you play baseball in the summer and hockey in the winter? You can find out this summer at _____ Library. Become a weather-watcher and learn about weather patterns in different parts of the world. Find out how storms are tracked. Build a weather vane and a thermometer. The forecast for this summer is fun. So don't be left out in the cold! Come to the library and **Read Up a Storm!**

Promotional Items

1. Sign reading "Weather Station" for check-out area
2. "Weather-Watcher" cards (membership cards)
3. Raindrop cut-outs (for books read)
4. Reading logs entitled "Weather Chart"
5. "Read Up a Storm" bookmarks
6. Meteorologist Awards (certificates of participation)
7. Sun visors, pinwheels (game prizes)

Activities

1. Bulletin Board. Draw a field scene. Over it, draw a huge tornado, starting from a speck on the ground and twisting into a giant black funnel. Throughout the tornado, paste cut-outs of books, smaller at the bottom and getting larger as the tornado expands. Caption: READ UP A STORM.

2. Reading Incentive Game: Across the Rainbow. Draw a giant rainbow. Mark the bottom left START, and the bottom right END. Pace off steps along the arc. Place a sun cut-out at START. Advance the sun one step for every X books read by the group. Readers will win a prize if the sun reaches the END by the closing ceremony.

3. Weather Words. Have children complete a crossword puzzle of weather terms (cloud, temperature, sunny, forecast, etc.).

4. Weather Maps. Show children a United States weather map from a current newspaper. Explain the different symbols. Compare this to newspaper weather maps from the spring, fall, and winter. Are the warmest and coldest areas the same? What is different? Let children color in a United States map with the current weather pattern.

5. Instruments. Display some weather-measuring instruments (barometer, rain gauge, etc.). Tell children how they are used.

6. Weather Vanes. Wind is an important feature of many kinds of weather. Have children make weather vanes to tell which way the wind is blowing. Glue a spool to a square wood base. Mark the compass points (N, S, E, W) on the base. Cut a large arrow out of heavy cardboard and glue or tape it near the top of a plastic straw. Stick the straw into the hole of the spool, making sure the straw turns easily. If desired, cut a picture of a rooster, horse, or whatever out of cardboard and attach it to the upper tip of the straw as a decoration.

7. Conditions. Show children pictures of extreme weather conditions (blizzards, droughts, hurricanes, etc.) and the damage they cause. Look at diagrams and aerial views of storms to show how they start and how meteorologists track them. Have children complete a word search puzzle of various weather conditions.

8. Snowflakes. Tell children that no two snowflakes are alike. Provide scissors and white paper to cut out snowflake designs. Mount snowflakes on colored paper and display in the library.

9. The Seasons. Read a book about the seasons. Then give each child a paper divided into quarters, each containing the same sketch of a leafless tree and a person. Have children label the seasons: spring, summer, fall, winter. Color the pictures to match the weather for each season, adding any appropriate features (clothes, rain, flowers, leaves, snowman, etc.). Have them write a short poem for each season. Display in library.

10. All-Weather Wear. Collect a pile of clothes in a large box. Pull out items one at a time, and let children identify what each item is and in which season or weather condition it is worn. (Shorts in summer, galoshes in rain, etc.) Or name a type of weather and let a child choose clothes to wear for it.

11. Seasonal Sports. Post a large 12-month calendar. Use stickers, stamps, or cut-outs to note the seasons of various sports (baseball and surfing in summer, etc.). How do these sports relate to the weather? What events are offered in the Winter Olympics? The Summer Olympics? Why?

12. Zippy Thermometers. Give each child an 8″ by 4″ piece of cardboard, and an 8″ by 4″ piece of oak tag in which a rectangular hole 7″ by 1″ has been cut. Glue a closed 8″ zipper to the center of the cardboard. Mark off degree lines on the oak tag, so that it will look like a thermometer. Then glue the oak tag onto the cardboard, so that the zipper will show through. Children can move the zipper up and down to match the temperature on the real thermometer.

13. Clouds. Explain that water vapor in the air forms clouds. When the vapor cools and comes together, drops form and it rains. Show this with a simple experiment. Fill a tin can with water and ice to represent a cloud. Set it down on a rack over a bowl of warm water to represent the earth. Soon water vapor in the air will form drops on the cold can, and "rain" down.

14. Weather Mobiles. Give each child two each of the following construction paper cut-outs: raindrop, lightning bolt, sun, cloud, rainbow. Staple the matching pieces together halfway around, stuff with newspaper, and staple closed. Hang the shapes from wire coat hangers to make mobiles.

15. Closing Ceremony: "What's the Weather?" Game. Divide children into teams. Give picture or word clues and have children identify the weather condition suggested by the clue. For example: picture of a *hurricane* lamp; or, "What kind of weather brought Dorothy to the Land of Oz?" (tornado). You may also use sound clues, by playing a part of a song ("*Wind* Beneath My Wings," "*Raindrops* Keep Falling on my Head," etc.). Prizes may be given to the winning team. Serve foods that are named with weather words (*snow* cones; *hot* dogs, etc.).

Theme-Related Books

For Younger Readers

Barrett, Judi. *Cloudy with a Chance of Meatballs.* Atheneum, 1978.
Berenstain, Stan, and Berenstain, Jan. *The Bears' Almanac.* Random, 1973.
Coombs, Patricia. *Dorrie and the Weather-Box.* Lothrop, 1966.
Dr. Seuss. *Bartholomew and the Oobleck.* Random, 1949.
Hutchins, Pat. *The Wind Blew.* Macmillan, 1974.
Keats, Ezra Jack. *The Snowy Day.* Viking, 1962.
Provensen, Alice, and Provensen, Martin. *The Year at Maple Hill Farm.* Atheneum, 1978.
Spier, Peter. *Peter Spier's Rain.* Doubleday, 1982.
Stoltz, Mary. *Storm in the Night.* Harper, 1988.
Wilks, Mike. *The Weather Works.* Holt, 1983.

For Older Readers

Bellairs, John. *The Dark Secret of Weatherend.* Dial, 1984.
Dickenson, Peter. *The Weathermonger.* Little, 1969.
Fleming, Susan. *Trapped on the Golden Flyer.* Westminster, 1978.
Moskin, Marietta. *The Day of the Blizzard.* Coward, 1978.

Nelson, Theresa. *Devil Storm*. Orchard, 1987.
Ruckman, Ivy. *Night of the Twisters*. Crowell, 1984.
Turnbull, Ann. *The Frightened Forest*. Houghton, 1975.

Nonfiction

Baker, Eugene. *I Want to Be a Weatherman*. Childrens, 1972.
Davis, Hubert J. *A January Fog Will Freeze a Hog and Other Weather Folklore*. Crown, 1977.
DeBruin, Jerry. *Young Scientists Explore the Weather*. Good Apple, 1983.
dePaola, Tomie. *The Cloud Book*. Holiday, 1975.
Fradin, Dennis B. *Disaster!* series. Childrens.
Gibbons, Gail. *Weather Words and What They Mean*. Holiday, 1990.
Sattler, Helen Roney. *Nature's Weather Forecasters*. Nelson, 1978.
Seymour, Peter. *How the Weather Works*. Macmillan, 1985.
Thomas, Robert B. *The Old Farmers Almanac*. Yankee.
Webster, Vera. *Weather Experiments*. Childrens, 1982.

Films and Videos

Animals in All Kinds of Weather. NGEO, 15 mins.
Bringing the Rain to Kapiti Plain. RR, 30 mins.
The Little Red Lighthouse. WW, 9 mins.
Wind. NFBC, 10 mins.
Winnie the Pooh and the Blustery Day. DIS, 24 mins.
The Wonderful Weather Machine. BARR, 13 mins.

—— A WHALE OF A TIME ——

(Whales)

*Want to go on a whale watch? You'll find them at _____ Library this summer. Join the Whale-Watcher's Club and find out about different types of whales and how they live. Chart the migration route of a school of whales. Learn about whaling and create scrimshaw designs. Make your own whale models and mobiles. This summer, you're going to have **A Whale of a Time** at the Library!*

Promotional Items

1. Sign reading "Whale University" for check-out area
2. "Whale-Watcher" permits (membership cards)
3. Whale cut-outs (for books read)
4. Reading logs entitled "Whaling Log"
5. "A Whale of a Time" bookmarks
6. "Graduate of Whale University" diplomas (certificates of participation)
7. Whale Watch items (game prizes)

Activities

1. Bulletin Board. Post paper ocean waves along the bottom half of the area. Post a large whale with the names of reading club members atop the water. Arrange whale cut-outs with names of fiction and nonfiction books about whales in the waves. Have the large whale spout the caption: A WHALE OF A TIME.

2. Reading Incentive Game: Whale Gallery. Along one wall, post labels indicating the names and full-grown sizes of several types of whales. For every X books read by the group, post a scale-sized picture of a whale above its label. Readers will win a prize if the Whale Gallery is completed by the closing ceremony.

3. Whales, Sharks, and Dolphins. Show children pictures or models of various whales. List some characteristics of these sea mammals vs. fish, sharks, and dolphins. How are they alike? Different?

4. Whale Search. Have readers complete a word search puzzle of different types of whales.

5. Whale Tales. Read a story about a whale. Let children write and illustrate their own whale stories. Collect and bind them in a book to keep in the library called "Whale Tales."

6. Stuffed Whales. Give each child two large construction paper whale cut-outs. Provide art materials so children can decorate the whales. Then staple the cut-outs together, leaving a hole at the top of the whale's head. Stuff with crumpled newspaper. Place a fringe-cut piece of white paper at the whale's spout to look like water, and staple the whale closed.

7. Whale Songs. Play a recording of whale sounds. Then play Raffi's song "Baby Beluga" and have children sing along. Let children write and sing their own whale songs.

8. Whale Mail. Give children 4″ by 6″ blank index cards. Have them draw a whale picture on one side. Then turn the card over and draw a line down the center to look like a postcard. Have children write, "I'm having A WHALE OF A TIME at _____ Library!" on the left half, and an address on the right half.

9. Whale Teeth. Show children pictures or actual whale teeth. Provide lumps of clay and let children make models of whale teeth.

10. Whaling. Read a book about whaling. Discuss: When was whaling a big industry in America? What was the life of a whaler like? Why was this an important job? Why is whaling no longer necessary today?

11. Whaling Terms. Give readers a fact sheet about whaling. Include terms such as blubber, scrimshaw, stove boat, harpoon, "thar she blows," etc. Have readers complete a crossword puzzle with these terms.

12. Scrimshaw. Give children 3″ by 4″ pieces of Scratch Etch Board. Let them scratch designs into the shiny side of the board with an opened paper clip. Color in the scratches with crayon and wipe off the excess with a towel. Children will have a scrimshaw-type artwork. Mount on oak tag.

13. Water Play. Give children plastic or wooden whale toys and let them play at a water table.

14. Sightings. Locate on a world map areas where various types of whales have been sighted. Trace the migration route of a school of whales.

15. Closing Ceremony: Whale Watch. Ahead of time, place various whale items around the library (stickers, erasers, stuffed toys, pictures, etc.). On one wall, post duplicates of the items that are hidden. Tell children to go on a whale watch. Everybody should find one of each whale that is posted. These items will be the reading game prizes.

Theme-Related Books

For Younger Readers

Day, Edward C. *John Tabor's Ride*. Knopf, 1989.
Himmelman, John. *Ibis*. Scholastic, 1990.
Johnston, Tony. *Whale Song*. Putnam, 1987.
McCloskey, Robert. *Burt Dow, Deep-Water Man*. Viking, 1963.
Reese, Bob. *Dale the Whale*. Childrens, 1983.
Steig, William. *Amos and Boris*. Farrar, 1971.
Wilson, Bob. *Stanley Bagshaw and the Twenty-Two Ton Whale*. Hamish Hamilton, 1984.
Wolcott, Patty. *Pirates, Pirates, Over the Salt, Salt Sea*. Addison, 1981.
Ziefert, Harriet. *Henry's Wrong Turn*. Little, 1989.

For Older Readers

Benchley, Nathaniel. *Kilroy and the Gull*. Random, 1973.
Chbosky, Stacy. *Who Owns the Sun?* Landmark, 1988.
Cole, Joanna. *Stranded*. Delacorte, 1989.
Landon, Lucinda. *Meg Mackintosh and the Case of the Curious Whale Watch*. Joy St., 1987.
MacGregor, Ellen, and Pantell, Dora. *Miss Pickerell and the Blue Whale*. McGraw, 1983.
Meader, Stephen. *Whaler 'Round the Horn*. HBJ, 1950.

Melville, Herman. *Moby Dick.* Silver, 1984.
Spinnelli, Jerry. *Night of the Whale.* Dell, 1988.
Stevenson, John. *The Whale Tale.* Random, 1981.
Thrush, Robin, editor. *The Grey Whales Are Missing.* HBJ, 1987.

Nonfiction

Adkins, Jan. *Wooden Ship.* Houghton, 1978.
Bright, Michael. *Saving the Whale.* Watts, 1987.
Gardner, Robert. *The Whale Watcher's Guide.* Messner, 1984.
Hurd, Edith. *The Mother Whale.* Little, 1973.
McGowen, Tom. *Album of Whales.* Macmillan, 1980.
McNulty, Faith. *Whales: Their Life in the Sea.* Harper, 1975.
Miller, Suzanne S. *Whales and Sharks.* Simon and Schuster, 1982.
Posell, Elsa. *Whales and Other Sea Mammals.* Childrens, 1982.
Stein, R. Conrad. *The Story of the New England Whalers.* Childrens, 1982.
Stidworthy, John. *A Year in the Life of a Whale.* Silver, 1987.

Films and Video

Dot and the Whale. FHE, 75 mins.
How the Whale Got Its Throat. COR, 11 mins.
Humphrey the Lost Whale: A True Story. RR, 30 mins.
Jonah and the Great Fish. WW, 6 mins.
The Singing Whale (from *The Undersea World of Jacques Cousteau*). CHUR, 24 mins.

—————— BOOKS: ——————
YOUR TICKET TO THE WORLD
(World Geography, Travel)

You have the world at your fingertips in the library. And this summer, our friendly travel agents will guide you on an international tour to exotic places. Get your passport and plan your trip. Design picture postcards and exchange them with your friends. Collect souvenirs. Learn dances and taste foods from other lands. Make a flag and join our international parade. Be a globe-trotter! Discover **Books: Your Ticket to the World!**

Promotional Items

1. Sign reading "Travel Agency" for check-out area
2. "Passport/Countries Visited" logs (membership cards/reading logs; see activity #3)
3. Ticket cut-outs (for books read)
4. "Books: Your Ticket to the World" bookmarks
5. Globe-Trotter Awards (certificates of participation)
6. Inflatable beachball globes (game prizes)

Activities

1. Bulletin Board. Display a map of the world. Number various locations across the map. Next to it, repeat the numbers in a column along with cut-outs of books. On each cut-out, write the name of a fiction or nonfiction book about the corresponding area. Caption: BOOKS: YOUR TICKET TO THE WORLD.

2. Reading Incentive Game: Complete the Map. Post a map of the world showing only the outlines of countries. For every book read by the group, color in one country (or more if necessary). Readers will win a prize if the map is completely colored in by the closing ceremony.

3. Passports. Fold a piece of construction paper in half, like a book. On the cover, write, "Passport for (child's name)." Glue a headshot of the child on the inside left page. Write name, address, and citizenship beneath it. On the right side, write, "Countries Visited." Place a sticker on that page for each book read. This booklet will serve as the child's membership card and reading log.

4. World Celebrations. Let children make a list of famous festivals and celebrations around the world (Chinese New Year, Octoberfest, etc.). Mark the dates on a large calendar. Which ones would the children like to see someday?

5. Travel Terms. Give children a fact sheet of travel terms (customs, passport, reservations, baggage claim, etc.). Have them complete a crossword puzzle with these terms.

6. Foreign Flags. Display stamps, coins, and flags of many countries. Let each child locate a different country on a world map. Then draw the flag of that country and tape it to a wooden dowel. Display in library and save for the closing ceremony.

7. World News. Travelers must know basic information about the countries they will be visiting. Show children how to use a gazetteer. Then tell them to plan their vacations by picking three foreign countries to visit. Make a chart listing the countries and the following information about them: monetary unit used, language(s) spoken, capital or chief town, and continent in which the country is located. What else should they know?

8. Music. Play recordings of music and songs from different countries. Teach children some dances from other lands.

9. Packing Up. Divide children into small groups. Assign each group a different country. Have them make a list of what they would pack if they were to visit that country for a week during the current season. What clothes and non-clothing items would they take? Let the groups share their answers.

10. Postcards. Distribute 4″ by 6″ blank index cards. On one side, let children draw a picture of a foreign tourist site, and label what it is. Draw a line down the center of the other side. Tell children to write a message on the left half, and the name of a club member on the right. Use stickers for stamps. Put a mailbox in the library and let children mail cards to each other.

11. Transportation. Ask children to tell you some types of transportation that may be used in tourist travel. Show pictures of these. Have children complete a word search puzzle of these terms. Include the obvious (airplane, train) as well as the exotic (gondola, cruise ship, pedicab).

12. Tourist Attraction Game Show. Post pictures of many famous tourist sites around the world (the Eiffel Tower, Taj Mahal, Big Ben, etc.). Divide children into teams. Use a TV game show format and ask children to identify the sites (1 point each) plus the countries and cities in which they are located (another point). The group with the most correct answers wins a prize.

13. Souvenirs. Provide lots of old magazines. Have children cut out pictures of various "souvenirs" from a pretend world tour. Glue them onto a sheet of oak tag and label where they came from (chocolate from Holland, perfume from France, etc.).

14. Speak the Language. Distribute dictionaries and phrase books that translate English into other languages. Have children look up traditional greetings ("hello") in other languages. Make a chart listing these. Note similarities among some languages. Have readers look up other phrases which are helpful to travelers, such as "thank you," "help," and "what is that?"

15. Closing Ceremony: A Small World. Set up a multi-national buffet and let children sample the foods. Play music from different countries. Invite a travel agent to speak to children and pass out travel brochures. Play the song "It's a Small World" and let children sing along while waving their flags in an international parade.

Theme-Related Books

For Younger Readers

Anno, Mitsumasa, editor. *All in a Day.* Philomel, 1986.
_____. *Anno's Journey.* Collins, 1978.
Baer, Edith. *This Is the Way We Go to School.* Scholastic, 1990.
deBrunhoff, Jean. *The Travels of Babar.* Random, 1985.
Demi. *The Adventures of Marco Polo.* Holt, 1982.
dePaola, Tomie. *Bill and Pete Go Down the Nile.* Putnam, 1987.
Fatio, Louise. *The Happy Lion's Vacation.* McGraw, 1967.

Kalman, Maira. *Sayonara, Mrs. Kackleman.* Puffin, 1991.
Remkiewicz, Frank. *The Last Time I Saw Harris.* Lothrop, 1991.
Scarry, Richard. *Busy, Busy World.* Western, 1965.

For Older Readers

Alexander, Lloyd. *The Remarkable Journey of Prince Jen.* Dutton, 1991.
Bond, Michael. *Paddington Abroad.* Houghton, 1972.
Bunting, Eve. *The Traveling Men of Ballycoo.* HBJ, 1983.
Cresswell, Helen. *Bagthorpes Abroad.* Macmillan, 1984.
Dahl, Tessa. *School Can Wait.* Viking, 1991.
duBois, William Pené. *The Twenty-One Balloons.* Dell, 1984.
Graham, Robin. *The Boy Who Sailed Around the World Alone.* Wester, 1973.
Keller, Beverly. *The Sea Watch.* Four Winds, 1981.

Nonfiction

Chiasson, John. *African Journey.* Bradbury, 1987.
Cole, Ann, et al. *Children Are Children Are Children.* Little, 1978.
Fowler, Virginie. *Folk Arts Around the World and How to Make Them.* Prentice, 1981.
Gerberg, Mort. *Geographunny: A Book of Global Riddles.* Clarion, 1991.
Haskins, Jim. *Count Your Way Around the World* (series). Carolrhoda, 1986.
Houston, Dick. *Safari Adventure.* Cobblehill, 1991.
Nelson, Esther L. *Musical Games for Children of All Ages.* Sterling, 1976.
Purdy, Susan. *Festivals for You to Celebrate.* Lippincott, 1969.
Smith, Samantha. *Journey to the Soviet Union.* Little, 1984.
Wilcox, R. Turner. *Folk and Festival Costume of the World.* Scribner's, 1965.
Willard, Nancy. *A Visit to William Blake's Inn: Poems for Innocent and Experienced Travelers.* HBJ, 1981.

Films and Videos

Bon Voyage, Charlie Brown. PAR, 76 mins.
My Little Island. RR, 30 mins.
Our World Series, Part III: Countries and *Earth.* NGEO, 2 films, 10 and 14 mins.
Portraits of the Continents Series. NGEO, 16–18 mins. each.
Tommy Tricker and the Stamp Traveler. FHE, 101 mins.

— READING TIME AT THE ZOO —

(Zoo)

We're bringing the zoo to you this summer at _____ Library.
Learn about the native habitats of different animals and design

zoo houses for them. Help make our zoo alphabet book. Take part in an animal show and play "Animal Peek-a-Boo." Find out where the best zoos in the country are. Design a souvenir pennant. Come to our own petting zoo. You'll have more fun than a barrel of monkeys during **Reading Time at the Zoo.**

Promotional Items

1. Sign reading "Curator" for check-out area
2. "Visitor's Passes" (membership cards)
3. Elephant cut-outs (for books read)
4. Reading logs entitled "Animal Food"
5. "Reading Time at the Zoo" bookmarks
6. Zookeeper certificates (certificates of participation)
7. Animal crackers and toy figures (game prizes)

Activities

1. Bulletin Board. In the center, post a picture of a large elephant holding up a book with its trunk. Post pictures of other zoo animals gathered around the elephant, as though they are listening to him read from the book. Caption: READING TIME AT THE LIBRARY.

2. Reading Incentive Game: Native Habitats. Post a large map of the world. Next to it, post pictures of various animals that may be found in a United States zoo. Each picture should be labeled with the animal's name and the country which is its native habitat. For every X books read by the group, post one animal on the map by its home country. Readers will win a prize if all the animals are on the map by the closing ceremony.

3. Zoo Alphabet Book. Let each child name a different animal that may be found in a zoo. Try to have at least one animal for every letter in the alphabet. Have children draw pictures of the animals. On each, write the animal's name and native habitat. Children may sign their names on the back of their pictures. Bind the pictures alphabetically in a looseleaf notebook. Title it "Zoo Alphabet Book, Summer (year)." Children may add to the book throughout the summer. If the book becomes too large, you may separate the animals by habitat and make several books.

4. Animal Peek-a-Boo. Post several pictures of zoo animals. On each one, cover most of the animal, except for its tail, nose, or ears. Let children try to guess what each animal is from the part that is showing. Reveal the entire picture to see if they guessed correctly.

5. Types of Zoos. Ask children what they think a zoo looks like. Explain that modern zoos display most animals in natural settings rather than in cages. Divide children into small groups and assign each group a type of zoo (African habitat, aquarium, desert life, aviary, etc.). Have them list some animals that may be found there.

6. Collages. Supply lots of old magazines. Let children cut out pictures of animals that may be found in a zoo and paste them onto pieces of oak tag. They may want to have a theme, such as rain forest animals or reptiles.

7. Monkey Word Search. There are many types of monkeys and other primates that may be found in a zoo. Have children complete a word search puzzle of monkeys. Other word searches on types of bears, reptiles, antelopes, big cats, birds, or other species found in zoos may also be given.

8. Animal Homes. Tell children to pretend they are going to build a zoo. Decide what animals will be there. Which animals can live together? Select a few animals or groups of compatible animals. Divide the children into teams and let each one design a home for one animal or group. Consider: How would you make the homes resemble the animals' natural habitats? What barriers would be needed to keep the animals safe without spoiling the visitors' view? How would you feed the animals? Look at pictures of animals in the wild to get ideas.

9. Aquarium Shows. Provide construction paper cut-outs of performing sea mammals (sea lions, killer whales, dolphins, etc.). Let children color their animals and glue them onto popsicle sticks to make stick puppets. Let children with similar animals form into groups. Have each group present a puppet animal act for the others. Groups may make props such as balls, fish, or drums, if needed.

10. Endangered Species. Zoos are often homes or hospitals for some rare and endangered animals. Show pictures and give children a fact sheet of some of these animals. Have children complete a word search puzzle of endangered species that are kept in United States zoos.

11. Play-Acting. Let children pretend to be different zoo animals. They can imitate the animals' motions and tell the group why they like living in a zoo.

12. Zoo Careers. Post a list of zoo careers. Include everything from the obvious (zookeeper, veterinarian) to jobs that may be overlooked (librarian, graphics designer). Ask each child to pick a career and explain how it relates to a zoo. Help children to understand that all these jobs are important in running an efficient zoo.

13. Souvenir Pennants. Visitors often buy souvenirs to remember their trips to the zoo. Give children paper pennants and let them design their own zoo logos. Display in library.

14. United States Zoos. Give children a list of some popular United States zoos (Busch Gardens in Florida, Mystic Aquarium in Connecticut, the National Zoo in Washington, D.C., etc.). Let children locate these zoos on a United States map. Pass out a list of zoos in your state and have children locate them on a state map.

15. Closing Ceremony: Petting Zoo. Invite animal trainers, farmers, or zookeepers to set up a petting zoo. Allow children to pet, feed, and ask questions about the animals. If the party is outdoors, perhaps animal rides can be given.

Theme-Related Books

For Younger Readers

Campbell, Rod. *Dear Zoo.* Four Winds, 1983.
Carle, Eric. *The Mixed-Up Chameleon.* Crowell, 1975.
Demi. *A Chinese Zoo.* HBJ, 1987.
Dr. Seuss. *If I Ran the Zoo.* Random, 1950.
Graham, Margaret Bloy. *Be Nice to Spiders.* Harper, 1967.
Knight, Hilary. *Where's Wallace?* Harper, 1964.
Lewis, Stephen. *Zoo City.* Greenwillow, 1976.
Lobel, Arnold. *A Zoo for Mr. Muster.* Harper, 1962.
Lopshire, Robert. *Put Me in the Zoo.* Random, 1960.
Sloss, Lesley. *Anthony and the Aardvark.* Lothrop, 1991.

For Older Readers

Baker, Betty. *Danby and George.* Greenwillow, 1981.
Dana, Barbara. *Zucchini.* Harper, 1982.
Fleischman, Sid. *McBroom's Zoo.* Joy St., 1982.
Howe, James. *Morgan's Zoo.* Atheneum, 1984.
Lively, Penelope. *The Voyage of QV 66.* Dutton, 1979.
Rietveld, Jane. *Monkey Island.* Viking, 1963.
Yolen, Jane. *Zoo 2000: Twelve Stories of Science Fiction and Fantasy Beasts.* Clarion, 1973.

Nonfiction

Anderson, Madelyn K. *New Zoos.* Watts, 1987.
Grosvenor, Donna K. *Zoo Babies.* National Geographic, 1976.
Lerner, Mark. *Careers at a Zoo.* Lerner, 1980.
Machotka, Hana. *What Do You Do at a Petting Zoo?* Morrow, 1990.
Meyers, Susan. *Insect Zoo.* Lodestar, 1991.
O'Connor, Karen. *Maybe You Belong in a Zoo!* Dodd, 1982.
Prelutsky, Jack. *Zoo Doings: Animal Poems.* Greenwillow, 1983.
Rinard, Judith E. *Zoos Without Cages.* National Geographic, 1981.
Thomson, Peggy. *Keepers and Creatures at the National Zoo.* Crowell, 1988.
Tongren, Sally. *What's for Lunch.* GMC, 1981.

Films and Videos

Dr. Doolittle CBS, 145 mins.
San Diego Zoo. DIS/COR, 16 mins.
Zoo Animals in Rhyme. COR, 11 mins.
Zoos of the World. NGEO, 52 mins.

Film and Video Distributors

Code	Distributor and Address
AIMS	AIMS Media, 6901 Woodley Avenue, Van Nuys, CA 91406-4878
BARR	Barr Films, 12801 Schabarum Avenue, P.O. Box 7878, Irwindale, CA 91706-7878
BNCH	Benchmark Films, Inc., 145 Scarborough Road, Briarcliff Manor, NY 10510
BRIT	Encyclopedia Britannica Educational Corporation, 310 S. Michigan Avenue, Chicago, IL 60604
BVV	Buena Vista Home Video, Burbank, CA 91521
CBS/FOX	CBS/FOX Video, Industrial Park Drive, Farmington Hills, MI 48024
CENT	Centre, Distributed by Barr Films, 12801 Schabarum Avenue, P.O. Box 7878, Irwindale, CA 91706-7878
CHUR	Churchill Films, 12210 Nebraska Avenue, Los Angeles, CA 90025
COR	Coronet/MTI Film & Video, 108 Wilmot Road, Deerfield, IL 60015
CTI	Children's Television International, Inc. 800 Forbes Place, Suite 201, Springfield, VA 22151
DIS	Walt Disney Home Video, Distributed by Walt Disney Telecommunications and Non-Theatrical Company, Burbank, CA 91521
DIS/COR	Disney Educational Productions, Distributed by Coronet/MTI Film & Video, 108 Wilmot Road, Deerfield, IL 60015

FHE   Family Home Entertainment, Distributed by Life Home
            Video, 15400 Sherman Way, Suite 500, P.O. Box 10124,
            Van Nuys, CA 91410-0124

FILM   Filmfair Communications, 10621 Magnolia Blvd.,
            North Hollywood, CA 91601

FIV   Films Incorporated Video, 5547 North Ravenswood Avenue,
            Chicago, IL 60640-1199

HI   Hi-Tops Video, a Subsidiary of Heron Communications
            5730 Buckingham Parkway,
            Culver City, CA 90230

LCA/COR   Learning Corporation of America, Distributed by
            Coronet/MTI Film & Video, 108 Wilmot Road, Deerfield, IL 60015

MAC   Macmillan Films, 34 MacQuesten Parkway South,
            Mount Vernon, NY 10550

MCA   MCA Universal Home Video, MCA Distributing Corporation,
            70 Universal City Plaza, Universal City, CA 91608

MGM/UA   MGM/UA Home Video, Inc., 10000 W. Washington Blvd.,
            Culver City, CA 90232

NFBC   National Film Board of Canada, 1251 Avenue of the
            Americas, 16th Floor, New York, NY 10020-1173

NGEO   National Georgraphic Educational Services,
            National Geographic Society, Washington, DC 20036

PAR   Paramount Home Video, 5555 Melrose Avenue,
            Hollywood, CA 90038

PHX   Phoenix/BFA Films & Video, Inc.
            468 Park Avenue South, New York, NY 10016

PYR   Pyramid Film & Video, Box 1048, Santa Monica, CA 90406

RH   Random House Home Video, 225 Park Avenue South,
            New York, NY 10003

RR   Reading Rainbow, c/o CPN, P.O. Box 80669
            Lincoln, NB 68501

WAR   Warner Home Video, Inc., 4000 Warner Blvd.,
            Burbank, CA 91522

WEST   Western Publishing Company, Inc., 1220 Mound Avenue,
            Racine, WI 53404

WW   Weston Woods, Weston, CT 06883-9989

VES   Vestron Video, Distributed by Live Home Video,
             15400 Sherman Way, Suite 500, P.O. Box 10124,
             Van Nuys, CA 91410-0124

Feedback Wanted

I would like to know your reactions to the units and other information contained in this book. After you have had a chance to try out some of these ideas, I would appreciate your writing to me, Martha Simpson, c/o McFarland & Company, Inc., Publishers, Box 611, Jefferson NC 28640. Please provide information along the following lines: Your name, position, and work address. Whether you are a public or school librarian (if public, are you in children's/youth services?), or a teacher (tell me what grade level/subject area), or otherwise!

Tell me your reactions to the introduction or general procedure suggestions. What, in your experience, adds to the success of your summer program?

What units in this book have you used?

What parts of those units worked particularly well for you?

What, in your opinion, did not work as well?

What would you like to see added or deleted in the unit?

Do you have suggestions for future themes? Future activities? Anything else?

I would enjoy very much hearing from you.

Martha Seif Simpson

Index

The Bad News Bears 18
Baer, Edith 164
Bagthorpes Abroad 165
Baker, Betty 168
Baker, Eugene 159
Baker, Olaf 79
The Balancing Act 7
Baldwin, Margaret 69
Balian, Lorna 116
Ballet Robotique 122
Balloons, Zeppelins and Dirigibles 59
Ballpark: One Day Behind the Scenes at a Major League Game 17
Bambi Meets Godzilla 92
Banana Twist 62
Bang, Molly 88
Banks, Lynne Reid 79, 145
Barbato, Juli 7
Barden, Rosalind 139
Barkin, Carol 106
Barkley 33
Barn Dance! 99
Barney and the UFOs 113
Barney Buck and the Phantom of the Circus 33
Baron, Nancy 17
Barrett, Judi 40, 62, 158
Barrett, Norman 27
Barrie, James M. 119
Barth, Edna 72
Bartholomew and the Oobleck 158
Barton, Byron 148
Barwell, Eve 116
Baseball 17
Baseball: You Are the Manager 17
Baseball Rules in Pictures 17
Baseball's Hall of Fame 17
Bash, Barbara 152
Basil of Baker Street 136
Bat, Ball, Glove 18
Bate, Lucy 155
Bates, Robin 47
Bates, Simon 47
Battle Day at Camp Belmont 24
The Battle of Bubble and Squeak 116
Bauer, Caroline Feller 20, 72, 142, 155
Bauer, Marion Dane 69
Baum, Louis 119
Baylor, Byrd 50, 78
Be a Dinosaur Detective 47
Be a Perfect Person in Just Three Days! 21

Be Nice to Spiders 168
Bea and Mr. Jones 106
Beadle, Jeremy 96
Beal, George 139
The Bears' Almanac 158
The Bears' Vacation 125
Bearymore 33
The Beast in Ms. Rooney's Room 89
The Beast in the Bed 88
Beatty, Jerome, Jr. 33, 122
Beauregard, Sue 125
Bedknobs and Broomsticks 83
Bee 44
Beetles Lightly Toasted 62
A Beginner's Guide to the Constellations 14
Behind the Circus Scene 34
Behind the Filmmaking Scene 92
Behind the Newspaper Scene 102
Behind the Scenes at the Amusement Park 8
Behind the Scenes of a Broadway Musical 143
Behind the Television Scene 139
Behrens, June 72
Beim, Jerrold 75
Beim, Lorraine 75
Being a Friend Means . . . 65
Beirne, Barbara 41
Beiser, Arthur 50
Beisner, Monika 82
Bell, Robert 113
Bellairs, John 82, 122, 158
Below the Root 152
Belville, Cheryl 142
Bemmelmans, Ludwig 148
Ben's Trumpet 98
Benchley, Nathaniel 79, 161
Bendick, Jeanne 125
Benedict, Rex 44
Benjamin, Carol Lea 11
Benny Bakes a Cake 72
Benson, Kathleen 148
Berenstain, Jan 105, 125, 158
Berenstain, Michael 82, 89, 128
Berenstain, Stan 105, 125, 158
Berger, Melvin 99
Bernstein, Bonnie 21
Bernstein, Joanne 72, 155
Berry, Joy 65
The Best Christmas Pageant Ever 142